IN THE
SEA OF
STERILE
MOUNTAINS

James Morton

IN THE SEA OF STERILE MOUNTAINS

The Chinese in British Columbia

1974
J.J. Douglas Ltd.
Vancouver

J.J. Douglas Ltd.
1875 Welch Street
North Vancouver, B.C. V7P 1B7

Canadian Shared Cataloguing in Publication Data

Morton, James W., 1922-
    In the sea of sterile mountains

        Includes bibliographical references
    and index.
        ISBN 0-88894-052-1
        ISBN 0-88894-142-0 pa.

        1. Chinese in British Columbia.
    2. British Columbia — Race question.
    I. Title.
    FC3850.C5M67   971.1'004'951
    F1089.7.C5M67

Printed and bound in Canada by the Hunter Rose Company
Cover design by Ben Lim

Acknowledgements

The staff of the Northwest Room, Vancouver Public Library, facilitated my research immensely. Others who helped were the Honourable E. Davie Fulton; Ainsley Helmcken; Roy Mah; General George Pearkes; the late Honourable H.H. Stevens; Peter Wing.

Contents

Prologue

"This Act is passed upon the express understanding that no Chinese, either directly or indirectly, shall be employed. . . . The offender shall be liable to separate and successive penalties for each and every day during which any Chinese shall be employed. . . . The term "Chinese", wherever used in this Act, shall mean any native of the Chinese Empire or its dependencies not born of British parents and shall include any person of the Chinese race."

It is difficult for British Columbians to realize that such clauses in provincial government contracts ever existed. Legislation against the Chinese has been attempted, both successfully and unsuccessfully, since the earliest of colonial days until the recent past. But the story of the Chinese in the colony and the province is not merely one of local legislation, local riots and the more subtle forms of local discrimination; it is one which touched—or should have touched—every citizen in the country; it is one which involved every Prime Minister of Canada, reflecting his bigotry, selfishness or apathy; it is one which resulted in disallowances of provincial legislation by courts of law, the Federal government and the Imperial Privy Council; one which resulted in the refusal of royal assent to legislation passed by a democratic government; one in which the unorganized workingman was manipulated by the industrial giants of the age —and one in which, through it all, could be seen the remarkable ignorance of British Columbia affairs by the unsympathetic Canadians living beyond the mountains.

It is not a necessarily sociological history of the Chinese in the sea of sterile mountains nor, for that matter, a particularly accurate or complete one. A considerable amount of the material has been obtained from newspapers, which had varying political loyalties. However, they reflected the thoughts of the citizens of the day—or the thinking to which the citizens were exposed.

Introduction

It did not start just in Victoria or just in San Francisco or just in Hong Kong, nor did it begin simultaneously in all these cities rimming the Pacific Ocean. Perhaps it began with Britain's expanding mercantile trade in the 19th century, or with the Industrial Revolution—and if this is so, one could blame it all on Mrs. Watt's tea kettle, rattling on her blackened kitchen stove in Greenock, across the Clyde from Glasgow, and on her son, James, who heard the rattle—and wondered. History is a chain of events, the first link of which is often obscured by the past; of the clearly defined links which determined the future of China and British Columbia—and the world—perhaps the first was Mrs. Watt's tea kettle and her son's musty, mid-18th-century laboratory in Glasgow.

And from there, many series of links created a chain: one series between London and the eastern cities of Calcutta and Hong Kong; another between Hong Kong and San Francisco; another between San Francisco and Victoria. There were links directly connecting Hong Kong to Victoria and yet others running from Britain to the Pacific Coast of North America via the great cities on the Atlantic. Three great chains looping round the world, linking lives in London to others in Calcutta, Hong Kong, San Francisco, Ottawa and Washington, all ultimately ending in Victoria. And in time, the millions of people affected by these chains forgot, or perhaps never realized that the links ever existed, nor that they began when James Watt heard his mother's tea kettle rattling on the blackened kitchen stove in distant Greenock.

The Portuguese had reached China as early as the 16th century, though they were confined by the Ming rulers to trade only in Macao. British, French, Dutch and American merchants appeared in the 18th century, but were also limited to a few coastal ports by the stubborn Manchus who had displaced the Ming Dynasty in 1644. It was exasperating to be so confined, but there was no real pressure upon the British traders until the Industrial Revolution spurred them on. Then they had to sell more and more of the products from their new factories, and to find new materials to feed the great steam machines in Birmingham and Manchester; inevitably the rattle of James Watt's tea kettle was heard in Peking.

There was the rattle of swords, too. The Chinese people, or more properly, their Manchu overlords, were an impossible group with whom to deal. They had swept down from the north 200 years earlier to demolish the Mings. They had treated the Chinese as a conquered people, requiring them to wear their hair in pigtail or queue style, but they ruled well. The boundaries of the empire were extended farther than ever before, the population increased and their fine Oriental culture advanced accordingly.

Culture? Why, China had produced fine paintings and ornate sculpture in bronze and jade and ivory a thousand years before Caesar silenced the mystical incantations of druidic Britons, hidden in the darkest groves and most secret recesses of their island. The Manchus considered the British an inferior race. They would not deal with them on a basis of equality. Chinese documents referred to the British as barbarians. Foreigners were not allowed to learn the language and Chinese were not allowed to settle in other lands.

But perhaps more galling than anything to the British merchants was the fact that the Manchu emperor forbade the importation of opium into his country. There were always corrupt officials who would allow it to be smuggled in, but after all, the British were growing field upon field of poppies in India and they had to have a market for their opium. The home market was relatively small. Certainly the 19th-century physician in London prescribed many opium based drugs, and certainly there were a number of opium addicts, notably Coleridge and De Quincey and the great slave abolitionist, William Wilberforce; but it was a relatively small market and one which was unlikely to increase, since the "opium eaters," though tolerated, were hardly admired. If the vice existed, the British preferred to keep it hidden. The millions upon millions of heathen Chinese were therefore a god-sent market on the other side of the world. If, however, there was some doubt in the British mind as to the evil qualities of the drug, there was none in the Chinese mind. In 1839 the Peking government sent a special commissioner to compel all foreign merchants to surrender their stores of opium for destruction. The British objected—and hostilities began.

1839—There was not much to be seen on the other side of the Pacific, at least if one was looking for civilization. There was a sleepy little Mexican settlement named Yerba Buena where San Francisco now stands. To the north, the redwood and pine forests yielded to fir and spruce and cedar, and the mountains, towering out of the sea, might for months be shrouded in mist and rain. There was a small trading post at Astoria at the mouth of the Columbia River and another, Fort Vancouver, near its mouth. Still farther north, where there was as yet no definite boundary between the United States and British North America, the lonesome sailor might sight only a small Indian village or an equally lonesome trader. Fort Victoria was four years in the future, and Fort Langley, though it had been established 14 years earlier, was far up the Fraser River. The coast was desolate and lifeless, too distant from civilization to be of any use except for otter furs which traders shipped to China, where man had reached a high cultural level centuries earlier, or to England, where Watt's tea kettle was now far more than a mere rattle and where the future of the world was being shaped.

1839—There were youngsters living in England quite oblivious to the fact that their futures lay on the distant, desolate shores of Britain's North America. Matthew Baillie Begbie, at the age of 20 years, was studying at Cambridge, and a 14-year-old youngster with an intriguing name, Henry Pelling Perew Crease, was about to attend the same university. John Sebastian Helmcken, at the age of 16, was being taught "to cup, bleed and otherwise physic" the London patients of an aging Dr. Graves. Robert Dunsmuir, in the Scottish county of Ayrshire, did not have education thrust upon him. He was just 15 years of age, but already he was learning the value of the coal business in which his father and grandfather were engaged. They would all find their way to that distant, desolate shore and help to mould its future—for better or for worse.

And there were many others in England, Scotland and Ireland, and even in Upper and Lower Canada, all youngsters in 1839, all staunchly loyal to the young queen who had succeeded to the throne two years earlier. Victoria, like Matthew Begbie, was in her twentieth year. She would never see the desolate coast, but a little hamlet on the tip of Vancouver's Island would be named after her and she, herself, would later name the capital of the mainland colony of British Columbia.

They were all youngsters in 1839. No one could blame them for the Opium Wars in far-off China. The British repeatedly defeated the Chinese, each time gaining new concessions, but were still not permitted to travel in the interior; they had only five ports in which to trade and they were not allowed to trade in opium. It was a most annoying situation. The British schoolboy could hardly be told that the White Knights of Downing Street would launch another war because Britons could not travel in the interior of China—and they certainly could not be told in Eton and Harrow and Winchester that the Chinese must be beaten senseless because they would not allow the importation of opium. Time after time, Britain found an acceptable cause, such as the violation of the British flag, and time after time she brought her mailed fist down upon a pigtailed Chinese head. And when it was all over, the Chinese were not only compelled to permit free trade, travel and the sale of opium but also had to pay for the privilege in pounds sterling.

The Opium Wars, 1839 to 1869—Historically speaking, 30 years is a very short period, though it is half a man's lifetime. In those three decades, many changes had occurred on the far west coast of North America. Mexico had ceded California to the United States in 1848, Yerba Buena was now San Francisco, and the state had passed through a wild gold rush which brought a huge influx of miners, adventurers, army deserters, gamblers and pirates. And Chinese. There were said to be 62,000 in California in 1868, and anti-Oriental riots were almost a daily occurrence.

There had been some remarkable changes, too, in the British colony above the 49th parallel. Many of the youngsters of 1839 had found their way there: men such as Matthew Baillie Begbie, Joseph Helmcken, Henry Pelling Perew Crease and Robert Dunsmuir; and many others who would shape the future of the colony and province in the tumultuous years ahead: the Davies, the Tolmies, the Robsons and an eccentric but intelligent gentleman named Amor De Cosmos. But his destiny did not start in 1869, as it did not start in Victoria or San Francisco or Hong Kong. If it started anywhere, it was in Greenock, where James Watt sat watching his mother's tea kettle back in the 18th century. But the rattle was not heard in Victoria until 1858.

CHAPTER I

1858-1871

"They May Be Inferior . . . Still Their Presence
At This Juncture Would Benefit Trade. . . . "
Amor De Cosmos 1860

The modern traveller considers the north-west coast to be one of
the most attractive corners of the earth. There are endless days of
summer sunshine, long, deep fjords, rolling green mountains and
striking, snowy peaks. There are limitless waters to sail upon, limitless fish to catch, limitless game to hunt and limitless shores to rest
upon in peaceful isolation. To the early traveller, however, it was a
dull, desolate land, a million miles from the comforts of the great
cultural centres of the old world. James Cook and George Vancouver, and even some of the Spanish explorers who were accustomed to desolation, considered it a most forbidding, inhospitable
land, fit only for savages and for those who chose to suffer untold
misery in order to become rich by trading in otter furs.

It was still a desolate land in 1843, when the fort was constructed at
the tip of Vancouver's Island; in 1846, when the western boundary
of British North America was chosen as the 49th parallel, and in
1849, when Vancouver's Island officially became a colony and was
transferred by royal grant to the Hudson's Bay Company. Indeed,
the colony's first governor, Richard Blanshard, resigned in 1851
partially because living conditions were unbearable for a young
English barrister and partially because Fort Victoria was the ultimate
in company towns. The new governor, James Douglas, was used to
bodily discomfort and isolation. He was 48 years of age in 1851 and
had survived the rigours of the fur trade in the most desolate parts of
the continent since the age of 16 years.

1

In the Sea of Sterile Mountains

When he became governor of Vancouver's Island and chief factor of the Hudson's Bay Company's north-west region—which included all the mainland, then referred to vaguely as New Caledonia—there were few more isolated places on the face of the globe. On the island, there was a fort and perhaps 200 company employees. On the mainland, there were a few trading posts sprinkled sparsely between endless ranges of mountains. The nearest to the tip of Vancouver's Island was Fort Langley, 80 ocean and river miles away; east of the Rockies, Rupert's Land stretched lonesomely to the Lakehead. To the south, Fort Vancouver was almost 200 miles distant and San Francisco, 800. There was no point in reckoning the distance to London in miles. London was reckoned in terms of time. The Hudson's Bay Company headquarters was perhaps two months away.

Vancouver Island's fort was there in 1849 when Douglas sailed into the inner harbour; it was there in 1850 when Dr. Helmcken arrived for a five-year stay; it was there on a sunny Sunday afternoon in April 1858 when the *Commodore* put in from San Francisco. That was when it began: on a sunny Sunday afternoon in April 1858. The bastions with their eight pieces of ordnance and the pallisade, constructed to protect the little settlement from potential Indian uprisings, in a matter of an hour became a relic of the past. The peace and solitude of the 300 souls who lived in and about the fort, too, were abruptly dissolved. Fort Langley was still 80 miles away, Fort Vancouver 200 and San Francisco 800, but in the time you could unload a boat, the population had risen from 300 to 700. By the end of the year, it was said, 20,000 human beings of all descriptions had slipped ashore on the inner harbour. Comparatively few had come to stay. In December of 1858, there were perhaps 7,000 living in wooden shanties, tents and hastily constructed hotels. The remainder had scrambled into boats of various sizes, shapes and degrees of seaworthiness, to sail, paddle or steam across the Gulf of Georgia and up the Fraser where they might sluice or pan the golden nuggets tumbling down from some untrammelled motherlode to the north. Perhaps these nuggets had been tumbling down through sand and gravel for centuries past, but in 1856 some nameless wanderer snatched a piece of shining yellow from a river bar. The news found its way to San Francisco by 1858 and there was a massive influx of miners to New Caledonia. Fort Victoria was just a port of entry, a source of supply, a point for re-embarkation to the gold fields. And it began on a sunny Sunday afternoon in April.

James Douglas was not taken completely by surprise. He knew

that gold had been found, he knew that such a discovery did strange things to men's minds, that the serenity of his little post was about to be destroyed; but he could have had no conception of the proportions of the changes about to take place. He had warned the imperial government that a gold rush similar to that so recently seen in California was likely to occur. In August 1858, New Caledonia became the Colony of British Columbia, and Douglas was offered the governorship of the new outpost of empire, provided he sever his relations with the Hudson's Bay Company. He accepted the proposition, perhaps reluctantly. It was the beginning of the end for the company. Settlement and gold mining were quite incompatible with trapping and fur trading.

The new mainland colony was completely dependent upon Fort Victoria for food and mining supplies—and soon Fort Victoria, which had survived alone for 15 years, found that it depended on the commerce brought by the miners of the mainland. The two colonies were so mutually dependent, one would hardly realize they were separate entities. And yet when Governor Douglas steamed across the gulf to visit his second empire, the local newspaper announced, "His Excellency is visiting British Columbia," as if it were a foreign land.

The mainland, however, gained a measure of independence and pride when the Royal Engineers carved New Westminster from the forests along the Fraser River in 1859. By then, rough bearded miners from California had been steaming or paddling past the site for over a year. They were mostly the white dregs of the earth. Following this first influx, however, the quality of immigrants improved somewhat. There were a few Englishmen and Canadians from Upper and Lower Canada (the latter of whom were considered by the Britons of the Island to be no better than the foreign Americans) who came in search of gold; there were more cautious types who came as merchants or land speculators; there was a sprinkling of professional men such as lawyers and engineers; and there were officials appointed by the imperial government. Matthew Baillie Begbie was one of the latter. He was a bachelor of 39 years when he sailed into the inner harbour in November 1858, to become the first judge of the mainland colony. Henry Pelling Perew Crease, now 35, arrived a month later. He was one of the professional men, the first barrister on Vancouver's Island.

But the earliest arrival of this group of men who appeared in 1858 was one who would mould the future of the two north-west colonies. Amor De Cosmos was born in Nova Scotia in 1825 as William

Alexander Smith, but as a young man he left eastern Canada, as so many did, to find his fortune in the west. He reached Sacramento in 1853 and, before he sailed northward five years later, he changed his name to the more flamboyant and suggestive Amor De Cosmos. He was neither miner, professional nor official; he was a reformer. And what better soil was there in which to germinate and cultivate the seeds of his genius than Fort Victoria in 1858—where the 200-year-old company had ruled unmolested for 15 years and the governor of the sister colonies had been a company man all his adult life; where his so-called government, then consisting of the seven members of a House of Assembly, were, in fact, his recent company surbordinates? And what better means was there to promote his revolutionary thoughts than to establish a newspaper? He named it the *British Colonist* (still in existence as the Victoria *Colonist*).

On December 11, 1858, his first edition appeared on the streets of Fort Victoria, such as they were. Amor De Cosmos, proprietor and editor, lost no time in attacking the establishment. The governor, Chief Justice David Cameron (Douglas' brother-in-law) and Dr. J.S. Helmcken (Douglas' son-in-law and Speaker of the House of Assembly) felt the bitter thrust of Amor's pen. The 53-year-old governor must have wondered what the younger generation was coming to. De Cosmos demanded the immediate union of Vancouver's Island with British Columbia and the resignation of Chief Justice Cameron. He accused James Douglas of discouraging the settlement of the two colonies in order to preserve the fur trade for the Hudson's Bay Company and described Helmcken in insulting, if not libellous, terms. The Victoria *Gazette*, established five months earlier, was a docile little journal beside the *Colonist*. It was not long before Amor had collected a sizeable number of supporters in the community—"independents," they liked to call themselves, in the sense that they were independent of the Company, not that they were non-partisan. They were pleased at the founding of an independent newspaper ". . . which fears not to be beard the lion in his den, the Douglas in his hall," as one of Amor's admirers put it.

The *Colonist*, however, did more than preach reform; it brought news from the outside world, pilfered selectively from the newspapers of Washington, San Francisco and London, and anywhere from one to six weeks old. Amongst the "California Items" in one of its earliest editions was a brief note stating that the miners of Mariposa had ordered the Chinese to leave within 48 hours. It is altogether likely that the Americans living in the vicinity of the fort noted this with considerable satisfaction. Perhaps the British settlers were shocked at this example of American bigotry. Perhaps they muttered proudly, "It could never happen here." But it did. And when it reached such enormous proportions that the government was forced to interfere, these same settlers could not recall when it all began.

There were several matters which stimulated the exodus of the Chinese from their homeland. First of all, their government, bruised and battered by one British and French attack after another, eased the emigration barriers. According to W.E. Willmott[1], the Chinese themselves admitted that one reason for their departure was the continual political instability of the Kwantung area, from which virtually all the immigrants to North America came. But perhaps of more importance was the poverty in which they lived. They were peasant farmers who laboured long and patiently in their fields. And when their crops were harvested, they plodded doggedly into the nearest village to barter and haggle for the best possible price they could get. They were aware that they had the ability to work hard and that they had a certain business acumen, both of which could be used to advantage in a more plentiful land.

The exodus of Chinese was also aided by their lineage system. They knew that they could safely leave their wives and children behind in the care of other members of the family while they remained in America for five years or so, to return with a few hundred dollars and live for the remainder of their lives in relative splendour. Their close family connections also were responsible for the "chain immigration" which followed: early immigrants spread the word of newfound riches and other Chinese from the same locality followed.

And so they came—at first in trickles, then in hundreds and finally in thousands. The year after the California gold rush of 1848, there were 300 Orientals in the state, but by 1852 this number had mushroomed to 25,000. Fortune may have smiled upon some, but for most the gold was not plentiful; as the years passed, they drifted into San Francisco to form an isolated settlement centred on Dupont Gai, the earliest Chinatown on the continent.

The first Chinese in British North America were undoubtedly the 30 Chinese artisans brought by Captain John Meares in 1779, but the seizure of his vessels by the Spanish caused an abrupt halt to his plans and an unknown fate to the 30 artisans. There is more certainty as to the date of arrival of the first Chinese immigrants to the two British colonies. The Victoria *Gazette* in its second issue (June 30, 1858) headlined an article "A Pioneer Chinaman."

"We have not yet seen a Chinaman in Victoria, though a small number of citizens of the Flowery Kingdom are known to have left California in the Frazer River exodus. From a sign which appears in our streets, however, it may be presumed that John is among us and bears the euphonius and suggestive legend, Chang Tsoo. Doubtless ere long the familiar interrogation of 'Wantee washee?' will be added to our everyday conversation library." (J.E. Vrooman, a Methodist missionary in China, later stated, "It was a conceit of the Chinese to call their land the Flowery Kingdom.")

"N.B. Since the above was penned, a batch of celestials have landed from the *Oregon* and are camped in the vicinity of the sign in question. Whether their efforts will be directed to the washing of gold or of clothing is a point yet to be ascertained, but we shall lay it before our readers at a moment as early as the grave importance of the subject demands."

Here, then, was the first mention of Chinese immigrants in a British North American newspaper. It was generally an inoffensive statement and yet it revealed an amused detachment on the part of the whites. The staunch old British residents were aware that Her Majesty's forces had been struggling with the stubborn Chinese emperor for almost twenty years, but surely this was not the reason for their immediate disdain. More likely it was a reflection of the Californian attitude. Many of the residents of Fort Victoria had lived in San Francisco and the remainder had all passed through that city on their journey to the north-west. They read San Francisco and Sacramento newspapers. They already knew the choice euphemisms of the day, such as "the Flowery Kingdom" and "John" and "the celestials." They were already aware of the typical Chinese predisposition to the laundry business.

Two weeks later, it was rumoured that the recently arrived Chinese were about to launch a business into the curing and exportation of fish products. Perhaps it was just a rumour. In a few months, at any rate, hundreds of Chinese could be found in the lower canyon region of the Fraser near Yale, where the quest for gold had begun. Beneath the perpendicular cliffs and sparsely treed slopes, every little patch of sand held its miner—and not far behind him, as he moved upstream, was a Chinese. There were Emory's Bar, Hill's Bar, Texas Bar, Boston Bar, China Bar, Ferguson's Bar, Horse-Beef Bar and Dancing Bill's Bar; each patch of sand had its name. But the movement was northward. To escape the long, backbreaking climb that had almost defeated Simon Fraser 50 years earlier, a new route to Lillooet was opened, up the Harrison River to a series of trails and lakes that brought the weary miner to "the upper Fraser," some 200 miles from its mouth.

In March 1859, the *Gazette* reported that one of the Chinese companies of San Francisco had arranged to bring 2,000 Chinese to Victoria, from which most of them would proceed to the upper Fraser. The newspaper also reported that the *Robert Passenger* would soon arrive from Hong Kong with a large number of Chinese immigrants. In the middle of the same month they described, in the disdainful style reserved for Chinese news, the departure from Victoria of a group of Chinese immigrants for the gold fields:

"A procession of moon-eyed Orientals 'might have been seen' yesterday afternoon on their way to the wharf of the steamer for Langley. The display consisted of sixteen individuals whose manoeuvres, although accomplished in Indian file, caused quite a scattering of bystanders on the line of march, as each of the immigrating army was his own pack animal and was loaded in true Chinese style, with a pole on his shoulder, dangling from each end of which were packages of provisions etc. In this instance, long-handled shovels were made to serve the purpose of poles, and it was cheering to witness the gay and airy manner in which the Johns, despite their burthens, bounded along the stony pavement as they passed . . . ."

The *Gazette*'s Fort Yale correspondent described the trek northward with more tolerance. He first came upon a group of whites with their Indian packers, but he soon met others: "Anon you meet throngs of Chinamen packing up the river; they pass and greet you in broken English with 'How you do, John;' we are all Johns to them, and they to us." (The *Colonist* of May 12, 1883 states, "John is the Christian name of all pale faces, so far as the Chinaman is concerned.") "Their bamboo canes and heavy loads are strangely singular to us. Next comes the Negro, with a polite, 'Good morning, sar,' or Chilano, Mexican or Kanaka each with his heavy load." (Ships rounding Cape Horn called at Chile and then took advantage of the prevailing winds to sail to Hawaii and then to the northwest coast. Frequently they carried with them Chileans [Chilanos] and Hawaiians [Kanakas].)

The first Chinese, then, appeared toward the end of June 1858, some two months after the momentous arrival of the *Commodore*. They came from San Francisco, but in the spring of 1859, others (if we assume that the newspaper reports were correct) arrived directly from Hong Kong. Many of them slipped away to the gold-flecked bars of the Fraser, while others settled in the growing hamlet at the tip of the Island. Some became washmen; others were eagerly accepted as house servants by the well-to-do. Some became merchants, and of these, the founder of the Kwong Lee Company of Cormorant Street was the most important. This company was said to have been established in 1858, though its advertisement did not appear in The *Colonist* until 1860. "Importers and Dealers in all kinds of Chinese Goods, Rice, Sugar, Tea, Provisions etc. etc.," it read. Walter B. Cheadle, the English physician who crossed the continent with Lord Milton in 1862-63, described Kwong Lee as "quite a gentleman of most polite manners and very intelligent." He spoke English fluently, "free from Yankee twang and slang," to Cheadle's delight—and he treated the adventurous English travellers to champagne and very good cigars. Kwong Lee's wife arrived on the *Pacific* in the spring of 1860, along with a child. "This," reported the *Colonist*, "is the first Chinese female that has ever set foot in the Colony." The Kwong Lee Company would become one of the leading merchants on both Vancouver Island and the mainland for many years.

The town around it was growing rapidly. In the summer of 1858, a reporter from the San Francisco *Times* had sailed northward to examine the latest gold rush. He described it as "the San Francisco of 1849 reproduced . . . the same hurry-scurry, hurly-burly, dust, inconvenience, bad living, cheating and lying . . . .The riff-raff of San Francisco . . . chiefly VERMIN of the masculine gender, has settled in Victoria." Amor De Cosmos was indignant over this generalization since, presumably, he was one of the vermin who had drifted northward.

Whatever riff-raff came from San Francisco did not stay long enough to prove just how verminous they were. Law and order were never great problems in the two colonies, though in August 1859, the *Colonist*'s Fort Yale correspondent reported a small incident of interest. "The Chinamen in the Little Kanyon," he said, "have occasional conflicts with their white neighbours, in which John is invariably worsted. The white men aver that the Celestials have pursued a most aggressive policy in jumping claims while the owners were in town buying provisions, pulling up stakes and tearing down notices, and behaving in an insolent manner generally, thereby meriting a sound trouncing."

In April 1860, there was a fight between "an Indian and a Celestial" opposite the Wells Fargo Building in Victoria. The culprits were brought before Judge Pemberton. "The Celestial conducted his own defense in an able and dignified manner," said the *Colonist*, "stating to the court that—'Him (the Indian) breakee me windee, me catchee him. Me say no good Mr. Injun, he strikee me once and skinee me nose and kickee me in back. No belly good Injun.' The Indian was fined ten shillings for assault and the Chinaman was discharged."

The legal problems of the day were largely concerned with the unfortunate natives of the land who were exploited, robbed and degraded by the white interlopers. In the late '50s and early '60s, Indians swarmed into the environs of Victoria. In addition to the local Songhees, there were Indians from Nanaimo, the Stikine River, Fort Rupert and the Queen Charlotte Islands. Perhaps it was their curiosity, or the white man's whiskey, which attracted them. Whichever it was, they frightened Amor half to death. "In broad noonday," he complained, "our streets are thronged with Indians carrying knives, pistols and guns with a recklessness perfectly terrifying." This, said the Lover of the Universe, was good evidence that "the red savage" or "siwash" was given privileges which white men were not allowed to enjoy. (The derivation of "siwash" is uncertain; it is said to be a variant of the French "sauvage.")

Though the Chinese were no threat to law and order, they were arriving in larger numbers. Over a period of three months in the spring of 1860, figures totalled from ship arrivals were 1,577, most of them directly from China. These figures may have been exaggerated, or there may have been other unreported arrivals, but certainly the influx was large enough to raise a few eyebrows. A census in May 1860 showed a total of 2,884 whites on the Island. Most of the immigrants would depart for British Columbia (whose population was unknown), but certainly 1,577 Chinese was more than half the total permanent white population of Vancouver Island. Commented the local newspaper, "At the rate at which they are going up the Fraser, the Celestials will soon outnumber the whites."

The citizens of Victoria were aware of the anti-Oriental feelings in California. They read of the Mariposa miners in 1858, and in 1859 the *Colonist* published an article from the San Francisco *Bulletin*: "It may do very well for the people in the cities, the merchants, the ship owners and steam boat men to talk in favor of the Chinese, but when a white man is placed alongside a company of these creatures, imported from abroad, and fed on rice and dog-fish, and made to measure the price of his day's work by the price of theirs, there will be complaining and dissatisfaction. And for our part, we sympathize with and take the part of the white miner when he is drawn to meet such unnatural competition. We say it is the prosperity of the white man in this state that makes up her prosperity; that the aggrandizement of the Chinese does not make us a particle richer—adds nothing to our fixed capital, builds no cities or towns, erects no churches or school houses, or, in short, does anything to advance us in wealth, power or greatness." San Francisco, 800 miles to the south, was Victoria's closest civilized neighbour. The sentiments of that community would mould Victoria's opinions for many years to come.

It may have been the influence of their southern neighbours which persuaded the seven-man House of Assembly to propose the first tax on Chinese. It came in 1860 and was in the form of a ten-dollar poll tax, but the good citizens of Victoria opposed it, not because it was discriminatory but rather because it was not exactly good for business. Victoria was a commercial depot and a point of embarkation for the mining districts, to which most of the Chinese were travelling. Said De Cosmos, "They may be inferior to Europeans and Americans in energy and ability; hostile to us in race, language and habits and may remain among us a Pariah race; still they are patient, easily governed and invariably industrious and their presence at this juncture would benefit trade everywhere in the two colonies.... Hereafter when the time arrives that we can dispose with them, we will heartily second a check to their immigration . . . ." Amor even complimented "the unmitigated muffs" in the House of Assembly. "it is pleasing to know," he said, "that the intentions of the government toward this immigration is just and reasonable. Invidious taxation, we are assured, will not be made . . . .Our prediction is that while British Columbia profits directly by their labor, indirectly our commercial prosperity [the Island's] is assured."

Thus, there were occasional words of caution over the large Chinese influx. But then, as now, the driving force in life was the search for wealth, and as far as Victorians were concerned, the Chinese brought commerce to the city.

"We learn from various Chinese firms," purred the *Colonist* in May 1860, "that a perfect fever exists in China in regard to Fraser river, and that an immigration of 8,000 to 10,000 coolies [An Anglo-Indian word from the Bengali or Tomil word 'Kuli' meaning 'burden bearer.'] may be expected between now and the first of August. Should these anticipations be verified, a very busy time is looked for during the coming summer. It is asserted by knowing ones that 500 Chinese left $10,000 with the merchants of this town last week."

The mainlanders were not so sure that they were profiting from the Chinese immigration. The New Westminster *Times* feared that the Orientals would become troublesome and drive whites from the mines. The *Colonist*'s Port Douglas correspondent (at the northern end of Harrison Lake) described the influx of hundreds of Chinese "by almost every arrival from below" and he expressed his belief that soon European and American miners would be outnumbered by the Chinese ten to one.

By the early 1860s, then, the blurred image of the north-west coast had focused into a very clear pattern. Fort Victoria, served only by a rare Hudson's Bay Company ship prior to 1858, now almost daily welcomed steamers, barks, brigs and clipper ships from the south and the Orient. From there, the little steam ships *Eliza Anderson, Otter, Governor Douglas* and *Emily Harris* constantly pounded back and forth across the Gulf of Georgia and up the Fraser to New Westminster, Fort Langley, Hope, Yale and Port Douglas. They carried supplies and miners to the Colony of British Columbia and returned with gold and news from Yale and Hope and Cayoosh Creek, from the Canoe Country and the hundreds of bars along the Fraser. They brought news of fabulous gold strikes, of murders, of drowned bodies floating down the river, of claim-jumping and of Chief Justice Matthew Baillie Begbie making his circuit through the north. British Columbians grumbled about his living comfortably in the civilized foreign Colony of Vancouver Island, but the judge enjoyed his soirees as much as he enjoyed his sallies into the wilderness where he dispensed justice with dignity and candour. Dr. Cheadle passed Begbie on the road near Clinton in 1863 and later played whist with him in Victoria until 4 a.m. The judge lived his life to the full.

But it was the gold mines, and to some extent the Chinese, that brought dollars and pounds into Victoria. The city was a great funnel into which was poured men and supplies, most of which flowed down the ever-narrowing neck to the gulf, the river, the canyons, the gorges and the untrammelled valleys of the interior.

However, the funnel was blocked in January 1862. The Fraser River froze solidly right down to its mouth and remained so for over two months. One ship from Victoria landed its passengers on the ice on a Sunday and they walked up the frozen river, arriving in New Westminster the following Wednesday. That same winter, James Batterton slid down the ice from Yale to New Westminster in three and a half days. There was only one way to solve the problem of moving supplies to the mainland; the tip of the funnel was shifted temporarily to Burrard Inlet. The little steamers from the Island then plowed through the First Narrows, past the present Stanley Park (first surveyed the following year) and up the wooded fjord where soon the logger's axe and saw would echo. The shivering passengers on those small steamers perhaps did not even glance through the icy windows at the desolate shore. They were far from civilization: far from the bustle of their great metropolis, Victoria; from the port with its ships pouring in from San Francisco and the Orient; from warm, comfortable rooms and from the theatre where that "charming little actress," Lulu Sweet, warmed the cockles of their hearts. (Lulu Island, in the Fraser River, is named after the popular actress.) They were probably more intent on keeping warm than on gazing out upon the southern shore where in 24 years a new city would appear, a city which would suck the commerce of the world away from Victoria and leave it just a little bit of old England. The passengers surely anticipated only their arrival at Port Moody, at the head of the inlet, and the five-mile wagon road to New Westminster.

It was a miserably cold winter on the mainland, but in Victoria's more salubrious climate the Chinese began to celebrate their New Year on January 29. The *Colonist* predicted that " . . . any amount of fire-crackers will probably be touched off by the Johns," and on the following day they commented further: "Yesterday our usually sedate Chinese residents engaged in ushering in their New Year in a noisy and jubilant manner. Hundreds of boxes of fire-crackers were set off, and the Johns exchanged calls and made themselves generally agreeable. Many white residents availed themselves of the opportunity thus afforded of by obtaining free drinks and eating chow-chow [pidgin English for Chinese preserve of orange-peel, ginger, etc.] with chop-sticks. Of course, on such a great and glorious occasion, this office was fully represented, especially in the chow-chow line." In future years Amor would be more careful with whom he ate.

It is not known how many Orientals lived in the city at this time, but those required to pay taxes for the half year beginning July 1, 1862 included Ah Foo (Fruiterer), Ah Sing (Trader), Du Quong (Trader), Fock Sing (Washman), Hong Sing (Restaurant Operator), Lee Yon Sin (Doctor), Lee Song (Apothecary) and Si Long (Chinese Trader). The heaviest assessment was levelled at the Hudson's Bay Company, to the amount of 25,000 pounds sterling, but next was none other than the Kwong Lee Company at 6,560 pounds, on which was paid a tax of 15 pounds. Janion and Green and J.J. Southgate were assessed at 6,000 pounds each, followed by four companies at between 2,000 and 6,000 pounds. At the 2,000-pound level were several establishments including De Cosmos (Printer) Government Street, Tai-Soong (Merchant) and the Yong-Wo-Sang Company (Merchants) each of whom paid a tax of six pounds. If this was any sign of the wealth of the city, the three Chinese merchant companies provided a remarkably large proportion of it.

The Chinese not only improved the commerce of the city but also contributed to the health and well-being of the good housewives of the town—or, more accurately of those households who could afford to own a Chinese servant. As Henry Pelling Perew Crease later pointed out, life in the colony had been rugged before the arrival of the Chinese. The lady of the house had to stand over a hot stove, clean her house and do the laundry. Occasionally she might acquire the services of a young English immigrant girl, but these were rare and unreliable. The Chinese proved to be ideal servants and the Oriental washman, trotting about the muddy streets with his bags of dirty linen strung across his shoulders on a bamboo pole, was a great boon to them.

No, the Chinese, as far as Victorians were concerned, were really quite useful and they promised to be more so, though always there were words of caution when further immigration was suggested. Amor De Cosmos pointed out that there were problems with the Chinese in Australia, and in March 1862, it appeared that the mining communities in California, which for the first time had a majority in the state legislature, would attempt to exclude the Chinese from the state. If this occurred, said De Cosmos, " . . . we see no substantial reason why this country—these colonies and the territory stretching from Fort Simpson [20 miles north of today's Prince Rupert] to the Arctic Ocean, may not provide an asylum for at least 50,000 Chinamen . . . . No one, perhaps, can be found in this country who would prohibit Chinese coming here at this early stage in our history; and whilst we are willing to invite them to this country to engage in every kind of employment, we cannot but forsee that a similar agitation must eventually rise in this country to what has occurred in Australia, or what is now going on in California, if we do not watch, guide and control the Chinese immigration from the beginning . . . ."

Amor always managed to protect his possible political future by covering all eventualities, though he did not forsee that within a few years it would be a distant government in Ottawa, rather than Vancouver Islanders or British Columbians, who would decide for or against restrictions on Chinese immigration. He continued to sally forth on his white charger to attack the Hudson's Bay Company, the House of Assembly and even the Commissioner of Police. The chain gang, it seems, was digging a sewer on Bastion Street and the stench was a most terrifying experience to the senses—"worse than a Chinese stink-pot," commented the quixotic editor of the *Colonist*. By now, however, he had been joined by another independent newspaper. In 1861, the New Westminster *British Columbian* rolled off its first issue. The editor was John Robson, a Canadian and the future leader in the fight against the Chinese. At the moment, however, Robson was more interested in attacking Governor Douglas. When His Excellency visited the mainland capital, Robson sarcastically headlined his report, "The arrival of the Czar," to which his fellow reformer in Victoria replied, "Rather expressive and more truthful than poetic."

But now the search for gold had shifted from the lower canyon and upper Fraser to Cariboo where, in August 1862, Billy Barker sank a shaft into the gravel of Williams Creek and Barkerville was born. In order to funnel the gold back to New Westminster and Victoria rather than across the unpatrolled border, James Douglas was blasting a road through the canyon which Simon Fraser had scaled 54 years earlier. By the end of the year, two and a half million dollars worth had tumbled down to Victoria, and the motley crew of miners were spreading along almost every creek in the mainland colony. There were diggings at the Stikine River, around Lake Okanagan, in the Shuswap country and even in the Peace River area. Not far behind them wherever they went were the ubiquitous Chinese, some working as labourers, some as washmen, some as restaurant operators and some actively working the diggings abandoned by whites or purchased from them. Five hundred Chinese were employed by Wright and Company at $40 a month, constructing the Cariboo Road.

1862 had been a prosperous year, but 1863 saw the beginning of certain changes in the two colonies. They were not happy ones for Governor Douglas, now 60 years of age. Perhaps the greatest project of his career, the Cariboo Road, was nearing completion by the end of the year, but the imperial government was not completely cooperative; it was curtailing its financial support, it was withdrawing its Royal Engineers and it delicately suggested that he should retire, to allow the appointment of two governors, one for each colony. Douglas borrowed huge sums to complete the Cariboo Road and sat back silently to listen to his critics. There promised to be detractors in the House after the summer's election; the bothersome editor of the *Colonist* was threatening to run for office.

When the brief campaign was over and the vote counted, Amor De Cosmos had won a seat in the House of Assembly, representing Victoria. He lost no time in leading the movement to unite the two colonies under one government, and in his newspaper he suggested many projects which would improve the efficiency and wellbeing of the colonies. His health, however, was suffering from overwork—or so he said—and on October 6, 1863, Amor De Cosmos wrote his last editorial for the newspaper he had established almost five years earlier. Island residents, however, could still read in the *Colonist* the long list of Caucasian names arriving on the *Sierra Nevada* ending, as did all passenger lists, with " . . . and five Chinamen." They could read, too, of the lawsuits against two young businessmen named Isaac and David Oppenheimer who, like the Chinese, would follow the trail of gold about the mainland, to settle 23 years later in a great city which in 1863 did not even exist.

In the spring of 1864, James Douglas ended a long and remarkable career as a Hudson's Bay Company official and governor. A magnificent banquet was held in the Victoria Theatre in his honour, he was knighted by the Queen, and he sat back to watch the "unmitigated muffs" who believed that they could govern better than he. The De Cosmoses, the Robsons and all the other "independents" were confident of better and more democratic times, now that he was out of the way. They would, in fact, do no better than James Douglas—indeed, perhaps no one has done better since.

The two new governors, however, were about to arrive, presumably full of zest and progressive ideas. Even before Douglas retired, a collection was being made for a reception for Arthur E. Kennedy, the new governor of Vancouver Island, the names of each contributor and the amount subscribed being duly published in the *Colonist*. The Chinese were not canvassed, but a letter to the editor in March testified to their generosity. "If the collectors appointed to receive donations for the governor's reception fund will call at Messrs. Kwong Lee and Co.'s Store on Cormorant street they may receive upwards of one hundred dollars contributed without solicitation by the Chinese residents of Victoria as a mark of loyalty to our Gracious Queen." It was signed, "Richard Hall, Sin Shang," and a few days later the gift of $103 was acknowledged by the reception committee.

After all the great preparations, Kennedy arrived quite unexpectedly on the *Brother Jonathan* from San Francisco on March 25, 1864, and the reception committee had to mobilize its forces in a hurry. The colonial secretary was the first to meet the governor and a parade was quickly organized, the Hebrews, French and Germans being well represented—but the Chinese were conspicuously absent, particularly in view of their unsolicited gift. There were floral arches, banners, stirring music, and hope, as ever, for a better future.

The new governor of British Columbia, Frederick Seymour, arrived on April 20 in New Westminster, where the citizens also bubbled with hope and great expectations. Perhaps they had more reason to do so than the Islanders; the axis of population and power was beginning to swing in their direction. The Island was said to have a population of 7,000; Cariboo alone had as many inhabitants, perhaps twice that number. The town that had sprung up around Billy Barker's claim had grown tremendously—some say to 10,000—and by the end of the year the Cariboo Road finally reached it.

By the summer of the following year, Barkerville had a weekly newspaper, the *Cariboo Sentinel*. It did not own as fiery an editor as the late proprietor of the *Colonist* in Victoria or the *British Columbian* in New Westminster. It was largely a mining newspaper, containing weekly reports from every creek and gulch for miles around. There were little groups of Chinese on almost all of them, but the greatest concentration of Orientals was at Quesnelmouth, where Kwong Lee had a store. He advertised in the *Sentinel*, as did several familiar Victoria firms, including the Oppenheimer boys and Arthur Bunster, the Victoria brewer who about this time was becoming interested in politics.

Barkerville was just past its peak in 1865, but its Chinese population was steadily increasing. "A large number of Chinese are building houses close to Barkerville with the intention of becoming residents of Cariboo," commented the *Sentinel* in the fall of that year. Justice of the Peace W.G. Cox noted the same tendency when he presided over the case of William Stewart against John Collins, Mary Boyle and "Sam (a Chinaman)." It seems that Stewart had entered Collins' bar where, in his apparently inebriated state, he found no one to attend him but Sam. He claimed he merely placed his hand on Sam's head and asked for a drink, whereupon Mary shouted to the Chinaman, "Take an axe and split open the——." Sam attempted to do so and a wild melee followed. Mr. Cox fined Stewart $5 for placing his hand on Sam's head and poor Sam got a 25-dollar fine "for the use of a deadly weapon or, in default, two months." Stewart agreed that since Mary was a lady, he would drop the charges against her. "I wish it to go forth," said Cox, "now that Chinamen are coming here in great numbers that they must not use deadly weapons . . . ."

But for its size and its strange conglomeration of people —Negroes, Chinese, French, Italian, British, Americans and Canadians—it was a fairly peaceful community. When Judge Begbie presided over his court in Richfield and Barkerville in June 1865, he noted that there was only one criminal case pending, "and that rightly belongs to 1864." The 46-year-old chief justice, "tall, well made and powerful, magnificent head, hair scanty and nearly white, with nearly black moustache and beard, full of wit"—as Dr. Cheadle[2] described him—was not overburdened with work. The *Sentinel* reported his hunting and fishing expeditions around Keithley Creek and Beaver's Pass.

Begbie was no doubt happy to escape the unpleasant political situation to the south. Governor Kennedy, after all the hopes that had been held for him, was not at all popular. There were terrible rumours that plans were being made to unite the two colonies and the Islanders feared their absorption by the growing giant across the gulf. New Westminster, with a trifling population of some three or four hundred, was beating its chest over the arrival of the telegraph from San Francisco in April 1865. Victoria could count 6,000 citizens, Nanaimo 800 at this time, but in Cariboo there was a population estimated as anywhere between 8,000 and 16,000. Indians and Chinese were stringing the telegraph in their direction, but Caribooites were not very happy: the usual rush of miners did not appear in 1865; there were few new, exciting gold discoveries; and they were most displeased with the new mining laws recently passed in their capital. They were pleased to hear that Governor Seymour was about to visit them, but after it had been announced that he had begun his journey northward, they learned that he had been given six months leave of absence. They were livid. "Our only object in desiring to see Governor Seymour here was that he might witness himself the disastrous results of his insane policy," roared the *Sentinel*. "We would advise His Excellency to remain in England when he gets there, as in the event of him returning here next year he will find the colony inhabited by Siwashes and Celestials alone...." The multinational citizens of Cariboo, many of them Canadians, were hardly enamoured of their English governor. When he returned, however, there were still a good number of whites about.

Seymour departed in 1865. The rumours of union persisted through 1866 until it was generally accepted that it was inevitable. Governor Kennedy slipped silently away, unlamented, before Seymour returned. His reception was cool on the Island but enthusiastic in New Westminster. Islanders waited despondently for his confirmation of union, and it finally came on November 6, 1866. "There was neither enthusiasm nor indignation expressed at the announcement," muttered the *Colonist* somewhat frigidly. The Islanders were a beaten people. Shower upon shower of humiliating conditions were poured upon them, not the least of which was that the capital of the single Colony of British Columbia (they even dissolved their ancient name) was the dismal little town of New Westminster. But the deed was done. All they could do was to complain. "This town of stumps," screamed the *Colonist*, "inaccessible in all seasons of the year . . . ," and it listed all the ships that had perished on the sands of the iniquitous Fraser.

The Chinese who had spread diffusely over the colony probably did not worry about the political problems in Victoria and New Westminster. It is difficult to indicate their numbers. Howay says there were "about 2,000" in the two colonies in 1864. This would appear to be a most conservative estimate if one considers the *Colonist*'s figures of 1860, when, in three months, 1,577 Chinese arrived in Victoria. There were no further significant newspaper reports following this one, though certainly some Chinese must have entered the country. Since there were no official records, no estimate could be placed on the number who walked across the border to or from Washington Territory, and no one bothered to keep an account of how many departed for China or San Francisco or, for that matter, of how many who simply died.

Whatever their numbers, there was no active agitation against the Chinese at the time of union. There was, however, some mild discomfort from the fear that they were taking over many of the diggings. Gold Commissioner Peter O'Reilly, in November 1866, gave a clear indication of this.

"Parties coming from Kootenay inform us that the Chinese have taken almost entire possession of that mining camp. When they first presented themselves in the diggings and purposed to purchase claims, the miners were informed by the commissioner that so long as they refused to sell out to the Chinaman, he would stand by them; but should any sell to the Chinese he would feel himself bound to extend all the rights and privileges to them which the law conferred upon free miners. The Celestials, however, bid high for claims and one after another sold out to them, receiving as high as $1,000 for claims which white men would not have paid one half of that sum for. Thus a large portion of the claims soon changed hands, and a Chinese population rapidly took the places of Europeans; we are told that next season will scarcely find a white man there, as the

Chinese are not only monopolizing the mines, but trade and commerce also. A short time ago they paid down $6,000 for a drove of cattle, and they are buying out merchants, butchers, bakers etc."

The Chinese continued to be treated with disdain, though when an Oriental was handled in an ungentlemanly fashion in Victoria, the citizens were appalled. Said the *Colonist*, "On Saturday an inoffensive Chinaman, while passing along Government street near O'Dwyer's bakery, was knocked from the elevated sidewalk into the street, and severely injured by a young white ruffian, who unfortunately made his escape although pressed by an eye-witness. The poor Celestial was assisted to his feet by passers by. It is to be regretted that the dastardly fellow cannot be traced and punished as he deserves." This same type of incident, with the same strange mixed response of condescension, sympathy and disgust, would be repeated many times over the next 20 or 30 years.

The Chinese, however, were sometimes more troublesome to each other than they were to the whites. There was a regular free-for-all amongst them in Quesnelmouth in October 1866. "A very serious riot took place here yesterday between the Chinese inhabitants," reported a *Colonist* correspondent. "The fight originated in a Chinese gambling house about some money, when the friends of each party adjourned to the street and fought it out. There must have been seventy-five in the fight at one time, using clubs, knives, hatchets, axes etc. None of them killed but about a dozen badly wounded. Had it not been for the great courage displayed by Chief Constable Trevor in quelling the riot, there would have been a great many killed."

In that warm but melancholy November of 1866, the First Nine, the Second Nine and the Cricketer's Nine were still playing "Base Ball" and W.J. MacDonald was being opposed in the mayoralty race by Arthur Bunster of ale fame. The *Colonist* supported MacDonald, since it felt Bunster was a businessman and his duties as mayor would clash with his private interests, though it conceded, "we know him to be a jolly good fellow and the brewer of an excellent article of beer." But Arthur's time had not yet arrived.

1866 was surely the saddest year in Victoria's existence. Perhaps one could not ridicule some citizens for speaking of the inevitability of confederation with Canada, but to others this was just another nightmare. They had had enough for one year; why worry about confederation now?—they might all be dead by the time it was forced upon them.

In 1840, the British government had passed an act of union

joining Upper and Lower Canada. This became "Canada," and from this country came the "Canadians" of Victoria, New Westminster and Barkerville. They were not especially admired on the Island, where most of the population was British. New Brunswick, Nova Scotia and Prince Edward Island were considering union in 1864 and, in the same year, Canada was urging the proposition. As the expanded Colony of British Columbia slid sadly into 1867, its citizens knew that confederation of the eastern provinces would soon occur, and they pondered the advisability of joining with them. Amor De Cosmos, a rabid promoter of the union between the two colonies, was an equally rabid confederationist; Amor was a Nova Scotian. John Robson, too, was in favour of binding the two coasts together, but of course John was a Canadian, born of Scottish parents in Upper Canada, as were many other citizens of the mainland. The loyal English and Scots of Vancouver Island were naturally more anticonfederationist. Split by such contentions, British Columbia was not yet ready to join the eastern provinces. To people like Dr. J.S. Helmcken (a "colonist" now for 17 years) and Attorney-general Henry Crease (a "colonist" for 9 years), home was still England.

The other popular subject of conversation in 1867 was the choice of a permanent site for the capital of the united colonies. With these disturbing problems on their minds, Victorians found no time to worry about the Chinese, though the New Year celebration could hardly be ignored. It burst upon them in early February that year, with the usual clamour—and they always seemed to enjoy it. "The Johns generally celebrate the event by snapping fire-crackers and calling at each other's houses," remarked the *Colonist*. In 1867, Pung Kee's celebrations were a little too vigorous for the shredded nerves of the depressed citizens.

"Pung Kee, a son of the Flowery Kingdom, was yesterday brought before Mr. Pemberton on a charge of setting off fire-crackers in the public streets, and also for assaulting Officer Ferrell when that officer came to arrest him. Pung pleaded that he had been making New Year calls; that he was elated in consequence of diverse drinks that he had imbibed at the houses of friends; that he was observing the New Years in an essentially celestial and thereby very proper manner and that the officer had no more right to interfere with his enjoyment any more than he (Pung) had to put a stop to the 'chlistmass' festivities of an Englishman. The accused, not with standing his eloquent, argumentative and logical defense was convicted, and ordered to appear for sentence."

On July 1, 1867, though no notice of it was prominent in New Westminster and Barkerville, the *Colonist* briefly commented on the confederation of Quebec, Ontario, New Brunswick and Nova Scotia, pointing out that some believed Canada would not accept a bankrupt colony such as British Columbia, while others thought it must, since "we are the western bulwark, as Nova Scotia and New Brunswick is in the east." The Islanders had become a pitifully submissive people, referring frequently to "the disagreeable past" and "this unfortunate colony."

Gold production improved slightly in 1867 and was expected to improve further in 1868. But the colony depended too much on the vagaries of this industry. " . . . a disaster at Cariboo is felt from one end of the Colony to the other," it was said, yet there was no other stable industry. The coal mines at Nanaimo were still comparatively small and the forest industry, which would sustain British Columbia over the next hundred years, was still in its infancy, though there were now two mills exporting lumber from Burrard Inlet.

That beautiful fjord on the mainland, however, was an isolated spot until the Fraser River froze again, most opportunely, in January 1868. The little steamer *Enterprise* once more turned to the inlet where its Victoria passengers saw the bark *Mercara* loading at Moody's Mill and the *Trebolgas* at Stamp's. It was this incident which all but condemned New Westminster to an icy death. Ten days later, when the *Enterprise* steamed out from Victoria, she met a number of Fraser River buoys floating out towards Asia, their chains ruptured by ice floes. "The government should not consume any more money in the vain attempt to convert an inland town into a commercial seaport," growled the *Colonist*.

On February 4, the Fraser opened again, and on April 2, the Legislative Council voted on the permanent site of the capital. Victoria was chosen, and the *Colonist*, barely suppressing its satisfaction, pointed out that citizens should not be excessively jubilant. It was only common sense to move "from a point so ill-adapted as New Westminster." The return of the capital could not possibly do much for the Island's tenuous state of economy, but its wounded pride was soothed.

The miners of Barkerville were not especially interested where the politicians placed the capital. They were very much in favour of confederation, what with all the Canadians about, but they did not grumble over the government's slow pace towards that event. They worked in their mines, drank in their saloons and whistled at the hurdy-gurdy girls in the Theatre Royal—until September 16, when the roof of Adler and Barry's Saloon burst into flames. It was almost in the centre of town, and the fire spread in all directions until it "swept past through Chinatown and exhausted itself for want of further prey." Within an hour and a half the destruction of Barkerville was complete.

The *Sentinel* listed the losses on both sides of the town. Included was $5,000 on the east side; $8,000 on the west side, for "sundry Chinese houses," the number of which totalled "about thirty." In addition, the Kwong Lee store, valued at $40,000, was destroyed, a loss topped only by the Hudson's Bay and Strouss establishments.

There were said to be many thefts during the panic, but they were soon forgotten in the great rush to rebuild the town. "The new Barkerville will rise . . . Phoenix-like, from the ashes," said the *Sentinel* a few days later. "Already buildings are being erected, amongst them ten Chinese houses." The Phoenix Brewery, so aptly named at this moment in Barkerville's history, was not required to rise from the ashes. It had been spared from the flames, along with the store belonging to the Oppenheimer boys.

With the capital now firmly established in their city, Victorians had at least regained some of their self-respect. Their little steamers bustled about happily and the great sailing ships slid silently up and down the coast. "The H.B.C. bark *Prince of Wales* sailed yesterday for London," reported the *Colonist*. "The steamer *Otter* towed the bark into the straits and left her to run out with a fair breeze." Victoria was a great shipping port. Arrivals and departures were always reported in great detail, as were ships overdue. In June 1869, it was H.M.S. *Sparrowhawk* that was a "non-arrival." Governor Seymour had been touring the coast on the British warship, and on June 15, Victorians were shocked to hear that he had suddenly died five days earlier, presumably of dysentery, in Bella Coola.

On June 17, it was announced that Anthony Musgrave was to be the new head of state. He appeared very quietly on August 23, joining Amor De Cosmos and Matthew Begbie as the most prominent bachelors in the colony.

Almost two months earlier, Canada had celebrated her second birthday. Under the heading "Dominion Day" the *Colonist* stated, "This is the anniversary of the birth of the Canadian Dominion. Throughout the interior there will be a general observance of the day, but here there will be no observance. Perhaps 'a change will come o'er the spirit' of our people before the first of July 1870."

Up in Barkerville, where the population was much less British and much more Canadian and American, preparations for Dominion Day and Independence Day had been going on for some time. There were races for everyone—children, adults, velocipedes—and for "Siwashes" and "Chinamen." The entrance fee for each was one dollar except for the boys' race, the Siwash race and the Chinaman race, for which there was no entry fee. First and second prizes for the latter two were six and four dollars, while for all others the prizes were ten and five dollars.

It was a great occasion; the British and American flags were both prominent, the French tricolour fluttered above the Hotel de France, and "over Mr. Cunio's establishment the flag of Italy quivered in the air." Dr. R. W. W. Carrall—another Canadian—led three cheers for the queen, followed by the same for the Dominion. In the next edition of the *Sentinel* the names of all the winners were listed, with the notable exception of the Siwash and Chinaman races. And just three days later it was all repeated, though true to tradition, Independence Day prizes were greater than those of Dominion Day.

The people of Cariboo were not only more interested in the Dominion, but were also more sensitive to the presence of Chinese than were the citizens of the southern portion of the colony. On July 24, 1869, the *Sentinel* reported very fully on the fire which had swept for several miles along the Quesnel River, with the death of ten Chinese, all "servants" of the Kwong Lee Company. On July 28, the same newspaper discussed a report on the evils of the Chinese in California. They believed it was exaggerated, " . . . but there is no doubt that the presence of a large body of Chinamen must be accompanied with a multitude of evils."

A week later, they attacked their own Oriental citizens. "Chinatown is universally voted a nuisance to Barkerville in every shape, sense or manner. Pigs are fed in the streets in front of the buildings; there is no regular sidewalk, the drainage is corrupted with animal and every kind of filth; in short, every inconvenience and disagreeable characteristic of a semi-barbarous race is present in Chinatown. Let the Grand Jury take the subject into consideration with a view to removing or modifying these evils. Pig-feeding in the streets ought to be stopped forthwith. A great many Chinamen have been sick lately, and no wonder. Let us compel them, however, for our own safety, to pay some attention to sanitary considerations. We have now a clean, neat looking town, but its neatness is marred by the causes above referred to."

The Orientals they had in their midst were peasants who were probably no more filthy or disagreeable than their white counterparts. They dressed differently, they wore their hair in pigtail fashion, they spoke little English and they did not mix well with the whites, unlike the Negroes and Indians, but they were generally law-abiding citizens. Indeed, it was occasionally the white boss who was brought to court by the Chinese labourer. In August 1869, for instance, Ah Gim brought action against none other than Oliver Cromwell, to recover $78 in back wages on the Eagle Creek claim. Unlike his 17th-century namesake, Oliver was a most submissive gentleman. He meekly agreed to pay Ah Gim from the declining profits of his claim.

Governor Musgrave had had a pointedly quiet reception in Victoria in August 1869. In September he set out on a Grand Tour of the colony. He received a much more hearty welcome in New Westminster, and when the townfolk of Barkerville heard that the governor would be paying them a visit in perhaps a week, they immediately held a general meeting; committees were struck and a grand celebration was prepared. Barkerville was always ready for another party, and on this occasion, the Orientals became involved. "The Chinese inhabitants, on this occasion, have acted well," said the *Sentinel*. "In that part of town inhabited by them there is every evidence of the slothful and repulsive habits of the Asiatics, but yesterday they set to work and, after cleaning the street, covered it with clean gravel and made the sidewalks and everything about them as tidy as possible under the circumstances. The celestials completed their attention to the occasion by the construction of an evergreen arch."

When the day dawned, Dr. Carrall, Thomas Pattullo and Isaac Oppenheimer rode out far from town to meet the visiting dignitary. A rider was despatched to warn the town of their approach and, as the governor passed beneath the four triumphal arches, "The Anvil Chorus Battery gave a Royal Salute and the Chinese burned myriads of fire-crackers, cheer after cheer rent the air and a general uncovering and waving of hats took place with continued cheering as the procession moved through town."

The governor, of course, dined in the Dominion Dining Rooms and later was serenaded by the Welsh Glee Club. There was certainly an international flavour to Barkerville. The most prominent emblem was that of the Dominion; a great pole had been implanted in the ground "on which the Union Jack with a beaver in red ground, was hoisted." But there were many British and American flags, as well as those of several other nations, including that of China.

"Three Chinese flags surmounted the pretty arch of the Chinamen," said the *Sentinel*, "and in large letters appeared, in English, 'Welcome to Cariboo', underneath some large Chinese characters expressing the same."

Numerous addresses were made to Governor Musgrave, amongst which was one by Dr. R.W.W. Carrall for the Chinese Committee. The address, welcoming the governor and expressing the Chinese residents' loyalty and devotion to the queen, was signed by six Chinese citizens, including Loo Cha Fan for the Kwong Lee Company.

Barkerville could not complain about its Oriental residents during this magnificent celebration. Indeed this was the closest to integration of the races that the colony had seen up to this point, and would see for many years to come. Said the *Sentinel*, "On this occasion the Chinese, having once commenced their part of the ovation, kept it up with enthusiasm, as if the Celestial Empress herself had come to Barkerville . . . . After the Governor arrived, the Chinese merchants and householders tried to outdo each other in exploding fire crackers and the rivalry increased so much that the Chinamen refused to work their regular night-shifts, in order that they might participate in the fun."

For some years, the British government had wished to rid itself of the responsibility of caring for its distant Pacific coast colony. The recipient of this gift would, of course, have to be an empire government, since a considerable amount of British capital had been invested in the colony. The young Dominion of Canada was the only candidate. There were, however, two obstacles. The first was that the Hudson's Bay Company owned all the land between Canada and British Columbia (Rupert's Land and the North-West Territories) and the second was that the truculent "colonists" of the west coast were not at all enamored of the Canadians. In 1870, Rupert's Land and the North-West Territories were acquired by Canada, and Governor Musgrave was given the task of persuading the colonists of the wisdom of joining confederation. There would be no trouble in Cariboo or the lower mainland, but on the Island there were old colonists such as Helmcken, Crease, Begbie and a host of others who outnumbered the Canadian hot-heads represented by Amor De Cosmos and John Robson—both of whom had been elected to the Legislative Council in 1866.

The loyal British colonists, however, were in a difficult position; they were deeply in debt, the gold mines were slowly declining, and their "home" government had publicly expressed the desire to abandon them. After a little sober thought, they had to conclude that their only hope of salvation would be to have some heavenly angel abolish their debt, construct a railroad from Canada and—if they had the courage to ask—construct a naval drydock at Esquimalt. There were only two angels available in 1870: Canada and the United States. The latter was an abhorrence to many. Confederation with Canada and annexation by the United States were discussed endlessly in the colony. Amor De Cosmos and a new face on the political scene, Robert Beaven, demanded confederation and responsible government, and Victorians gradually succumbed. A delegation of three was chosen to discuss the terms with the Canadian government: Dr. J.S. Helmcken, now 47 years of age; Joseph Trutch, the English-born engineer who had constructed much of the Cariboo Road and who was now 44 years of age; and Dr. R.W.W. Carrall, the 31-year-old bachelor from Woodstock, Ontario, and member of the Legislative Council for Cariboo.

They found the Canadian government in a most expansive mood. Before they knew it, their one million dollar debt was wiped out and they had the promise of a railroad which was to be started within two years and completed in ten. They also had the government's promise that it would use its influence to persuade the British government to maintain its naval station at Esquimalt and that Canada would provide a loan to construct the drydock. There were a few minor concessions they had to make, including a grant of land 20 miles on each side of the railway, for which they would be recompensed. It was that easy. On January 5, 1871, the Legislative Council of British Columbia met to discuss the terms of confederation, and a few days later accepted them. The Canadian and British governments completed the last details for the dissolution of the colony, due to take place formally on July 20, 1871.

During the year's negotiations over confederation, the Chinese received little attention. In May 1870, however, Victorians were no doubt amused to read the *Colonist* report, written in its usual derisive style, on the launching of a Chinese ship in the capital city.

"An oddity in the shape of a veritable Chinese junk, built near Mr. Lenevue's residence by Celestial junkbuilders was launched on Sunday. A good many Johns were present with a band that discoursed celestial (but by no means heavenly) music as the craft glided from the ways and rested on the bosom of the harbour. A feu de joie of snapping crackers and a bottle of medicated wine completed the ceremony. The junk will be rigged and placed in the local fish trade."

A bill introduced into the Oregon Legislature was received in Victoria with an equal touch of humour. The bill made it a penal offense for any person to wear his hair more than six inches in length. It was aimed, patently, at the Chinese queue; but, asked the *Colonist* puckishly, "What will become of the ladies should that law pass? Pigtails and Chignons must vanish together."

There were occasional reports of Chinese assaulting each other in gambling houses and on one occasion "a heathen Chinee" was caught stealing a pair of boots. "He was seized by the tail and dragged off to prison," said the *Colonist*. The Chinese New Year, of course, always brought at least one transgressor to the courts. In 1871 it was Ah Kee, who was fined $2.50 plus one dollar costs for setting off firecrackers in the street.

In January 1871, the *Colonist* printed two small but very significant items in its pages. The first was that Chinese were about to be put to work in the coal fields at Nanaimo and that the *Shooting Star* would bring an "invoice" of about a hundred on her next trip. The second item read, "We are glad to hear that Mr. Dunsmuir has been eminently successful in his search for coal in close proximity to the water. . . within half a mile of the steam boat landing and he expects to find it still nearer. Mr. Dunsmuir has, without a doubt, got a good thing, and we know of no man more deserving of it."

This was Robert Dunsmuir, the Scot whose father and grandfather had preceded him in the coal mining business in Ayrshire. He and his family (a son, James, had been born at the mouth of the Columbia River on the way north from San Francisco) arrived on Vancouver Island late in 1851. Robert, with his uncle, searched for and found coal deposits for the Hudson's Bay Company; then he had managed the London-based Vancouver Coal Company, which bought out the Hudson's Bay coal rights in 1852. Following this he prospected for the rival Harewood Company, and after that set out on his own. In 1869 he discovered "a splendid seam of coal at Wellington," not far from Nanaimo, and now in 1871 he had made a new discovery. The Dunsmuirs were on their way to becoming the great coal entrepreneurs of the country and were ultimately to set the style for gracious living in the future province.

James Watt's steam engine needed coal. This mineral was not as glamourous as gold; there were no stampedes to the coal fields, no overnight millionaires, no exotic champagne orgies to celebrate finds. Coal brought dusty, backbreaking labour to many, wealth to a few and a certain stability to the economy. It also brought to the future province the problems of the worst labour-management struggles in its history; strikes, riots, marshal law, court proceedings and anti-Oriental legislation.

In 1871, however, these disasters were still a few years away. There was another matter of interest to consider as the colony swept headlong toward confederation. In 1860, a motion to place a ten-dollar head tax on Chinese had been discarded on the grounds that it was not good for business. In May 1865, a similar motion had been defeated, since "in the present state of the colony at least, Chinese immigration was a thing to be encouraged." Now, in the last session of the colonial Legislative Council, the big, rough Irish brewer, Arthur Bunster—who had just defeated the mighty John Robson in Nanaimo—rose and moved an address "imposing a Poll Tax of $50 per head per annum on all Chinese engaged in any occupation in this colony." This was received by laughter, but Arthur pointed out that there was more pressure for such a motion from the citizens of the colony.

"It's going to be a test question at the next election—see if it ain't," he said. " ... I want to see Chinamen kept to himself and foul diseases kept away from white people....Why when I drive my wagon along the Esquimalt road past the hovels, the stench is enough to knock me off my seat....Everybody knows the Chinese don't pay any taxes if he can help it. Only forty-two have paid the school tax and there is no getting at them either. You go to one of them for taxes and see what he'll tell you. 'Me no go; no money. Me work for Kwong Lee!' Nine-tenths of the Chinamen work for Kwong Lee and the balance work for Sing Sing or some other Sing."

Arthur claimed that most of the crime in town was committed by Chinese; they blocked the streets with their smelly baskets hanging from long poles and "if you come along with your wife they say 'Gettee out, John, gettee out, John' and they shove you and your wife into the gutter and there ain't any law to prevent them."

This description was followed by roars of laughter, but it was typical of Arthur Bunster. He had always been followed by laughter in the past and would continue to be for many years in the future. Arthur was a big, heavy-set Irishman with thick, black hair parted carelessly down the left side of his massive head. He had fierce black eyes and a heavy, solid black beard and moustache. Since leaving Ireland he had wandered over the world, to settle in Victoria in 1858. He was an agent for the Colonial Brewery in 1860 and later became its owner. But Arthur could hardly be termed one of the more genteel aristocrats of the city. In 1860 he was charged with keeping a public bar room without a licence. In 1863, he was arrested for violently assaulting Terrence Monaghan; he was fined five pounds, but he got his money's worth by filling Mr. A.F. Pemberton's court with gales of laughter and making poor Monaghan look quite ridiculous. Two years later he was back before Mr. Pemberton, charged with driving over James Bay Bridge "faster than a walk." Arthur blamed his horse: "a peculiar one who could not be held. It once pulled a whole verandah down," and again the court roared with laughter. But Arthur Bunster had managed to win a seat on Victoria's City Council in 1869 when Mifflin Gibbs, a Negro alderman, "overstayed his leave of absence," and the following year he demolished John Robson in Nanaimo.

This then was the rough, Irish Arthur Bunster who would bring shouts of delight and merriment to the people of Victoria and Ottawa—and shudders of fear to the Chinese of British Columbia. In January 1871, his motion provoked laughter, sarcasm and criticism from the majority of the Legislative Council. Amor De Cosmos cautiously pointed out that the Chinese interfered with whites and monopolized the vegetable trade, but Arthur, on the advice of the attorney-general, withdrew his motion.

On July 7, Joseph Trutch was appointed lieutenant-governor of the new province. A huge committee including such luminaries as Bunster, Beaven, De Cosmos—and two Chinese, Kwong Lee and Ty Soon—made preparations for a massive celebration. One second into July 20, 1871 "bells were rung, guns fired, blue lights and Roman candles burned and crackers snapped," the *Colonist* reported. "And people met on the street and shook hands and congratulated each other, and cheered and cheered and cheered . . . ." It was a most unseemly display for old Victoria. But perhaps it was just the Canadians who were out there on the streets.

Helmcken and Crease and Begbie almost certainly were not there. Nor was the man who had spent the better part of a year tramping between Fort Vancouver near the mouth of the Columbia River and York Factory on Hudson's Bay, 36 years earlier; the man who had begun it all; the man who had guided the colony in its earlier years better than anyone had since—Sir James Douglas, now 68 years of age. Perhaps they were all fast asleep at one second after midnight on the 20th, or perhaps they patiently awaited the hour to raise their glasses in a sombre toast. It would be a sombre one. None of them was the type to enjoy a public display on the streets; none of them was particularly enthusiastic about confederation, but at least it was better than annexation. The De Cosmoses, the Carralls and the

Robsons were Canadians again. And they had their railroad—at least the promise of one—but there were loopholes in the Terms, and many unknown complications which, in the future, would bring strife to the new province.

CHAPTER II

1871-1880

*"Let This New Empire Be
For Our Own Race...."*
John Robson 1871

There were three matters to settle in the new province. The first and most immediate was the election of its political representatives and the appointment of their senatorial appendages. The other two matters were not urgent, but they were present and would become chronic: the construction of the railroad and the restriction of the Chinese.

In colonial days, elections had always been very informal affairs, and they were no less so when the colony became a province. There were no political parties, no demonstrations for favourite sons, and the perfidious heads of public relations men had not yet appeared. Voters would gather at a designated spot (in Victoria, the Police Barracks), candidates were nominated and seconded and a number of speeches were made. Voting would then take place by a show of hands; and, if the gathering was not satisfied, a poll would be demanded and a date set by the sheriff. Furthermore, elections were not held on the same day in the different districts. In the first provincial election, for instance, Victoria City chose her four members on October 16, 1871, while Nanaimo did not elect John Robson until October 19. On October 22, Victoria District elected Amor De Cosmos and Arthur Bunster, but Comox and Yale did not elect their members until October 26 and November 4 respectively. From this group, Joseph Trutch chose John Foster McCreight as the province's first premier.

Dominion elections, too, were pleasantly informal affairs held on various dates in different localities. In November, British Columbia's six members were elected, the most notable being the flamboyant Nova Scotian and former editor of the *Colonist*, Amor De Cosmos himself. He now held both a provincial and a Dominion seat.

Elections and appointments were all very interesting, but the railway was of much greater importance. Surveyors had actually arrived before July 20, and there was a great deal of discussion about the route the railway would follow to its terminus, which Victorians assumed would be at Esquimalt. Even at this early date they were a little impatient, especially with Sandford Fleming, the Dominion engineer, who was lolling about in New Brunswick with Charles Tupper. "Why don't he hasten to the shores of the Pacific where the great engineering problem awaits solution at his hands?" asked the *Colonist* on August 2, 1871. However, Fleming would not make his appearance for another year—and there were still almost fifteen years of impatience ahead.

As for the Chinese, there was a notable increase in newspaper reports concerning them in the latter half of 1871. Up to this time they were mentioned only occasionally. Perhaps this was natural. They took no part in public life and they lived in a tight little community near the waterfront, centred on Comorant Street and bounded loosely by Johnson, Fisgard and Store Streets. Apart from well-to-do merchants such as Kwong Lee, they were labourers of the peasant class—market gardeners, peddlers, woodchoppers and washmen. A few achieved the dignity of becoming house servants in aristocratic Victorian homes, but they were a greatly appreciated few. Although most scurried back to Chinatown each evening, some lived in those ornate mid-Victorian homes set in neat little gardens of pansies and hollyhocks, shaded by beech and oak trees. Sideboard houses they were, with spacious verandahs stretching all along their width and long Roman columns supporting their roofs. There were gables—numerous gables—and perhaps a tower or two coated with scalloped shingles, pointed at the top. There might be a balustraded balcony, sometimes covered, sometimes not. And every edge and every eave of every roof was outlined with fluted, elaborate, Victorian trim. In the cluttered drawing rooms there were high-backed wicker chairs and hand-sewn cushions and tinselled lamps and tea wagons and tea services and tea cosies. There were pianos and desks and dim photographs in ornate frames. And potted plants beneath tasselled drapes.

If you knocked on the door it might be opened just a crack, and then an inch or two, and a strange oriental tongue might ask who you are and what you want. That would be Gee, if you knocked on Mrs. W.A. Baillie-Grohman's door. And if you happened to bear the tall, imposing figure of Judge Matthew Baillie Begbie, wearing a top hat on your head and showing the bowl of your pipe sticking out of your waistcoat pocket, you would be admitted immediately. The judge often dropped into the Grohmans' for lunch on the Sabbath, after raising his voice in praise in the choir of St. John's Anglican Church. Gee was most impressed with the judge; but if you happened to be a mere naval lieutenant or even a close friend such as Mrs. Drake, Gee might just be a little difficult.

Florence Baillie-Grohman came to Victoria from England with her husband, the sportsman and author, who, in 1889, completed the canal joining Kootenay River and Columbia Lake in the area now known as Canal Flats. They had taken a furnished house; with the furnishings came the 18-year-old houseboy, Gee. It was a novel experience for the young London aristocrat, who, of course, was quite familiar with well-trained English butlers and chambermaids, but completely unfamiliar with those household tasks which today's housewife would consider routine. In the very first week of her residence, for instance, Mrs. Grohman found a broom and dust pan in the drawing room. She told Gee to remove it. "O I tink you sweep out dlawing loom today, velly good," he answered. ". . . I no do that loom; missus she do him evely week; I no time." Since Gee had already proven that he was a magnificent worker, Mrs. Grohman set to the task, though she had never cleaned a room in her life. Gee watched for a few minutes and then he said, "Missis Gloman, you go out walk, I tink.... You no know how, you give me bloom, you go lunch with Missus Dlake."

But her relationship with Gee was a pleasant one. Certainly she made him aware that, next to her husband, she was the "boss." Perhaps she was a trifle condescending, as she was with her occasional white chambermaid, but she was also very kind to Gee. She taught him to write, she sewed him little articles for his pleasure, and on one occasion when the local police expressed complete disinterest in a group of small boys who threw stones at Gee every time he passed a vacant lot, she personally escorted her Chinese servant past the danger area. And in return, not only did Gee provide remarkable service as a cook, a washman and a housemaid, but also chattered away incessantly to his "boss," much to her interest and amusement.

Like so many whites, Mrs. Grohman had the impression, only partially correct, that the Chinese believed in—and even saw

—spirits and devils, often stimulated by the use of opium. She argued these matters extensively with Gee who always seemed to conclude the discussion with a shrewd and subtle statement. She once asked him why, if he believed in joss, did he not go to the joss-house more often.

"It cost me two bits," he answered.

"Why do you have to pay to go to the joss-house?"

"All the same you pay in church, to keep debil away."

When Mrs. Grohman asked why he took chickens and wine and cakes to graveside ceremonies and then brought them home and ate them himself, he answered by way of a pretty and perceptive metaphor. He picked up a cup and held it in front of a lamp so that a sharp shadow fell on the white table cloth. "You see that?" he asked, pointing to the shadow. "Dead men all the same that, he eat all the same that (shadow) of food and wine. I this," and he flicked the cup with his finger. "If I no get all the same this food and wine, me pretty soon die quick."

And then there was the matter of wives. Mrs. Grohman was filled with righteous Victorian indignation when she discovered that the two Chinese ladies with whom she was sitting (they were Gee's friends) were wives of the same husband. She was also shocked at Gee's sympathizing with his friend, Ah Wan, not because Wan had just lost a wife through suicide, but rather because he had paid a considerable sum for that wife just a year ago.

"How much boss he give your father for you?" Gee asked. When Mrs. Grohman explained that her father had been paid nothing, Gee considered this the height of foolishness. He was there in Victoria hoping to save a few hundred dollars, at which time he would return to China where his mother would arrange a suitable marriage at a cost of $250 to $300. Gee was willing to play a servile role in white society in order to achieve his ambitions—to return to China with money, to marry and to sire a son. He achieved all three goals. Some time after his departure, Mrs. Grohman had letters from Gee telling of his good fortune, but he would not return in spite of her entreaties. It was a disappointment. ". . . As an average they are good," she remarked, in reference to the Chinese house servant, "comparing more than favourably with the ordinary Western help. . . who expects to be treated as an equal."[4]

All the Chinese intended to return, like Gee, comparatively wealthy to their homeland, not out of patriotism, but because of a cult of ancestral worship. They were indeed not returning to China but rather to an ancestral graveyard where they expected to be worshipped, just as they had worshipped their ancestors. The Chinese companies who brought their countrymen either to California or to British Columbia were bound to return the remains of deceased Orientals, about seven years after burial. Victorians were always fascinated by the festivity of a Chinese funeral but somewhat disgusted with the Oriental habit of exhuming the bones, which sometimes included particles of flesh from long-deceased countrymen.

One of the earliest examples of the increase in anti-Chinese sentiment following confederation was the report of a fire in a "Chinese Dead House" on Store Street. The mortal remains of 50 Chinese lay there, awaiting shipment. They were not destroyed, though it was assumed they were meant to be. "Dead or alive, the Chinaman must put in an appearance in his native country or the company suffers a heavy pecuniary consequence," reported the *Colonist*. "Women are considered mere chattels and may lie where they die. There is only one excuse that will be accepted as valid for the non-production of a man. Should his remains be destroyed by fire, the responsibility of the company ceases. Therefore, if the building set on fire yesterday morning had been burned down, fifty dead bodies would have been consumed with it, and the company would have been spared the expense of shipping the ghostly remains to the Flowery Kingdom .... There is abundant evidence that the fire was caused designedly."

Reports of Chinese crimes—embezzlement, burglary, assault—also increased significantly and the lynching of 50 Chinese in Los Angeles was described in considerable detail. The most remarkable reference to Orientals, however, was carried in a despatch from London where there had been a bitter struggle between labour and capital. "We should not be at all surprised," the despatch read, "in these days of excessive competition, rapid locomotion and the Suez Canal if before long we saw John Chinaman and party hard at work over here."

John Robson's newspaper was incredulous. "This from England?" the editor asked in dismay. "Britain has set a noble example by freeing slaves from her dominions....She has suppressed the slave trade in Africa and the Coolie slave trade in China. . . . Is it possible that England, Christian, philanthropic England, is going to turn round now and tarnish her brightest escutcheon, give the lie to her best professions and stultify her noblest acts by introducing coolie slave labor—for that is what Chinese labor really means—to compete with her own struggling sons—to snatch the last morsel of bread from the already half-famished millions of her own flesh and blood? We cannot believe it.

"Two thirds of the population [of England] are kept in grinding and unrequited toil that the remainder may roll in luxury and wallow in accumulating wealth.... Let labor be fittingly rewarded .... Let this new Empire be for our own race, and for free and requited labor and let it be our earnest aim from the first to give labour its true position and its fitting reward. So shall we succeed in building up a great, free and enlightened commonwealth in British North America."

This was the material which Victorians and many other British Columbians read as the day for the meeting of the first provincial Legislative Assembly approached. It came on February 15, 1872, and on the fourth day of that first session, John Robson gave notice of two motions he would place before it. One week later, he moved that a bill be sent to the Dominion House during its present session, providing for the imposition of a per capita tax of $50 per annum upon Chinese in the province. It was almost the exact motion that Arthur Bunster had proposed, and was persuaded to withdraw, at the last session of the colonial Council.

John Robson suspected there would be constitutional objections by the attorney-general, but, he said, "after all, constitutions are very much what people make them." Premier and Attorney-general McCreight had to agree that the Chinese did not pay their fair share of tax, but like the true lawyer, he quoted the British North America Act and stated that the resolution was unconstitutional. It was a word which would haunt British Columbians for many years—and one that would always bring forth recollections of Robson's observation on the fallibility of constitutions.

There were several men who sat and listened or spoke that day, men who would play an important role in the future of the province and of the Chinese. Amor De Cosmos unfortunately had departed to take his seat in the Commons on February 24, but there were others: Robson, Beaven and Bunster, who voted in favour; George A. Walkem, Charles Semlin and William Smithe, who voted against it. The latter, perhaps in jest, perhaps not, suggested a tax on queues rather than heads, "Chinamen being more willing to lose their heads than their tails." The resolution was defeated 14 votes to 6.

Editorial response to this precipitate attack on the Chinese varied. The Victoria *Standard* (published by Amor De Cosmos since June 1870) protested the Robson motion, saying it was "unmitigated buncombe, a bid for cheap and nasty popularity that might win the admiration of the unwashed." Robson was represented as "catering to an unreasonable prejudice existing against the Chinese population . . . ."

The *Colonist* angrily answered that it was not "buncombe" and unreason. The per capita tax "is based on the assumption that the Chinese do not now contribute their fair quota toward public revenue. Will our contemporary [the *Standard*] contend that they do? Almost the only tax that reaches them is the indirect one imposed under the Customs Tariff; it will hardly be contended that they are anything like as large consumers of dutiable goods as are the Caucasian race. . . . Can Englishmen, Scotchmen, Irishmen and Americans live as Chinamen do—packed together in a smoked hole, like sardines in a can? The Chinese trader's outfit is a bamboo stick and two baskets. The Chinese laborer's his chopsticks. How is it possible to place the two classes on a level? No general system of taxation can do it, for what is sauce for the Mongolian goose is sauce for the Caucasian gander. The habits and modes of life are essentially different and they must be exceptionally dealt with.... The Caucasian laborer keeps a house, raises a family and does his part toward maintaining all institutions of a civilized Christian community. The Mongolian laborer emerges from his sardine box in the morning, consumes his pound of rice and puts in his days work, baiting naught from his earnings, save the veriest pittance he subsists on. No wife and children to feed and clothe and educate, no church to maintain, no Sunday clothes to buy, he saves nearly all he earns, is a useless member of society and finally carries with him all his hoardings home to China. . . ."

In 1872, one could hardly deny such an argument—barring the characterization of the Chinese as "a useless member of society"—but the motion failed, and on February 27 Robson rose again in the Assembly to move "that effectual measures be adopted for the purpose of preventing the employment of Chinese labor upon the public works of this Province, or upon any Federal works within the same . . . ."

The railway was a federal work and British Columbians all wanted the railway, but virtually no one wanted the Chinese. It had been found necessary in California to use thousands of Orientals to build the railroad there, and British Columbians knew that the same would happen in their province. If, however, it came to a question of "no Chinese, no railroad," they would grudgingly accept the Oriental. The railroad was an economic necessity for their development and a buffer against the vague possibility of annexation by the United States.

The members of the local house all spoke against the Oriental, and yet the majority opposed the motion. The premier himself said it would give their opponents (largely in Ontario) an excuse not to build the railway and that it was "impolitic and illegal." Said T.B. Humphries, "The resolution is pure buncombe."

Robson did his best to persuade the Assembly of his wisdom, and they would dearly have loved to accept it, if it were not for the railroad and that old bugbear, "the constitution." Though aware that his motion was unconstitutional and would be defeated now, Robson was assured of its inevitable acceptance. His final words in the debate were paraphrased in the *Colonist*: "Although voted down today, the principal was as certain to triumph as Truth itself. He and the seconder might . . . stand alone; but he would prefer standing alone, even without a seconder, in a good cause, to going with a majority against it." He also asked that the names of all those who voted "aye" and "nae" be recorded "as we are writing history now." This was followed by laughter, but John Robson, a first generation Scots-Canadian, a British Columbian resident for 13 years and now 48 years of age, had the insight to foresee a future problem and the courage to express it with restraint. There were only 5 "ayes" (Robson, Beaven, Robertson, Semlin and Bunster) and 17 "naes," including McCreight, Walkem and Smithe.

The business of the Assembly continued that day with Arthur Bunster presenting a bill for the registration of births, deaths and marriages. When asked if it included native Indians, he answered that it included neither Indians nor Chinese.

The first session of the first Legislative Assembly had seen the presentation of two anti-Oriental bills, both defeated. It was the impending construction of the railroad which obsessed the members. The railway was on everyone's mind. The railway made the news. Victorians might note that Dr. Livingstone, who was always getting lost somewhere in Africa, had been found again, this time by a New York newspaperman, or they might read the usual reports of an imminent "find" in Cariboo or Omineca. But it was the railway, not mines nor missionaries, which drew their undivided attention. "THE TERMINUS! ESQUIMALT SELECTED," the *Colonist* headlined in April 1872. They had known it was coming; surveyors could be found in almost every valley, pass and water course in the province. They were not at all sure when it would come; but when it did, those with any foresight knew that Chinese labour would pour into the province. They had only to look to the south.

British Columbia was closer to California both in terms of geography and in terms of communications than it was to Ottawa. One needs only to read the account of Milton's and Cheadle's journey across the continent, or that of Sandford Fleming and George Grant, to realize how impossibly distant Ottawa was from Victoria. There was even a closer spiritual affinity to California. The histories of the state and province were remarkably similar—a peaceful, isolated corner of the globe suddenly stirred into frantic activity by a gold rush, each followed by peaceful immigration of Chinese. Both had united with the older, more civilized regions in the east, yet both had remained isolated. Both were separated from the federal seat of government by thousands of miles of sparsely populated prairie and impassable ranges of mountains. Each required a railroad if it were to progress. California got hers in 1869, but she got it with Chinese labour. Chinese were recruited from all over the state and thousands more were shipped from Canton, crowded together like cattle, below decks. To the surprise of many, the Oriental toiled as well as the white; to the delight of Leland Stanford and Charles Crocker, he toiled cheaply; to the horror of many, he was a threat to labour, morals and state economy—or so they said. He became the scapegoat of society, especially in times of depression, and this had led to demonstrations, riots and lynchings.

British Columbia was about to get its railroad, and John Robson meant to avoid the complications, which history had taught him were inevitable, should the Chinese construct the railway. Neither he, nor anyone else at this time, spoke of Chinese crime, opium dens or the health hazard. Neither he, nor anyone else, spoke of the Opium Wars, of British troops slashing through the countryside to open China to James Watt's steam engine and the grasping paws of British industrialists.

There was no observable increase in anti-Oriental sentiment following prorogation of the Legislature, though the Chinese were always referred to in an imperious and contemptuous manner as "almond-eyed pedlars," "rascals," "Celestials" or "Heathen Chinee." Occasionally they made the news in matters unrelated to gold mines, crime and potential immigration. One of the hazards in life before the automobile made its appearance was that of the runaway horse. Over the space of a few months, there was a major epidemic of such accidents in Victoria, all involving Chinese draymen. On such occasions, the *Colonist* took great delight in describing the incident in terms of a wagon running away with a horse. When a correspondent asked, "Why do horses driven by Chinese display so extraordinary a penchant for running away" the answer was, "Because in the first place, John always buys the cheapest animal and he either gets 'sold' with a broken-winded, spavined brute or a 'tricky' one that is sold because of its failings; and secondly, because Chinamen, as a rule, know as little of managing a horse as elephants do of climbing trees."

And in March and April winds, their kites caused no end of trouble. "We beg to draw to the attention of the City Council," said the *Colonist*, "to this nuisance. Both whites and Chinamen are in the habit of flying kites in our public streets, and are the source of a great annoyance to passers-by and of fright to horses. It was a Chinese kite which started off Mr. Piper's mare on Wednesday and was the cause of her death. The council ought to prevent the flying of kites in the streets. There is plenty of room for such amusement at Beacon Hill. In San Francisco, a person convicted of kite flying in the streets is fined $100."

There was some interest in the establishment of a boot factory in Belmont, using Chinese trained in San Francisco, but in late 1872 and early 1873 there were more fascinating matters to consider. These began in June when it was rumoured that John Hamilton Gray was to be appointed as British Columbia's third judge. "Who is Colonel Gray?" asked the *Colonist*, and proceeded to reveal that he was born in Bermuda of English stock and had been a member of the Executive Council, attorney-general, premier and speaker of the assembly in New Brunswick. When that province united with Canada, Gray sat in the House of Commons. It was not mentioned, but he was also a Father of Confederation before those venerable gentlemen, by the passage of time, were elevated to the stature of saints.

This was the province's introduction to political patronage. De Cosmos' newspaper, the *Standard,* began to speak of "British Columbia for British Columbians" and continued to do so into 1873, when another easterner, L.T. Dupont, was made internal revenue collector. Matthew Baillie Begbie growled in his beard over Gray's superfluous appointment, but he and Henry Crease took their seats on the bench with Gray in October 1872, listened patiently to the reading of his commission and swore in the political appointee. Sir John A. MacDonald looked after his friends.

There was also a Dominion election in 1872. The six members from British Columbia had travelled by ship to San Francisco and across the continent by train to attend only the last session of the House. By the time they had returned by the same slow, circuitous route, elections were already under way in the east. Indeed, on nomination day in Victoria, shocking news reached the city. Sir Francis Hincks, minister of finance in Sir John's Conservative government, had been defeated in his Ontario riding. British Columbia still had no political parties, but its citizens had naturally polarized themselves to Sir John's side, since he had been so gracious in the Terms of Union, while Alexander Mackenzie, leader of the opposition "Grits," had been most unpleasant. It was an absolutely beastly thing to defeat Sir Francis, and the *Colonist* had the audacity to suggest that Mr. Wallace and Mr. Bunster withdraw their names in Vancouver District (that electoral district of the Island north of Victoria) and allow Sir Francis to take the seat unchallenged.

Surprisingly, the fiery, ambitious Arthur Bunster withdrew, as did Mr. Wallace, and Sir Francis, without being closer than 3,000 miles to the Island, became member for Vancouver District and the province's first cabinet minister, though the Conservative victory was a narrow one. "Mr. Bunster M.P.P. [Member of the Provincial Parliament] ... showed true patriotism," said the *Colonist*—suggesting, of course, that to be a "Grit" was treasonous.

In due course, Amor De Cosmos again won the Victoria seat, and in Yale District a rising star and one of the province's many great engineers, Edgar Dewdney, was elected. Thirty-seven years of age at the time, he would later become involved in the Chinese problems. The House of Commons, however, produced nothing in regard to the promised railway, but the provincial legislature, meeting in mid-December 1872, was notable for two events. The first was that McCreight was defeated and replaced by Amor De Cosmos as British Columbia's second premier. The other was the passage of a bill to abolish dual representation. De Cosmos was the only individual who sat in both provincial and federal Houses, but for the moment, he was safe. It would not come into effect until after the present sitting.

Although there was a distinct lull in the harassment of the Oriental during the first seven months of 1873, an Anti-Chinese Society made its appearance in May of that year. There were to be others in future, all with similar names and composed largely of the same people. The 1873 organization passed resolutions demanding a revision of the treaty that permitted the immigration of Chinese, the withdrawal of the subsidy from China's ships, and the passage of a law that would forbid men working more than eight hours a day. It appeared to be a most inappropriate time for such a group to organize, though through all this period the newspapers were full of reports of increasing immigration and an increasing number of assaults, riots and anti-Oriental legislation in California. The infamous Queue Ordinance, requiring all prisoners to have their hair cut to within one inch of the scalp, was passed in the state at this time. By June, it was believed that these incidents were driving Chinese from

California to British Columbia, and by August there was considerable concern felt in Victoria. In that month, the *Colonist* printed a long editorial on "The Mongolian Race."

"Bret Harte made himself famous by his 'Heathen Chinee' [in a widely read poem entitled "Plain Language from Truthful James"] but he left the Heathen where he found him," the article read. "If one might venture to judge, the signs of the times indicate a less agreeable and poetic inspiration on the part of the Mongolian race, on this coast. It is now considerably more than a twelvemonth since we endeavored to impress the reader and legislator with the duty of guarding the labor interests against the intrusion of this race, and at the same time, having recourse to such special taxation as would compel these peculiar people to contribute something like an equitable ratio toward the public revenues of the country which gave them a home and protection to life and property . . . ."

The situation in California, Oregon and Washington, the editor said, was explosive. "Indeed the increasing volume of Chinese immigration (to British Columbia) for some months observable, may in a very great measure be traced to the expulsion policy of our neighbors. Those who are in the habit of resorting to our wharves will be aware of the increase. The time seems to have arrived when this question can no longer be blinked and we are glad to see a growing recognition of its importance."

The *Cariboo Sentinel* also spoke of "the evil effects of the employment of Chinese, or what might rightly be called slave labor." Even the Ottawa *Citizen* noted the presence of Chinese in the distant Pacific coast. "We dare say the time is not too far distant," they said, "when we shall see in British Columbia a very considerable Chinese population. The moment the Canadian Pacific is commenced, there will probably be an influx of Chinese into the labor market to meet the large demand that will necessarily arise for servants, navvies and laborers of all classes."

There was no doubt that anti-Oriental sentiment was again gathering momentum. A former resident of Australia suggested the adoption of a law passed in that country. It charged every ship carrying Chinese $50 a head and, in addition, each Chinese had to pay a tax of $20 a year. "The ladies of Australia," said the former resident of the Antipodes. "have a higher sense of delicacy than to allow a Heathen Chinese to make their beds or wash their body linen, for I never saw, during a residence of between four and five years, a Chinaman employed as a domestic servant or one peddling with baskets."

As 1873 drew to a close, there were ever-increasing complaints of firecrackers being set off in the streets, the blocking of sidewalks with Chinese merchandise and of "A Pagan holiday." Said the *Colonist*, "On Friday night a Chinese laundryman married an almond-eyed beauty. On Sunday the fellow countrymen of the bride and groom passed the day setting off firecrackers in the public streets and beating tom-toms. Such a scene would not be tolerated in any other town on the coast, and if a white man were to set off squibs or firecrackers even on a week day he would be stuffed into gaol instantly. Why Chinamen should enjoy immunity, and on the Sabbath, too, we cannot imagine."

With this constant barrage of anti-Chinese commentary, it was perhaps to be expected that John Robson would raise the matter again in the provincial House. He did so in January 1874, two years after his first motions had been defeated. In his constituency of Nanaimo, he said, there were 250 Chinese who were gradually monopolizing all the light occupations, taking bread out of the mouths of whites. They were there to the injury of the white miner, merchant and artisan; their occupation as domestic servants was a very great evil as it prevented female domestics entering the field; and he advocated his tax as an act of justice to every white citizen.

Arthur Bunster, in seconding the motion, "held it quite competent for the House to go after an obnoxious class as these Chinese," reported the *British Colonist*. "He said a doctor should examine all immigrants to see their hair was cut the orthodox length—six inches. Also that they be vaccinated."

George A. Walkem, the attorney-general and acting premier, of course said that it was all most unconstitutional, though he was obviously in favour of the tax, as were all others who spoke. Before the matter was voted upon, Arthur Bunster made a motion to impose a tax of $5 on all persons wearing queues, and John Robson enforced it with a plea not to worry about legal opinions—they were often wrong. Vote now and let the legal opinions come later, he said.

Robson's arguments were always hopefully logical, never insulting to the Chinese. Arthur of Bunster Ale managed to be much more obnoxious. Neither approach succeeded. In spite of general sympathy to the tax, the resolution was defeated.

Following this, politicians were so occupied with affairs in Ottawa that they had no time to worry about immigration, coolie labour and pagan holidays. "The Pacific Scandal," as it was known, had begun in the spring of 1873, when there were accusations of bribery and corruption in the Conservative hierarchy in awarding contracts for the eastern portion of the railway. British Columbia's darling, Sir John A. MacDonald, was in a very precarious position. Indeed, the attack upon him by the evil Grits was so intense (the *Colonist* referred to it as "un-British") that he was forced to prorogue parliament and appoint a Royal Commission to investigate the matter. When the House opened again in October 1873, Sir John valiantly defended himself, but it was a losing battle. He resigned, and the opposition, under Alexander Mackenzie, formed a government.

This was a cruel blow to British Columbia's hopes for an early start to the railway. Mackenzie had violently opposed the concessions made to the western province, and just a few days earlier his Grits had complained that British Columbia had only 925 voters but six M.P.s. Mackenzie won a comfortable victory in the ensuing election—and Amor De Cosmos had to hurry back from England to campaign. He announced that he would resign from the provincial legislature, but before he could do so he became involved in the Texada Island Scandal and in an insurrection led by Dr. J.S. Helmcken. Amor, however, won his old seat in Victoria.

Arthur Bunster took the Vancouver District seat formerly held by Sir Francis Hincks. Arthur was an ambitious man, both politically and professionally. His brewery was a great success and now he was constructing a flour mill on Johnson Street—indeed, blustery Arthur Bunster had been promoting agriculture as hard as he was able. An Ottawa newspaper described him as a brewer and agriculturist. "He is also a great anti-pigtail champion," they said, "and is pretty sure to bring the 'Heathen Chinee' question under discussion."

George Walkem replaced De Cosmos as premier. In 1863, at the age of 29, he had delighted Dr. Cheadle with his humorous tales of western justice, and later that year the diminutive bachelor accompanied the two English adventurers, Cheadle and Lord Milton, to San Francisco, where he showed them the merrier sights of the city. Eleven years later he was premier and much more serious. It was the railroad. The Dominion had promised a start by July 1873 but it was now July 1874 and nothing had been achieved except a multitude of surveys and hours and hours of arguments. Furthermore, there were no prospects of anything being achieved in the near future. Walkem set off for Ottawa, threatening to travel to England to place his complaint over the delay of the railroad before the imperial government—who had more or less forced his province into confederation. Walkem dallied in Ottawa for weeks—threatening, negotiating and hoping. Finally he gave up and sailed for England, where he arranged for Lord Carnarvon to arbitrate British Columbia's opposition to relaxing the Terms of Confederation. Mackenzie, however, would have nothing to do with arbitration.

There were no people dancing in the streets on Dominion Day 1874, as there had been in 1871. "To the Pacific province," said the *Colonist*, "the day is painfully suggestive of broken promises and blasted expectation, and will not, on that account, be celebrated with as much loyal enthusiasm as might otherwise have been the case...."

But the First of July was still a holiday. Most citizens of Victoria found their way out of town to picnic, though "some parties" remained behind to lower the flags of the city to half-mast. One enthusiastic gentleman, when he saw this proud display of British Columbia independence, rushed off across James Bay to the Provincial Buildings where he broke a window, climbed to the top of the cupula and lowered the flag to half-mast. There was even less enthusiasm in Cariboo, though they still had their quoit matches, horse races and foot races, again with a special entry for Siwashes and Chinamen.

"Unfortunate Columbia!" sighed the *Colonist*. It was worse for the Islanders since it became more and more apparent that, should the railway ever appear, it would not end in Esquimalt. H.J. Cambie and John Trutch were surveying the Fraser River route to Burrard Inlet and those unhappy terms "Secession" and "Annexation" were being heard again. The situation was almost as gloomy as the days just before and after the union of the two colonies.

The Chinese of Victoria, never actively persecuted, went unobtrusively about their business in what was now being referred to as Chinatown. Some slipped out into the white community to peddle vegetables, chop wood or act as servants. Several of them advertised quite freely in the newspapers:

"Kim Win, Washing, Ironing and Fluting, Yates street opp. Wells Fargo. Has had 15 years experience in the best laundries in the U.S. on the most difficult work. Satisfaction guaranteed at very low rates."

"Hung Gay, Grocer and Intelligence office Keeper. Has removed to Yates street, opposite Mr. Chadwick's International Hotel."

"Chong Kin. Store street between Johnson and Cormorant streets. Manufacturer and wholesale dealer in CIGARS."

"Dr. Ma Choo Tsung (from Canton) Surgeon and Physician. Cormorant street opposite Orleans Hotel. Certified by English and American Consuls at Canton as being duly qualified; solicits the attention of the afflicted."

"Dr. Ying. From the College of Medicine, Canton. Lately arrived. Cures consumption, bleeding of the lung, paralysis and other diseases. Johnson street next door to On Ming's."

On one occasion, to dispel temporarily the gloom hanging over Victoria, the *Colonist* printed a long humorous tale on the death of a cat.

"All Chinamen took a holiday yesterday to attend Judge O'Reilly's levee at the Police Court where they watched the proceedings with lynx-eyed interest. The cause of the examination was a cat, and a dead cat, at that. A charge of cruelty to animals was preferred by one Chinaman against another. . . . Mr. Courtney stated that the cat, when alive, was invaluable. It had caught rats and mice beyond the power of man to count, within a reasonable number of years. Other Chinamen saw that cat and envied the fortunate possessor. They offered him large sums of money for it; but he refused to part with the household treasure. In one evil hour, the cat's owner 'fell out' with another Chinaman and the latter cast about him for revenge. Presently he thought of the unfortunate cat, and he went out and bought a bit's worth [12¹/₂ cents] of poison and cannily concealed it in some meat and dropped it just where the cat came and gobbled up the meat, and laid down immediately and died. And then the per-fidious poisoner hid and watched till the owner appeared and revel-led in his great grief and then went to bed to sleep the sleep of the just. But suspicion fell upon the guilty man. The owner suddenly found that the cat was worth $700 and went and lodged a complaint . . . but the magistrate held that the case was one for the City Court and dismissed the charge with costs. And one half of Chinadom cheered the follower of Lucretia Borgia and the other half hooted him."

A leprous Chinese also received a great deal of attention. In 1873 he had been reported as taking up his quarters on the road near Webster's Tannery. "He is a most repulsive looking object and should be placed in confinement," said the *Colonist*. "He is said to be more expert than a fox in robbing hen roosts." He appeared again in 1874. "The leprous Chinaman is in custody upon a charge of steal-ing chickens," said John Robson's newspaper. "It appears that this wretched being has a strange weakness for chicken flesh. He robs roosts and devours the fowls raw."

But the greatest annoyance to British Columbians was that the Chinese were not only a strong labour force, but also a cheap one. There was no concern about railroad construction at this time, but the Grand Trunk Road from the mouth of the Fraser to Hope was being built, much of it with Chinese labour. One of the arguments in favour of the road-building programme at this time was that it would lift the province from its doldrums. If half the labour force were Chinese, said the *Colonist*, this purpose was defeated. In true Robsonian style the newspaper concluded, "This grievance is as yet only in the bud. Depend upon it, if not nipped there, it will attain dimensions that are certain sooner or later to demand attention. It cannot, in the nature of things, be otherwise."

The *Mainland Guardian* argued along the same lines. Money earned by Chinese was promptly sent off to China. The *Standard*, on the other hand—"The Government Organ"—pointed out that Chinese labour was cheaper and more reliable. They cited a New Westminster contractor who hired a white crew. They "did well enough until the first pay day, but no sooner did they get their money than they marched off to New Westminster—this was on a Saturday evening—and on the following Monday more than half of them were absent from duty, drinking and carousing in the city and his work was nearly suspended in consequence."

The tide of anti-Orientalism was again in flood by the end of 1874. In a by-election in Lillooet it was discovered that eight "disciples of Confucius" had cast a vote. The Legislative Assembly had excluded Chinese and Indians from the franchise, though there was some confusion, since the Chinese in question were from Hong Kong, a British protectorate. The bitterness engendered by this event had hardly healed when the Victoria civic elections were held. The *Standard* supported Councillor Drummond for mayor while the *Colonist*, by a process of elimination, supported Councillor Charles Morton. "Belly good man for mayor," remarked Robson's newspaper. "Councillor Drummond's friends boast that he has secured the vote of Chinamen by promising to give them Railway work. Think of that, white electors!"

Drummond won by a majority of 67, but it was discovered that there were the names of 92 Chinese voters on the list. It was believed that 77 Chinese votes went to "Lummond," enough to elect him.

The *Standard* claimed a magnificent victory. However the *Colonist* stated, "The Heathen Chinee has elected a Mayor, and our contemporary and its party are very welcome to all the credit of the achievement . . . .We have said the Chinese vote has elected the Mayor. No honest man acquainted with the facts will seriously question the correctness of the statement." Ratepayers have a right to vote, said the newspaper, "but the Heathen Chinee are an exception to the rule. Chinese do not vote in respect to any bona fide interest. A poll tax, a hawking license or trading license, at best, constitutes the voting qualification with these people . . . .

"On general principle, we contend that the Chinese ought not to be admitted to the electoral franchise, either municipal or parliamentary; and we have no hesitation whatever in going farther and advocating that they should be debarred from coming into direct competition with free labor on the public works of the country. This is a question that must soon force itself upon the attention of our Legislature. It is simply idle to argue against exceptional legislation. These people are exceptional in every respect and their case can only be met, justice can only be done, by exceptional legislation and, we may add, by exceptional taxation . . . ."

But the matter of the civic election did not end there. In January 1875, Councillor Hayward moved that the Municipality Act of 1873 be amended to prevent Chinese from voting. "He explained that a Chinese paying a $2 road tax could vote . . . .He alluded to the voting of Chinese who might have been in the city only five minutes and said that it would be possible under this state of things that Kwong Lee might be mayor next year (Hear, hear and general laughter) . . . and that next year all the council will be filled with gentlemen with pigtails." The motion was defeated, "six Chinamen" voting against it.

At this meeting, Councillor Gerow stated that the Negroes of the city had the right to vote and there was therefore no reason to exclude the Chinese. "To couple Chinamen and the colored man as was done on Wednesday evening," wrote the editor of the *Colonist*, "is not only in the worst possible taste but it betrays ignorance of the principal ground upon which the question rests. Colored persons differ only from the white in point of color. In language, religion, habits of life and thought, they are the same. They are not less intelligent, enterprising, industrious, orderly, benevolent. They own as much property, pay as much taxes. In a word, they are no less citizens and no less capable of making good use of the electoral franchise on account of their color. But in all these respects the Chinese are essentially different and are likely to remain so. Without any interests and sympathies in common with bona fide citizens, they are precisely the element to be desired and used at an election by the designing and unscrupulous."

John Robson's arguments—if indeed he wrote the editorial—were usually based firmly in logic, and perhaps this one was too. With the exception of a few well-to-do merchants, many Chinese could not speak English and still fewer could write the language. They lived in a separate community, had little understanding of the laws of the white society—indeed they frequently took the law into their own hands—and they had no interest in politics. But John Robson attacked the Chinese on the grounds, by inference, that they were less intelligent, less enterprising, less industrious, less orderly and less benevolent than whites and Negroes. He failed to note, perhaps for the convenience of his argument, that the Negroes had been in the same position when they were brought as slaves from Africa, that they had lived in North America for two centuries and that there were only perhaps 50 or 60 to be found in the Province.

The matter of the civic election went to the courts, where it was found that Mayor Drummond did, indeed, add the names of the Chinese to the voters list and he did, in some cases, pay the taxes of the Chinese. Drummond resigned, but in the ensuing election he defeated Councillor Hayward by 235 votes to 133.

They were bitter days in the young province—the Pacific Scandal, the Texada Island Scandal, the Helmcken insurrection, the hoplessness of the railroad situation, the appearance of the words "secession" and "annexation," the rising anti-Oriental sentiment and, to top it all off, the unseemly quarrel between Bishop Hills and Dean Cridge, resulting in an unpleasant cleavage in Episcopalian Victoria. The individual citizen, however, survived happily enough. The miner sluiced for gold in Omineca, Cariboo, Cassiar or Kootenay, and drank his leisure hours away. Victorians attended the theatre or symphony—where they discussed the knighthood recently bestowed by Queen Victoria on Matthew Baillie Begbie. And in the summer they still enjoyed their picnics and excursions. "Our colored fellow citizens, accompanied by their lady friends and children, went to Van Allman's Farm yesterday and enjoyed a most agreeable picnic," reported the *Colonist* in July. At the same time, over a hundred excursionists sailed on the *Maude* from Nanaimo at 4 a.m., spent the day on Burrard Inlet and arrived back at 3 a.m. the following morning.

One might as well ignore the politicians, who discussed the railroad endlessly and produced nothing. In 1875, Premier Alexander Mackenzie finally agreed to allow Lord Carnarvon to arbitrate the dispute, resulting in "The Relaxed Terms," one of which was that the Esquimalt and Nanaimo Railway (E. & N.) would be constructed. A bill to this effect was passed in the House of Commons but, alas, was defeated in—of all places—the Senate, much to the annoyance of the Islanders.

British Columbia's M.P.s did their best in Ottawa. Of the six, the great showman, Arthur Bunster, drew most of the attention. Edward Blake, the strongest and most intellectual of Mackenzie's cabinet, and an avowed opponent of concessions to British Columbia, had insulted the western province by stating to his South Bruce, Ontario, constituents that British Columbia was "an inhospitable country, a sea of sterile mountains." It was a statement Blake would not be allowed to forget till the end of his days. Irish Arthur Bunster had read a report of this speech before leaving for the east. When he departed for the House, he carried with him a bag of fall wheat raised by Robert Brown of Saanich. Arthur, before the assembled representatives of the country "in defense of Blake's remark, hauled the sack of wheat from under his desk, took a handful out of it and indignantly tossed it toward the member from South Bruce as the best answer to his statement that British Columbia was an inhospitable country, a sea of sterile mountains . . . "

This little deed surely did nothing to soften Blake's dislike for British Columbia, but it was great for home consumption, for the press and for Arthur Bunster, whom the Hamilton *Times* described: "His complexion is dark, and his hair and whiskers, which are abundant, black. Mr. Bunster has the accent of the men of Leinster, although he has probably not seen Ireland for many a long year . . ." It was not Arthur's last scuffle with Blake.

George Walkem's government managed to survive an election in October 1875. When they met in January of the following year, they were in a surly mood. Edward Blake had recently accepted the post of minister of justice on the condition that the E. & N. would be merely a local work, for which taxes could not be raised. The new provincial government rejected this and unanimously voted to send a petition to Queen Victoria, outlining their grievances and threatening secession. A month later, Walkem was defeated in the Assembly, and British Columbia, not yet five years of age, had its fourth premier, Andrew Elliott.

In the meantime, the attacks against the Chinese ebbed and flowed. In January 1875, Nanaimo had her first election as an incorporated city. "Chinese were not permitted to approach the Ballot-box," said the *Colonist*. "True, the Act does not exclude these people; but so sensible were the Freemen of Nanaimo of the impropriety, the degradation of allowing these heathen slaves (as the great bulk of them undoubtedly are) to stand side by side with themselves at the Ballot-box and have an equal voice in the management of affairs which they little understand and in which they have still less interest or sympathy in common, that they, with one accord, decided to exclude them."

The Chinese were now referred to bitterly as "our rulers." During the New Year celebration, "Tong Sang, one of our rulers, for throwing a pack of firecrackers in the face of officer Black, was fined $2.50," reported the *Colonist*. On the following day there was a further denunciation of the Orientals. "Our Celestial Rulers made things hot about town last evening. The dangers of a conflagration from the indiscriminate use of firecrackers is not to be thought of for a moment. A hundred happy homes might be laid in ashes, a hundred happy families reduced to beggary on this bright Sunday morning; but of what consequence would these calamities be compared with the proper celebration of a Chinese New Year in this British city. We have seen a white man incarcerated for burning a blue-light on Yates street but, bless you! he hadn't a vote. The Chinese have, and therein lies the difference. Great is Joss. Let us set him up in our high places and bow down and worship him."

John Robson retired from politics and gave up the editorship of the *Colonist* in 1875 to become paymaster for the C.P.R. Surveys. The policy of the newspaper, however, did not change. It complained of Chinese brothels and it printed several editorials on "The Chinese Evil" and "Mongolian Slave Labor." It pointed out that over $800,000 a year was sent back to China and that there were 2,500 white families in the province averaging four per family while not one of the 3,000 Chinese labourers had a wife. There were only five lawfully married Chinese women in the province, the newspaper believed, presumably married to Chinese merchants.

If it was not the railroad about which British Columbians complained, it was the Chinese; they were making no progress with either. Amor De Cosmos in March 1875 made his first careful approach to the Chinese question in the Commons, asking if the government was planning to introduce "European or Canadian" immigrants to that far-off foreign country, British Columbia, in order to supply labourers other than Chinese for railroad construction. Mackenzie replied that the government was not planning to introduce any class of immigrants.

Apparently, if any anti-Chinese legislation were to be passed, it would be on a local level. That day dawned on July 21, 1875, in the city of Victoria when Councillor Noah Shakespeare proposed that no Chinese be employed on city works, a suggestion that resulted in a magnificent quarrel amongst the city fathers. "The council accused one another of buying greens from Chinamen and after a long and disorderly discussion, a resolution was carried to instruct the city surveyor to insert in all specifications and contracts, a clause to the effect that no Chinese labor shall be used on any labor for the City Council or the City Water Works. The resolution was carried four votes to three."

"The city council have at last made a sensible move toward lessening the evils of the Chinese nuisance," said the *Colonist* the following day. "It is estimated that there are 2,000 Chinese laborers in the Province and, as one of the councillors expressed it, they are brought to our shores in steamers and landed like so many hogs. A more undesirable class of people could not be encouraged, and we are glad that the City of Victoria has set an example to the municipalities elsewhere in the Province for forbidding their employment on city works. The local government, which has done all in its power to sustain this kind of labor to the exclusion of white labor, might profitably take a leaf from the Council Minutes in this respect."

The following month, however, the city surveyor neglected to include the anti-Chinese clause in his tender for blasting a rock at the corner of Humbolt and McLure Streets, and there was another disorderly argument in city council, resulting in new tenders being called.

Perhaps it was the new municipal legislation which stimulated the formation of a laundry in Victoria. The new firm was given a remarkably large amount of free publicity by the *Colonist*. "An establishment in this branch of industry, which has heretofore been monopolized by our fellow Mongolian creatures, has been started by Messrs. Doscher, Murphy and Company, who have determined to try whether the improved appliances of the Caucasian and superior capacity of the European for the organization of labor on a large scale, will not enable them to compete successfully with the cheapness which is the result of that superfluity of mere manual labor in which the Celestials excel the world . . . ."

The full tide of anti-Orientalism began to ebb in September 1875, not to rise again for another seven months. The endless railway surveys of the province continued, and Andrew Elliott carried on the equally endless fight with "Canada." British Columbians still referred to the east as "Canada." Politically they were part of it; spiritually they were not, and perhaps would never be. Economic union, which was all they were interested in, could only come with a railway, and there were no prospects of its being constructed in the near future. "It is useless now," said the *Colonist*, "to refer to the oft repeated warnings of such men as Dr. Helmcken, Mr. McCreight,

Mr. Robson, Dr. Tolmie, Mr. Humphries and Mr. Smithe and others that, should Canada once get us into her power, she would then dictate her own terms for railway construction."

In the House of Commons, De Cosmos, Dewdney and Arthur Bunster were active in the debates, but they could do nothing for the railroad. Irish Arthur Bunster was the only one who left his mark. On St. Patrick's Day, 1876, he rose to speak and, when he was completely drowned out by members beating their desks, he removed two heavy kid gloves from his pocket and threw them into the middle of the chamber, daring any or all of the opposition members to pick up the gauntlet and meet him outside. It was said that Edward Blake later procured one.

Before the tide turned again in April, the Chinese of Victoria opened a temple. A *Colonist* reporter described it for the edification of both its contemporary and future readers in January 1876: "A Chinese Joss house or temple of worship has been erected on Government, just beyond Cormorant street, and was dedicated Friday night and yesterday. Joss means god or idol, and the over-devout children of the Celestial Kingdom have set up two gods and a goddess in the new establishment.... Crowds of Chinamen of every rank and condition filled the place and the din of the instruments and the scent of opium and foul clothes was so great that the few whites who ventured in were soon glad to beat a retreat."

But in April 1876, "The Chinese Evil" began to appear again in the editorials, the only difference from those preceding them being that now they could add, "They worship strange gods." And on the first day in May, a public meeting was held in the Theatre Royal with Mayor Drummond in the chair, to discuss the Chinese problem. Robert Smith, provincial member for Yale, moved that steps be taken toward preventing the country from being flooded with a Mongolian population. This was seconded by Alexander Edmund Batson Davie, member for Cariboo since the previous year's election. The motion was supported wholeheartedly by the mass of Victorians who filled the theatre—except for one small but courageous voice, that of James Fell who, it seems, felt responsible for the predicament of the Chinese. The mob, however, did not relish the truth.

Fell stated that there was no proof that the Chinese of the province were slaves. "He maintained that England at first sought trade with China and forced that deadly drug—opium—upon the Chinese; they must remember, too, that today Hong Kong was a British Colony and that many Chinamen were just as good British subjects as many present. (Cries of No! No! hisses and groans). If they did not like to hear facts, why had they asked him to address them? Where was their intelligence? (Groans) They were cowards if they said they could not compete with Chinamen. (Groans) . . . They had thrown down the barriers of China and now expected the Mongolian to stay home. (Cries of Time! Time! Put him out. . . . Sit down. Get somebody else. Pass the rice around! And other confusion.)"

They had a rollicking evening in the Theatre Royal. James Fell did not win any converts, but perhaps he gained some satisfaction in expressing the truth to those who did not wish to hear it. The meeting contributed nothing. "A practicable way out of the difficulty should have been shown," remarked the *Colonist* the next morning. "The Government should employ only whites on public works . . . .As to keeping the Mongol out of the mines, it cannot be legally done; neither can an exceptional tax be placed on him. Nor can private individuals be prevented from employing him. BUT HE NEED NOT BE ALLOWED TO DRAW A SINGLE DOLLAR OF PUBLIC MONEY and it ought to be the duty of every citizen to see that he does not do it."

The tide of anti-Orientalism was in full flood again. In the legislature, a petition was presented from Cassiar miners praying for the imposition of a tax on Chinese. The House went into committee to discuss the matter of "preventing the province from being flooded with a Mongolian population" and a $10 queue tax was proposed. Former premier George Walkem, now in the opposition, insisted that everything was unconstitutional. Even a $100 or $500 tax would not stop them, "and even if Canada [Canada again] allowed the imposition of the tax, England would not."

Such an argument always irritated the editors of the *Colonist* beyond endurance. They lengthened their usual editorial headline to "The Chinese Evil and the Constitution." Walkem, they commented, "seemed to be suffering from a severe attack of the Constitution. He would not interfere with the Chinese lest the Constitution should suffer. The Chinese were a great evil; but the Constitution sustained the evil. If it were not for the Constitution he would be happy to protect the poor workingman and his family; but —really—the Constitution was so sensitive that the slightest legislation in favor of one's own flesh and blood would be disastrous—to the Constitution . . . ."

There had been a great deal of dialogue over "the constitution," though Canada did not have one. It did, however, have the British North America Act, which forbade discriminating taxes, and it gave to the Dominion government the power to control immigration. This was "the constitution." As John Robson had said in 1872, "constitutions are very much what people make them," but few had the courage to test the B.N.A. Act, and perhaps the time was not yet ripe. In spite of the entire legislature's being of one mind against the Chinese, they were encumbered at every turn by their own democratic process of government. It would have been a much simpler problem for James Douglas. He had no provincial politicians, he had no "Canada" and he had no constitution. He made decisions. But the people of the colony had clamoured for responsible government and many had clamoured for confederation. Now they had both; however, the sordid realities of life, were, at least for the moment, more important than democratic ideals.

Anti-Oriental legislation foundered and was soon forgotten with the news of an event which brought great joy to the hearts of loyal British Victorians: the governor-general was about to pay a visit to his recalcitrant western province. There had not been such excitement since the ill-fated arrival of Governor Kennedy in 1864. Committees were struck, tours organized and the usual triumphal arches planned. There were, however, ugly rumours spread about town that "some people with more zeal than knowledge have talked seriously about placing ungracious and seditious mottoes upon the arches under which the Vice-regal visitor is expected to pass." Such mottoes usually dripped with patriotic sentimentality, but occasionally they were barbed with critical comment. On this occasion, the Indian motto "Hias Klahowyou" (Chinook for "a big hello") was, for some strange reason, particularly offensive to the mayor, as was "Empress of India," referring to Queen Victoria. "Such a title is repugnant to British subjects," said the *Colonist*. As it later developed, they objected to the wrong mottoes.

The celebration committee, however, was pleased with the preparations of the Chinese who had brought lanterns and other "parapernalia" to decorate Cormorant Street. There were to be three arches, and "on both sides, the sidewalks are being lined with evergreens to hide the shanties which would possibly prove obnoxious to the eye . . . .The residents of Cormorant street intend to have that thoroughfare thoroughly cleaned and swept. The grass also is to be cleared away."

H.M.S. Amethyst was expected to arrive from San Francisco on August 16, but alas, the telegraph lines were "again prostrate" and the ship slipped into Esquimalt harbour unannounced on the evening of August 15. The next day, however, the new lieutenant-governor, A.N. Richards (an immigrant from Canada two years earlier) boarded the warship to welcome Lord Dufferin, while Sir James Douglas, who had first stepped ashore on the Island 33 years earlier, awaited his turn on the dock.

With the completion of the usual formalities, the procession wound through the city beneath the endless triumphal arches, each adorned with various mottoes. The first Chinese arch at Government and Cormorant Streets read "Glad to see you here," the second read "English law the most liberal" and the third, at the end of Cormorant, "Come again." Said the *Colonist* in their next edition, "These three arches were erected solely at the expense of the Chinese population and with a variety of other decorations in their district did much to render the line of march attractive."

"The Empress of India" managed to survive a petition to remove it, but neither it nor such mottoes as "Our Railway Iron Rusts," "We Welcome You to the Sea of Mountains," (in reference to the villain Blake's insulting speech) "United Without Union" and "Confederated Without Confederation" seemed to concern the mayor or vice-regal party. However, the onlooker on Fort Street must have been somewhat dismayed when, just before Lord Dufferin's carriage approached yet another arch, it hesitated, then veered off in another direction. His Excellency refused to pass beneath it. The Fort Street motto read, "Carnarvon Terms or Separation." It was an embarrassing moment, especially since some staunch patriots in the procession insisted upon marching defiantly through the arch while others "rushed forward and endeavored to force His Excellency's carriage to pass beneath the inscription." Said Malcolm Sproat sadly, "It was the only shadow across the sunshine of the magnificent welcome."

This was not the only—or darkest—shadow. Lord Dufferin, on another day, refused to accept an address which indicated that the province was prepared to leave confederation. At the Great Railway Meeting in Philharmonic Hall two days before Dufferin's departure, Robert Beaven referred to the refusal as "a peculiar course" for a governor-general to take, and, before the evening was over, a unanimous vote in favour of separation was completed. British Columbians were becoming more serious about it now; the promised date for the commencement of the railway was three years past.

Although the vice-regal visit ended on a discordant note, it had given the Chinese an opportunity to improve their public image, winning them some surcease from verbal persecution for several months. There was the occasional editorial on the Chinese situation in Australia, California and Oregon, and the odd question on Mongolian immigration in the legislature, but the anti-Orientalists had lost their vigour temporarily.

In the last week of February 1877 an event which was to affect many citizens of the province, including the Chinese, began in Nanaimo. The miners who toiled for Dunsmuir, Diggle and Company went on strike. Dunsmuir requested aid and was granted the gunboat *H.M.S. Rocket* and the use of 12 deputy sheriffs from Victoria—who were promptly met by a volley of sticks, stones and fists. Thirty-eight miners from San Francisco, brought up by Dunsmuir to help break the strike, were repulsed, and finally the militia was called out. It ended after three months of violence with Robert Dunsmuir, American strikebreakers and Her Majesty's forces the victors. The Chinese were not involved, but it was an event which demonstrated the power of the great coal magnate and the lowly position of the labourer in the 19th century. And it foreshadowed events of the future.

Perhaps the old governor watched the events of that spring with distaste. Perhaps he considered how much happier the Island was when there was no province, no Canada, no politicking and no gold. There was just one authority and one company, and employees were satisfied and loyal. He had been forced to use the might of the British Navy on a rare occasion for apprehending murderers—but not for strikes. Times had changed.

Victoria celebrated Dominion Day quietly with picnics. It was British Columbia's sixth and Sir James Douglas' last. He died suddenly on the evening of August 2, 1877, at the age of 74 years. He had first crossed the Rockies in 1825, less than 35 years after the expeditions of George Vancouver and Alexander Mackenzie. When he died, Bunster and Blake were sparring over mining regulations (Arthur had a coal business in Victoria now), Sir Matthew and Henry Crease were continuing their circuits over the mainland, and the citizens of the capital were amused in September to read of a new townsite on Burrard Inlet. "The chief thing that can be said in favor of 'Hastings' is that it is distant, as the crow flies, 40 miles from Esquimalt, the richly endowed natural terminus of the Canadian Railway on the Pacific." They still had not surrendered their hopes for the railroad, and continued to act courageously even when Mackenzie, backed by the demon, Blake, announced in December that the route would be by way of the Fraser River, not by Bute Inlet, Seymour Narrows, Vancouver Island and Esquimalt.

There were great hopes, too, for an improvement in the general economy of the province; the fishing industry was growing rapidly and there appeared to be a rebirth of gold mining in Cariboo with the development of quartz mines. Economic recovery, however, brought visions of a certain evil to the inhabitants of the province—a "Chinese Evil." Since May 1876, the Orientals had been virtually free of abuse. In October 1877, the canker of anti-Orientalism burst forth again. It began with a report from Queensland, Australia, where new mine discoveries brought a great influx of Chinese. The government placed a tax of 100 pounds sterling on every immigrant, and the licence to dig gold was raised from ten shillings to three pounds a year. This differential tax on Chinese was ultimately accepted by the imperial government. It was referred to as the Queensland Act by British Columbians and was destined to be quoted frequently in the future.

"The Chinese Evil" began to appear regularly in the *Colonist* editorials. It was said that of the $400,000 to $500,000 provincial debt, about two thirds was paid to Chinese labour and was sent out of the country. "How many of the 1,000 and odd Celestial laborers who worked on the Yale-New Westminster road in 1874 and 1875 and were paid $300,000 for their labor, became permanent settlers?" asked the *Colonist*. "Not one," they answered. "They came like locusts and so departed."

Anti-Oriental articles were now daily fare for the Victoria reader. Dr. Yuen Sung, recently arrived from Hong Kong, was the subject of a long and lurid description when he cut his throat and allowed his life's blood to run tidily down the drain of his brother's kitchen sink. In Cariboo, quartz miners had agreed not to employ Chinese labour while whites were available. "Celestial sports" were continually being arrested for gambling; warnings of a new Chinese influx as the result of lawlessness in California were being sounded; the application of the Queensland Act was being recommended to the local government.

But even the most rabid anti-Orientalist opposed violence. This was always one of the few differences between the histories of California and British Columbia. In January 1878, the Nanaimo *Free Press* reported, "On Tuesday morning some evil disposed persons smashed the door in the Chinese store of Si Song & Co. on Winfield Crescent. Although the Chinese are anything but a desirable element in our midst, yet while here, they should be no more treated with abuse than other inhabitants. We trust the culprits will be caught and punished." And when "a well-dressed boy of 12 or so" threw a stone and seriously injured "an inoffensive Chinaman," his name was taken by a passerby and the *Colonist* stated, "These brutal assaults must be checked by the strong arm of the law."

Attempts were made in Ottawa to restrict the Chinese in the spring of 1878; as might be expected, they were made by Arthur Bunster. He delighted easterners by suggesting, with unaccustomed subtlety, that the House meet only every two years, thus saving $350,000 which could be spent to speed the construction of the railway. There was, of course, no sign of it yet. He then swung his attack to the Chinese, proposing that "no persons be employed on the Pacific Railway, in any capacity, whose hair is more than five inches long." Premier Mackenzie answered that this might militate against the seconder of the motion, J.S. Thompson of Cariboo, who had long, flowing locks. The flustered Mr. Thompson answered that he had no intention of seeking employment on the Pacific Railway, and if he had, he did not think anyone would be likely to do much work on that road while the present government was in power. This led to an amusing debate, but Mackenzie finally brought it to an abrupt halt by stating, "It would not be becoming to the House to legislate against one class of people." Arthur Bunster provided great entertainment, but British Columbia was too distant for "Canada" to worry herself over such matters as railroads and Chinese.

Until election day on May 22, 1878, the *Colonist* printed anti-Oriental material almost daily, and each political camp accused the other of actions favouring the Chinese. It was the first time this had been an election issue and it presented itself in a strange fashion: each candidate accused the others of having sympathy towards the Chinese and then defended himself against the same accusation by other candidates. Robert Beaven was the most severely criticized. "John Chinaman's friend," they called him.

"We are informed on good authority," said the *Colonist*, "that there are now 2,000 Chinamen in town and that the number is being augmented by every arrival from Puget Sound and California. The Legislature adjourned without taking any action to check the evil. . . . Once a Chinaman's hands close on a dollar he gives no rest to the soles of his feet until he has carried it to the Celestial Kingdom. He has no sympathy or taste in common with a civilized population. He is not a patron of local industries, arts or sciences. His clothes and most of his food are brought from China. He ignores hygenic laws. A small house will shelter twenty Chinese who will sleep four in a bed in an atmosphere that would stifle a white person. . . . Mr. Bunster's recent resolution in the Ottawa House was attacked by the Premier of Canada and lost, but had Mr. Mackenzie been compelled to compete in his early days with a Chinese stone-cutter [Mackenzie's first occupation in Canada], he would scarcely have earned wages sufficient to feed him; his education would have been neglected and the country would have been deprived of his great services . . . ."

The newspaper again recommended the Queensland Act, and on April 27 it ominously announced, "Three hundred and twenty Chinese coolies have left Hong Kong on ships bound for Victoria. What shall we do about it?" The anti-Oriental propaganda continued until the last day before the election. It was a smashing victory for George A. Walkem and his "Opposition" party, which then became the "Government" party. In the following week, while the *Colonist* and the "Opposition" party were recovering from the shock of their defeat, there was quiet on the Chinese front. By the end of May, however, the newspaper had recovered sufficiently to discuss the Queensland Act again, though in a much more repressed manner, and on June 9, they described some new arrivals in the city:

"The bark *Quickstep*, Captain Barclay, 48 days from Hong Kong, arrived in Royal Roads yesterday and was hauled alongside Rhodes and Co.'s Wharf last evening by the steamer *Etta White*. She brings 400 tons of general merchandise for Chinese firms in the city and 355 Celestials as passengers . . . .On arrival of the vessel alongside the wharf a large number of people assembled to witness the landing of the Chinamen, and since their presence is not desirable in our midst, the welcome they received was not of the most flattering nature. Notwithstanding the large number of citizens in attendance and the comments passed derogatory to Chinamen as a class, the new arrivals encountered no violence . . . ."

The Chinese firm to whom the vessel was consigned stated that the Chinese came on their own responsibility and that most were going to Cassiar and Cariboo, while others would remain in Victoria. "Had these 355 Chinamen landed in Queensland yesterday instead of British Columbia," growled the *Colonist*, "a tax of $50 per head would have been collected on every one of them. What an acceptable gift to this country $17,750 would have proved in this particular instance."

There was no end now to the propaganda against the Chinese. The argument centred around the Queensland Act, which some said was unconstitutional. It was pointed out in response, however, that this Australian legislation had been disallowed on three occasions by the imperial government before it was finally accepted and furthermore, the Franchise Act of earlier years (forbidding Indians and Chinese to vote), though expected by the legal profession to be refused by Ottawa, was actually accepted.

The first session of the third legislature was opened on July 29, 1878, and on the 31st, Finance Minister Beaven presented a bill which stated "that this house is of the opinion that Chinese should not be employed upon the public works of the Province and that a clause should be inserted in the specifications of all contracts awarded, to the effect that contractors will not be permitted to employ Chinese labor upon the work and that, in the event of their doing so, the Government will not be responsible for the payment of the contract."

V.W. Williams seconded the motion and made a brief speech, Forbes Vernon asked one question, and, with no further debate, the motion passed unanimously. It was as easy as that. Victoria City had passed a similar act applying to their public works in 1875. The province, in 1878, now had their own.

But this was not the end. On August 2, Premier and Attorney-general George Walkem introduced a bill which would prevent Chinese from escaping taxes in the future. All Chinese would be required to take out a licence every six months from which $30 would be paid in advance. Collectors were to be appointed and employers made responsible for supplying a list of Chinese employees. A Chinese without a licence and the firm employing him could each be fined up to $100.

This bill, entitled "An Act to provide for better collection of Provincial taxes from Chinese," resulted in a considerable amount of criticism and embarrassment to the government. The opposition-oriented *Colonist* referred to it as claptrap and stupidity. "It is not intended to become law," they said. "Nothing so incongruous, so monstrously unjust and absurd, could run the gauntlet of the masterminds in Ottawa, even should it escape the legal eye of the Lieutenant-governor, which is not probable."

On August 10, while the bill was still being debated, the cannery workers of New Westminster met to protest the Act. The Chinese were the only available labour, they said, and the canneries would have to close; no class of people except the Chinese would be satisfied to work for just a month or two and remain idle the rest of year. It was unjust to make the employer pay for the defaults of their employees, and canneries should be fostered rather than have obstacles thrown in their way. The Act, they claimed, would deprive 1,500 whites and Indians of employment. But it passed its third reading on August 12, it received the lieutenant-governor's assent, and Noah Shakespeare, the city councillor, was appointed collector of "the head tax."

Noah's task was not an easy one. He met with a considerable amount of resistance, culminating on September 16 in a dreadful turmoil in the Chinese district. "Chinatown was in a state of commotion yesterday," reported the *Colonist*, "occasioned by the seizure of goods for non-payment of the head tax imposed by the local government." The goods of Sam Gee on Yates, On Hing on Johnson and Tai Yune on Cormorant Streets were seized and on the latter street all the Chinese put up their shutters and suspended business. "After the drays were laden they were driven to the police barracks and there, chests of tea, bales of cloth, packages of opium and other effects were deposited to await public sale. . . . It is said there will be a general strike today of the Chinese hands at the boot and shoe factories, the Chinese cooks at the hotels and the laundrymen etc."

The Chinese go on strike? Surely it was just another rumour. But on September 17, 1878, not a single Chinese appeared at his work. "Ladies are doing their own kitchen and housework," said the *Colonist*, "restaurant and hotel keepers their own cooking; heads of families sawing their own wood and blacking their own boots. . . . This is all very well and good. The Chinese no longer mongrelize the labor market... some 250 situations are vacant in this town alone. Cooks, housemaids, chambermaids, laundresses, woodsawyers, boot and shoe makers and tailors are in demand. The need is pressing and good wages will be paid. This the day and this the hour to prove that Chinese are an unmixed evil and that if debarred from employment, white men and women will spring to fill their places. The system is fairly on its trial. What say the white laboring classes?"

The Belmont boot and shoe factory announced it would have to close, since without cheap Chinese labour it could not compete with San Francisco manufacturers. Hotels were also having difficulties providing meals and services. But the *Colonist* was ecstatic. The best jobs, it said, were now being taken by whites. "John imagines the white community cannot get along without him. He will shortly discover, to his cost, that such is not the case." The strike, however, lasted only five days. The government compromised. They agreed to return the seized goods and await the action of the Dominion government. Wealthy housewives, hotel men and boot manufacturers breathed a sigh of relief and settled back into their worn, comfortable routines.

The matter was solved much sooner, and in an unexpected way.

Tai Soong, a Chinese merchant, had applied for an injunction to prevent his seized goods from being sold at public auction. On September 27, Mr. Justice John Hamilton Gray, the Father of Confederation and Sir John A. Macdonald's first political appointee in British Columbia, granted the application on the grounds that the Act was unconstitutional, since it interfered with the authority of the Dominion government. The provincial body could have appealed this decision, but they never did—and were later severely chastised for not doing so. The Act was not enforced thereafter. Indeed it ended on a somewhat farcical note when the new tax collector, John Maguire, ignored Gray's injunction, sold Tai Soong's goods and was rewarded with a $40 fine.

For a year now, the Chinese had been under attack. It was not yet over, but in mid-September 1878, Victorians were overjoyed to hear that the Dominion elections in "Canada" were completed and that the Conservatives had swept to magnificent victories in Nova Scotia, Quebec and Ontario. And, as if this were not enough, evil Edward Blake himself had been defeated—but, alas, so had Sir John A. Macdonald. That news was indeed sobering. Their great friend and benefactor of the past, and presumably in the future, had been defeated ignominiously in the midst of a massive victory by his own party. There was some hope, however.

These were still the days when eastern Canada held its elections long before British Columbia. Indeed the composition of the House was virtually set, before the western province had even nominated its candidates. It was a convenient arrangement for defeated eastern politicians. Sir Francis Hincks had taken advantage of it before, and now, on September 18, a telegram arrived at the home of Arthur Bunster. It was from none other than Sir John A. himself, and it requested that Arthur "secure" him a seat in British Columbia. "There is no doubt that Sir John will be triumphantly elected in Victoria City," purred the *Colonist*, "and under the circumstances, it is the duty of Victorians to elect him."

Former premier Andrew Elliott accordingly withdrew, but Judah Davies, a local auctioneer, declined to do so—perhaps because of a not uncommon antipathy to Amor De Cosmos, the third candidate, rather than from any dislike of carpetbaggers from the east. Despite the strong opposition of the *Colonist*, Amor obtained 538 votes to Sir John's 896 and Judah's 480, in the two-seat riding.

For the second time, then, British Columbians had grovelled at the feet of the mighty eastern politicians. But they were not about to do it for a third time—not at least, for such an insignificant person as

Hon. H.L. Langevin, one of Sir John's former cabinet ministers who had been defeated in Quebec. Langevin sought the seat in Vancouver District, but the five candidates there, including Arthur Bunster, declined to capitulate. Langevin then attempted to obtain the New Westminster seat but was again greeted by a cold refusal. Dr. T.R. McInnes won the seat, while Bunster was the victor in Vancouver District, Dewdney in Yale and J.S. Thompson in Cariboo.

For several years, anti-Oriental sentiment had waxed and waned, somewhat paralleling the activities of the politicians. Now it was a continuing attack, and a new power was beginning to make itself felt—the Workingman's Protective Association (W.P.A.). This body was presided over by Councillor Noah Shakespeare who, since his failure to collect the head tax, was now the collector of the school tax. Indeed, Noah was becoming more prominent on the Victoria scene. He had arrived from England in 1863 and for several years had worked as a photographer in Gentile's Gallery on Government Street. He was tall, lean and bearded with piercing, clear blue eyes and black wavy hair, a handsome, youthful man of 39 years. In the City Council he had not been paid much attention until he began his forays against the Chinese, and now he was the Oriental school tax collector and the driving force behind the W.P.A.

The W.P.A. held weekly meetings in Victoria and later established a branch in New Westminster. Its agenda was concerned almost wholly with the Chinese problem and its guest speakers, chiefly politicians, supported its goals completely. On October 4, the names of all the firms and families who employed Chinese were read out to the audience, which usually numbered between 50 and 100, and Premier Walkem and Finance Minister Beaven expressed their thoughts on the best methods of suppressing "the evil."

In November the W.P.A. announced that its members were sending a petition to Ottawa praying for relief of Chinese immigration, and named all those who refused to sign it. It reported that the I.O.O.F. would not employ Chinese in the construction of their new building and it passed a motion to notify all architects that if Chinese were employed in a project, the Association would withhold its patronage from that business. In December the Workingmen stated that they were starting two laundries, that they "were going in for the growing of vegetables" and that they were about to start a newspaper.

Under Noah Shakespeare's vitriolic direction, the W.P.A. was beginning to influence politicians. Newly elected as president (though defeated for the 1879 council), Noah took credit for the act passed to cut the hair of long-term prisoners in the province. The *Colonist* made the announcement of the first cutting on January 5, 1879. "In accordance with the Act, the long-term prisoners had their heads shaved yesterday. Amongst the number operated on were some seven or eight Chinamen who had their queues cut off. The Celestials, however, resisted strongly, without avail. It is hoped that this will be a warning to others not to breech the laws of the country where they are well treated." This was said to be a health measure. It included white prisoners, but it was directed at the Chinese, amongst whom the queue had been a badge of honour ever since their Manchu overlords had forced it upon them in the 17th century.

In the W.P.A. meeting of January 6, Noah stated that it was his influence on the city and government officials which provoked this measure "more particularly for the Chinese, several of whom, he was happy to say, had, in accordance with this ordinance, been deprived of their queues. He had taken great pains to obtain one of them (which he produced) and which he intended keeping as an heirloom in his family."

There were no protests in Victoria over this degrading action, but the New Westminster *Guardian*, when the cutting was repeated in their city jail, claimed it to be illegal. Though the practice soon died a natural death, the issue remained for some time to come.

At this time, there was probably very little Chinese immigration. It was later stated that over the five years between 1876 and 1880, 2,326 Chinese landed from Hong Kong. By the end of the decade, however, several firms refused to employ Orientals. They were prevented by laws from working on municipal and provincial projects, and they were continually being hounded by "Brother Shakespeare." There were also an increasing number of incidents in which Chinese were beaten, hit with snowballs or, in one instance in Nanaimo, pelted with chunks of coal. Such incidents were always strongly condemned as being "disgraceful" or "barbarous," yet there was no doubt that anti-Oriental sentiment had markedly increased. To further intensify feelings, there was a growing public awareness of secret societies among the Chinese. Reporting on the funeral rites of one such society, the *Colonist* betrayed a tone of uneasiness lurking beneath the age's general fascination with the mysterious and bizarre.

"Many Victorians yesterday witnessed a most imposing Chinese ceremony—the funeral of Yip Jack, a partner in the firm of Wha Chung, restaurant keepers, Cormorant street. At noon about 1,000

Chinamen and a large number of white people collected opposite the store when the coffin was brought out and placed on a bier with an umbrella to shade the head. The corpse was then surrounded with all kinds of eatables—roast pig, sheep, etc., after which the head man and friends appeared and after going through certain ceremonies, the coffin was placed on a hearse and, headed by two men carrying flags and a number of others attired in yellow and white garments, proceded to the cemetery, when Yip Jack was finally interred. The deceased was a member of a Society here called by some Free Masons, but which is really an offshoot of the Tae Ping Company. . . . The society here seems to be nothing but an offensive and defensive organization and has some 300 or 400 members."

There can be no doubt that the Chinese were organized; they could not have carried out their strike of 1878 without close cooperation. They had Free Masons in both Victoria and Barkerville. It would also appear that some companies took responsibility for the welfare of their "servants." The Kwong Lee Company, for example, were concerned over the fate of their "servants" during the Quesnel River fire of 1869. This is reminiscent of San Francisco's "Six Companies," which were benevolent societies who cared for the welfare of Chinese immigrants from the six districts of Kwantung province, from which all Chinese came. They had no connection with the notorious Tongs of San Francisco. They were organized, all right, and Victorians experienced a little twitch of discomfort at the thought.

In distant Ottawa, British Columbia members had two matters on their minds: the railroad and the Chinese. The primary one was still the railway. Although surveys were continuing, no real progress had yet been made. The provincial government had sent its second "Separation Memorial" to the queen, by way of Ottawa, in August 1878. (It stated that if the terms of union, notably that of the railway, were not carried out by the end of April 1879, they would withdraw from confederation.) After an inquiry from Amor De Cosmos, it was discovered that the memorial "lay about unnoticed" in Ottawa and was not sent on to the imperial government until January 1879. "Unpardonable," growled the *Colonist*.

British Columbia M.P.s were becoming increasingly disenchanted with the casual treatment their province was receiving from the Dominion government. It was not merely the contempt they showed the memorial; absolutely no progress was being made on the railway, other than yet another survey, this time, of all places, on the Skeena and Peace Rivers. On April 8, 1879, Amor De Cosmos rose in the

House of Commons, in a great temper, to introduce a bill for the peaceful separation of British Columbia. This was greeted by cheers and laughter. Amor was told he was out of order and to take his seat, but he stuck to his ground. "He said that he had heard the grossest attacks on British Columbia. It had been called an excrescence, an incubus and a burden to the Dominion that yielded no return. He made the motion to test the hon. gentlemen. They wished to get rid of that province and he asked them to second his motion but there was not a single one, from the Premier down, who would second the motion." He was again ruled out of order "and obliged to take his seat."

It was quite a subtle challenge on Amor's part. It was apparent that Canada did not want to lose British Columbia, and it was equally apparent that British Columbia did not want to lose Canada. There had been ample opportunities to do so if they had wished. But Amor, for one, was becoming more and more disillusioned with the confederation he had promoted so strenuously. Little had been done about the railroad; furthermore, he had raised the question of the Chinese in the House several times but had always been asked to postpone it.

Now it was Arthur Bunster's turn, and Arthur would not be denied. He urged that a committee be formed to investigate the matter of the Chinese, British Columbia's second great concern. If the Chinese were not employed in Dominion works, he suggested, it would be of great benefit; certainly no international treaty would be broken. The Chinese, furthermore, should not be naturalized, and the Shipping Act should be changed to prevent them from working on Canadian ships. Finally, the Immigration Act should be altered to bar their entry, and Canada should join with Britain in preventing Chinese from leaving Hong Kong.

Again no action was taken, but in mid-April, Alexander Mackenzie asked Sir John what the government was doing about the Chinese question, and the premier no longer deferred the matter. He rambled on interminably. Would he ever come to the point? It was a masterpiece of political circumlocution. He stated that the matter interested not only Canada but all the continent and "our sister colonies in Australia" and that he sympathized with British Columbians, but it was "contrary to the laws of nations to stop people coming in and excluding them." This, of course, was patently untrue. Immigration was later restricted and finally discontinued. "Laws of nations," like constitutions, are only what people make them, and at this moment, regulation and restriction were unsuitable to Sir John. But he did agree to the formation of a Select Committee on Chinese Labor and Immigration.

It was one of the few concessions British Columbia had obtained in eight years of confederation, and it was achieved through the intervention of the leader of the opposition, Alexander Mackenzie—Sir John's and British Columbia's sworn enemy. The railway, six years past its promised starting date, was still a vision of the future, but now there was a committee to investigate the Chinese situation. Not that committees meant much; Sir John, the senior member from Victoria, could let it die quietly when it was politically expedient to do so. But it was the first small step. Railways and Chinamen, Chinamen and railways.

Parliament did not close on a happy note for its western members. Dr. R.W.W. Carrall complained bitterly about the failure to carry out the terms of union, and on the last day of April, Arthur Bunster rose in the House amidst good-natured cheers, but he spoke of secession. He was quoted as saying, "tomorrow the contract will be up," in reference to the mislaid memorial, "and all members of British Columbia will perhaps have to bid goodbye to some warm friends. (Oh no—Oh yes—laughter)." Merriment always followed Arthur Bunster, no matter what he said. But matters had reached a climax which even a select committee could not satisfy. Virtually every level of society in the province had become bitterly disenchanted with the treatment it had received from "Canada." In New Westminster, a public meeting was held "to consider the propriety of celebrating Dominion Day." The *Colonist*, in reference to the worldwide publicity the railway squabble had received, said, "If no other good has flowed from the Union of the Province with Canada, it at least enjoys the advantage of becoming widely known." Said Arthur Bunster on his return, "She [Canada], it is true, gave us a custom house, a lunatic asylum and a governor [Lieutenant-governor A.N. Richards, an easterner and brother of the Chief Justice of the Supreme Court of Canada] and, in my opinion, they are all three a pest to the country."

The Select Committee had met in Ottawa in April and May, before prorogation of parliament, with that great reformer of past years, Amor De Cosmos, in the chair.[5] He was not the most impartial of chairmen; he continually asked leading questions and, when the answers were not sufficiently anti-Oriental, he badgered the witnesses unmercifully. Those who gave evidence were all British Columbians by adoption, and all were M.P.s or senators, with the exception of F.J. Barnard, who just happened to be in town. Barnard has been a stagecoach operator since the early days of the gold rush. He was not a politician, though he would soon be.

The majority of witnesses agreed that Chinese immigration should be stopped, largely on the basis that they occupied jobs which whites would otherwise have. They were able to obtain these jobs largely because they provided cheap labour, which they could afford to do since they lived so cheaply. They occupied crowded quarters, ate cheap food and had no families to support. Whites, it was said, lived on 50 cents a day, Chinese on 25. This was probably true. It was also probably true, as alleged, that Chinese were not reliable witnesses and that, with the exception of the wives of a few well-to-do merchants, the women were imported prostitutes. The Chinese were, predictably, accused of draining money from the country. They were not, it was asserted, the least bit interested in settling permanently. They were not interested in politics nor in becoming part of the social structure of the province. Counteracting this, however, was their value as labourers in fish canneries, market gardening, laundering and as household servants. Much of the evidence, however, was hearsay, rumour and unadulterated Prejudice. But they were the opinions of the men who represented the colony and the province, opinions which reflected the types of men they were.

Arthur Bunster, at the age of 52 years, was, as usual, the most interesting voice to be heard. There were 6,000 Chinese in the province, he said, and British Columbians were strongly against them, with the exception of what he referred to as "the snob aristocracy." Said Arthur, "There are a few would be aristocrats who like to put on frills, and they are fond of having Chinese servants. They think that it is something grand and something away up. They do not care about employing Sewash [sic] though these, who are Indians, are equally as good servants as are the Chinese, in my opinion. The Indians ought to be encouraged more, and if this were done, we would not have Chinamen amongst us in such numbers. Chinamen will come in and do some things about a house, chores etc., which a white man is not supposed to do. For instance, the lady of the house wants to take a bath, and they will think nothing of going and scrubbing the woman of the house in a bath tub—as I have been told."

Mr. Trow, an eastern member, then asked, somewhat incredulously, "They are not male but female servants who do this?"

"No," answered Arthur, "I mean male Chinamen."

"Does the mistress like it?" asked Trow, obviously taken aback.

"Well, you wouldn't think so, if you saw Joe Murphy on the stage," answered Arthur. (Bunster later admitted he had seen a skit of this description on the stage in San Francisco and the actor, Joe Murphy, had "made $10,000 out of it.)

Bunster had always been the greatest promoter of his adopted western province. He appeared now to be bitter and somewhat disillusioned. In his concluding remarks, he stated that he had given his anti-Oriental testimony "as one who has been a resident of the Province of British Columbia for the period of 20 years, and as the father of a family, and I say it sincerely and honestly, and if their coming into the country is not checked, I sometimes seriously think of emigrating from British Columbia on account of their presence in the country. Indeed, I have brought my boy to Canada (Arthur still referred to the east as "Canada") to educate him, in consequence of the Chinese being in our country, and fearing that during my absence he might get astray with the Chinese. It has been remarked that what are called the hoodlums are down on the Chinese who live in the Province, but they have brought a great deal of the sort of treatment in question on themselves. The Chinamen take advantage of young boys whom they meet unprotected to insult them, and the white boy naturally retaliates. In fact my boy has come to me and told me that a Chinaman has insulted him, and I have asked him—are you ready to take care of yourself; thrash a Chinaman that insults you, when you can; and he has done it."

J.S. Thompson of Cariboo was almost as anti-Oriental as Arthur Bunster. He complained that the Chinese miners produced no new diggings but merely followed in the steps of the whites. He also described the oaths taken by the Chinese in court. "They write their names on a piece of paper, and burn it.... It is supposed that if they speak falsely, their souls will be burned in the way that the piece of paper in question was consumed. They have another way of taking an oath—they break a plate; and there is still another mode—in this form they cut off a fowl's head." [The *Colonist* later related a tale in which a Chinese was asked how he wished to be sworn in. "Me no care," he answered. "Clack 'im saucer, kill 'im cock, blow out 'im matchee, smell 'im book, allee same." Added the *Colonist*, "He was allowed to smell 'im book."]

When the interrogation touched upon the numbers and occupations of Chinese, an eastern member was surprised to hear that there were relatively few Chinese servants—and these were employed mainly by wealthy Victoria families. Amor De Cosmos just happened to have a set of statistics on hand. He presented them to the committee as the figures for the province, though there was no accurate account of the numbers and occupations:

Domestic servants	300
Shoemakers	150
Laundrymen	300
Tailors	100
Laborers	700
Gold Miners	1800
Peddlers	50
Gardeners & Farm Hands	1500
Fisheries	1100

This conveniently totalled 6,000 Chinese.

Dr. T.R. McInnes was the third of the string of anti-orientalists to be heard. His city of New Westminster, he said, contained about 300 permanent Chinese, by which he meant they remained five to ten years before returning to China, with an additional 1,000 to 2,000 migratory workers who left after the salmon canning season. Dr. McInnes also condemned the Chinese for bringing in an especially virulent form of syphilis and spreading it to the Indians—an allegation impossible to prove.

Senator W.F. Macdonald, the former mayor of Victoria, was a more moderate witness. He was against further immigration and against the employment of Chinese on the railroad, but he would not accept the hearsay evidence of earlier witnesses. To Arthur Bunster's utter disgust, Macdonald said that Chinese were "not more immoral than the people of London, England." The senator could afford to be more honest in his statement of opinion. He was no longer a politician, a fact which deeply irritated Arthur Bunster, who later stated that Macdonald was "pitch-forked" into his position and therefore did not represent the people.

F.J. Barnard perhaps knew the Chinese, on a province-wide basis, better than anyone else. He condemned them in certain ways, praised them in others. Of the 200 Chinese women in the province, he said, there could not possibly be more than five who were married; the remainder, including some who appeared to be ten years old, were imported from China for the satisfaction of the 6,000 males.

When Edgar Dewdney, the great road builder, appeared, there was an obvious chill throughout the room. He was a reluctant witness and would not answer questions about which he was not familiar. He pointed out that there was no way of knowing how many Chinese were in the province. All estimates were useless. Even when pressed by De Cosmos he would not make a statement unless he knew it to be fact, not merely rumour. He waffled a bit on the Chinese immigration question, possibly because, on general principles, he did not wish to agree in any way with Amor. Perhaps, he said, there should not be too many come into the country. When asked if he thought the labouring class was against the Chinese, he answered very pointedly, "Yes; so also is the feeling of some politicians." And did Chinese ever marry Indian women?

"No," Dewdney answered, "they just live with them."

"Do you consider that a good state of society?"

"No; I do not."

"Do you think it speaks well for the morals of the community?"

"No; I do not. But white men do that, too, you know."

Edgar Dewdney was certainly the most honest, the most objective and least bigoted of the witnesses. Perhaps the worst that could be said of him was that he could afford to be honest. He knew that the general feelings of British Columbians were against the Chinese, but he also knew that he was about to retire from the field of politics. The announcement had not yet been made, but he had been appointed Indian Commissioner for the North West Territories.

There was only one more witness: the Clinton rancher, Senator Clement Cornwall, a very English gentleman. His great love appears to have been his fox hounds, which he ran, in true English tradition, over the wild ranch land of the interior; his great dislike appears to have been the lower classes, in which category he placed politicians.

When asked the general feeling of British Columbians on the Chinese question, Cornwall answered, "I should think the feeling against Chinese is widely spread. The employers of labor and the better classes in British Columbia recognize the advantage of having Chinese there; but the working classes, aided by politicians, have raised this cry against them." Amor would not let such a statement escape unchallenged. "If that statement goes abroad to the public," he said, "it might be thought that the better classes of society were against them."

Answered Cornwall, "What I said, I said quite simply, and I cannot help the construction that may be placed upon it. I should not place what I call politicians among the better classes."

The senator placed no importance on a petition Noah Shake-speare had sent on behalf of the W.P.A. He said the signatures were from the labouring class of the migratory type. When questioned on crime amongst the Chinese, he said they were largely law-abiding but occasionally committed a violent crime on impulse. "I have never known a case of that kind malciously premeditated," he said. "The offence of a Chinaman is seldom overlooked."

J.S. Thompson then asked, "Nor would it be overlooked in the case of a white man, if a white man were subject to the same charge?"

Senator Cornwall answered, "The class who have signed the petition would not overlook the case of a Chinaman charged in that way, while they continually do so when one of their own numbers so offends."

De Cosmos then interjected, "That is the class on which society is built."

"I should say, so much the worse for society."

Clement Cornwall, like Dewdney, was no longer a politician. He could say what he wanted.

The Select Committee's report was dated May 14, 1879. It recommended that Chinese immigration should not be encouraged and that Chinese labour ought not to be employed on Dominion public works. It was actually labelled the "First" report. Amor De Cosmos had planned for more meetings and was most annoyed when Sir John did not allow them.

Conspicuous by his absence was Senator R.W.W. Carrall. Perhaps he was on his honeymoon—he was married in May 1879. In the autumn of the same year, Victoria was saddened to hear of his death at the age of 40. A street in the Gas Town section of Vancouver, not then in existence, perpetuates his name.

From the prorogation of parliament in May 1879 until October of the same year the Chinese thankfully received no publicity except for the remark that "the political trinity across the bay" (Walkem, Beaven and Humphries) had apparently abandoned further legislation on the subject of "the Yellow Agony." They continued to drift into Victoria in thirties and forties from New Westminster, the *Isabel* was frequently reported to have arrived with three or four from Puget Sound, and the *City of Chester* usually brought four or five, occasionally more, from San Francisco. On June 20, 1879, the American bark *Thomas Fletcher* arrived, 57 days from Hong Kong, with 282 Chinese passengers. The figure was printed without comment. All that summer, G.A. Keefer and H.J. Cambie surveyed a possible railway route through the Skeena and Peace River areas, and on October 7, 1879, the *Colonist* printed a headline of considerable significance. "The Long Agony Over," it said. The government had called for tenders for four sections of railway between Emory's Bar, two miles south of Yale, to Savona's Ferry, near Kamloops.

It appeared certain now that British Columbia's greatest problem—the long-broken promise of a railway—was about to be solved. This, however, did not solve her second great problem, the Chinese. In fact, the solution of one threatened to aggravate the other. Railroads and Chinamen, Chinamen and railroads. They were about to meet headlong.

The *Colonist* lost no time in bringing the situation before the eyes of its readers. On October 8, one day after the announcement of the calling of tenders, the campaign began: "The workingman must look to it that the Chinese do not pluck the labor plum from the Canada Pacific fruit tree. As far as possible, the money expended on the railway construction in the Province should be paid to white laborers. Within the next few months the hum of industry will be heard throughout the Province. What steps are the Workingmen taking to secure the preference in the labor market?"

The W.P.A., now known more commonly as The Anti-Chinese Association, was indeed busy. Noah Shakespeare was working closely with the New Westminster branch to arrange a petition to the Dominion government requesting the prohibition of "Mongolian labor" on the railway. They had no difficulty obtaining newspaper publicity. In their meeting of October 27, Noah stated that he would rather vote against the transcontinental railway than see Chinese employed upon it. "Hear! Hear!" shouted the audience. Arthur Bunster was still in a surly mood when he addressed that meeting. Instead of being the flamboyant, witty champion of British Columbia rights, he appeared morose, disgruntled and bitter. If he had known the Chinese would have met with so much success and encouragement in the province, he said, he would not have adopted it as his home. When he was asked about the Select Committee, he answered that they had "received a stab from a Senator and a member from this country." The wild audience shouted back at him, "Names! Names!" and Arthur bitterly pointed out, wrongly, that Senator Macdonald had stated he would rather have a Chinaman than a white woman for a servant. "Oh! Oh!" screamed the audience. And Mr. Dewdney, cried Arthur, had said the Chinese were a benefit to the province. "Scalp them!" shouted Clement Cornwall's lower class—or, in De Cosmos' words, "the class on which society is built."

Arthur had changed. He was fighting everyone now—even his friendly morning newspaper, the *Colonist*. There was a wild exchange of letters through the columns of that organ, between Arthur and the Senator Macdonald whom Arthur had misquoted. On November 10, they met each other face to face at a meeting of the Anti-Chinese Association. Macdonald asked Bunster to admit that he was mistaken, but Arthur stubbornly refused to do so. He announced grandly that he was elected by the people, while Macdonald was appointed—he knew not how. "And where are all the other representatives of the people tonight?" he shouted. "Where is the carpet bag governor who has been pitchforked into his position. ..?" He was referring, of course, to Queen Victoria's representative, Lieutenant-governor A.N. Richards.

"Tell us about the wash tub!" cried the audience, and Macdonald jumped up to say that Arthur's reference to Chinese scrubbing the back of the lady of the house was "vile slander to every woman in the country." It was at this point that Bunster weakly pointed out that he had seen the incident on the stage of the Bella Union Theatre in San Francisco.

The meeting ended with much shouting, confusion and disorder, much of it directed at Arthur Bunster. It was sad to see this colourful personality decline, though perhaps it would be only temporary. He did not appear to have a friend at this time. Even his beloved workingmen had deserted him. He faded from the scene for several months.

The four contracts for the 127 miles of railroad were announced on December 12, but by the end of the year a gentleman named Onderdonk had purchased three of them from the successful tenders. Later he purchased the fourth. "Who are Onderdonk and Company?" asked the *Colonist*. All they knew was that he had built the San Francisco sea wall, and it was believed that he was backed by the great American railroaders, Stanford, Crocker and Towne. It was not an uncommon practice to purchase tenders; it was always looked upon, rightly, with suspicion, but when it was stated that David Oppenheimer was involved with Onderdonk, westerners, for some strange reason, felt better. It was, however, only a rumour, though David Oppenheimer was in Toronto at the time—indeed the Oppenheimers always seemed to appear suddenly wherever there was any monetary action, whether it was Victoria, Barkerville, San Francisco, Toronto or, later, Vancouver.

On the last day of 1879 it was announced that Premier Walkem had married the previous day and had left for Ottawa to discuss some drydock business, but the greatest news was the railway. "All aboard for the west! Vast preparations in progress in Canada," was the *Colonist* headline. And all the quick-money seekers were well aware of it. David Oppenheimer was in the midst of it all. Emory's Bar was now referred to enviously as Emory City, and a sale of town lots was about to take place. It had 13 streets, the *Colonist* reported, and listed all of them for the reader's benefit. "One thing may be accepted with absolute certainty," said the newspaper "Emory City will be the liveliest business place on the mainland for some years to come." Foreign capital had bought up much of the land, and Captain John Irving was building two ships to sail to Emory City. The stampede was on.

There were a few notes of caution, however. There was still some suspicion about the reliability of Andrew Onderdonk. The Toronto *Globe* objected to his purchase of the contracts and, perhaps facetiously, mentioned that a member of his firm was "president of a Chinese Company with 60,000 Chinamen at his beck, who he intends, like another Moses, to lead to the Promised Land of British Columbia." In a more serious vein, the Seattle *Post* said, "British Columbians may resign themselves to all the evils of Chinese competition, for but little short of a miracle will prevent these San Francisco contractors from employing Chinamen on their work."

But the *Colonist* had its head in the clouds. "We have reason to believe that such will not be the case," it answered. "In all cases where practicable, we understand the preference will be given to white labor, the object of railway construction being to colonize the country and induce permanent settlers to take up their abode within its borders." In their manic state of excitement, the editors seemed to believe that the American contractor and his San Francisco backers might be benevolent enough to allow Chinese to stand in the way of a profit. And colonization in a Canadian province? Would San Francisco capitalists worry about colonization? The *Colonist* was indeed so euphoric that it complimented the Chinese for the manner in which they conducted themselves in the celebration of their New Year early in February 1880.

That spring, Amor De Cosmos presented another petition from the Anti-Chinese Association to the House of Commons, and Arthur Bunster again had the members rocking with laughter at the expense of his old enemy, Edward Blake. Arthur himself, however, was the butt of a practical joke at this time, reported in the Hamilton *Times*. Wong Wo See, "a Celestial from the Flowery Kingdom," had recently opened a laundry in Ottawa. Someone had convinced Wong that Bunster was "the friend of the Heathen Chinee on the

Pacific Slope" and that he, Bunster, could obtain the laundry contract of all the House of Commons for Wong. The Chinese innocently visited the House and asked for "Mr. Blunster" who was called out of the session. When Arthur discovered the object of the Chinaman's mission, "in language more strong than elegant, he ordered the Chinese to get out."

And on his return from Ottawa, Premier Walkem reported that he had tried to persuade Sir John to insert a clause in the railway contracts prohibiting Chinese labour, but Sir John said that the country was straining every nerve to complete a gigantic undertaking, and the government could not adopt the unusual course of dictating to contractors how their work should be done so long as it was well done.

Excitement began to mount as April approached. "On the mail ship now nearly due at this port," said the *Colonist*, "is the advance guard of what we have reason will prove a mighty host, coming to people this vast and rich Province and lift it from the depths of gloom and despondency to a position of brightness and prosperity . . . .The fancies of yesterday have become great facts today and no amount of scepticism will alter them. The railway is coming."

The 'mighty host' arrived on April 2, 1880, on the *Dakota*. Included were G.A. Keefer, H.B. Smith, M.E. Eberts (all of whom would remain in the province), Andrew Onderdonk and the usual "two Chinese." Onderdonk registered at Driard House with his wife, and on April 11 he met a deputation from the Anti-Chinese Association, including Noah Shakespeare and F.L. Tuckfield. They requested information on the class of labour to be used on the railway. Onderdonk answered that he would give white labor the first chance, and when British Columbians were all occupied, he would fall back on French Canadians. If he still could not obtain sufficient labour, he would, "with reluctance, engage Indians and Chinese."

Before the month ended, Robert Beaven somewhat belatedly attempted to get his rendition of the Queensland Act passed by the provincial legislature, while in Ottawa Edward Blake did his best to postpone the construction of the railroad. Both attempts failed, but Blake attained some measure of success; he became leader of the opposition when Alexander Mackenzie resigned on April 29. "British Columbia has nothing but ill treatment to expect at his hands," commented the *Colonist*, "and must take her stand with the conservatives."

By the end of April 1880, then, the stage was set for the construction of the railroad, nine tempestuous years after British Columbia's confederation with Canada, seven years after the promised date of commencement. The players, too, had been selected. Sir John A. Macdonald was firmly entrenched in Ottawa, Edward Blake had a minor opposition role, George A. Walkem and Robert Beaven appeared to be safely ensconced in the British Columbia Legislature, and all the mighty engineers were in attendance—Onderdonk, Keefer, Cambie and a host of others. New faces would appear as the drama played on: speculators, capitalists, engineers, and of course, Chinese. A cast of thousands.

The old pioneers of the '50s were the audience. Roderick Finlayson, Dr. J.S. Helmcken, Sir Matthew Baillie Begbie, Henry Perring Pellew Crease, Robert Dunsmuir, Edgar Dewdney, Joseph Trutch—they were all still active. Sir James Douglas and Dr. R.W.W. Carrall did not live to watch the plot unfold. Nor did J. Spencer Thompson, the first Cariboo M.P. Like the others, he had arrived in 1858. He died in December 1880 while the right-of-way was still being cleared and blasted in the deep canyons of the Fraser.

CHAPTER III

1880-1883

"John Chinaman is Putting on Airs."
The British Colonist, 1881.

Politicians have a great penchant for cutting ribbons, turning first sods or driving first spikes. Invariably they choose a day of national rejoicing to perform their annointed task, a day when patriotic glands are functioning at their maximum. Sir John was to turn the first sod on May 24, the Queen's Birthday; then Sir Charles Tupper was assigned the mission for July 1, nine years after British Columbia had joined Confederation. Both found more urgent business in Canada. It was not a very encouraging start, though Andrew Onderdonk did not particularly care. The descendant of a Dutch settler, Van De Donk, who had come to America in 1672, he was still four months short of the age of 35 when he scrambled through the stunted forests at Yale and stumbled up the rocky bluffs to the north.

Andrew surely did not consider sod-turning ceremonies—nor colonization, nor Chinese labour—of any importance, unless they resulted in political pressures being placed upon him. He had to fulfill his contract, which said nothing of sod-turning, colonization or Chinese, and he had his San Francisco backers to satisfy. Chinese labour was certainly cheaper, though when the Union Pacific was built it was said that two whites did the work of three Chinese. He would require perhaps three or four thousand labourers, but there were only some 10,000 souls in this whole benighted province, most of them fully occupied in gold or coal mining, fishing or commerce. Andrew must have known from the beginning that he would be forced "with reluctance, [to] engage Indians and Chinese."

Nevertheless, he opened a labour office in Victoria, advertised in the *Colonist* and constructed an office in Yale, adjoining Oppenheimer's new store. Supplies were a greater problem. Shallow-draft sternwheelers such as the *Western Slope* had to pound 65 relentless miles across the gulf from Victoria and up the narrowing Fraser to Yale, inside the sharp, grey teeth of the canyon.

Yale was now the centre of activity. Its old Chinese residents were forced to move their buildings off Front Street to make way for the railroad, but they were soon joined by more of their countrymen. On June 14, exactly one month after the first blast of dynamite shook the canyon, 40 white and 160 Chinese labourers arrived from San Francisco. On July 10, less than two months after the first blast, the British iron bark *Strathearn* arrived in Victoria from Hong Kong with 473 Chinese: 336 for British Columbia, the remainder for Portland. They were assigned to Sun Yee Chan of Victoria. Ninety-five of the consignment arrived in Yale on the *Western Slope* on July 20. "Many of them seem mere boys," said the Yale *Inland Sentinel*, "a very poor lot for railroad work, we should think. A large number of Chinamen shook the railroad dust off their feet and left by the returning *Slope*." Further arrivals from the current gold mining hope on the Skagit River caused the *Sentinel* in mid-September to conclude that "the Chinese will build most of the road." By then they were numerous enough to have their own physician. A Dr. McLean was appointed by the Chinese High Commissioner to attend the Chinese working on the railroad.

Above and below Yale, hills were being cut away, the waste material being used to fill ravines. This grading work was done almost completely by the Chinese, while the white labour force did the lumber work, largely on bridges and tunnels. Accidents began occurring at the construction site, in numbers sufficient to stimulate the *Colonist* to suggest that an inquiry be made. Chinese labourers were frequently involved. In August, a heavy charge of dynamite was set off below Yale. "Through a misconception of orders," the *Colonist* reported, "nine Chinamen were standing on the rock immediately over the charge when the explosion occurred. They were hurled high in the air and fell maimed and bleeding to the earth." The friends of the victims immediately started after the white foreman with pick axes, chasing him high up on the side of a hill. Fortunately they failed to catch him.

There was no inquiry into this incident, but a few days later when a cow wandered into a Chinese garden to gorge herself on Oriental cabbages, the Chinese owner struck the beast with an axe and was immediately charged with cruelty to animals. "From what transpired at the trial," said the *Colonist*'s Yale correspondent, "as well as from what I hear outside, there appears to be little doubt that the Heathen Chinee constitutes at once the most cruel and least lawabiding element in the community." The correspondent also complained of the lack of 'Sunday Observance' amongst the workers of Yale, particularly those who blasted on the Sabbath.

In contrast to the unfortunate owner of the Chinese cabbage patch, a white man was let off rather easily from another misdemeanor during this period. Queen Victoria brought charges against none other than Andrew Onderdonk for failure to supply a list of employees who were liable to pay the school tax. Justice of the Peace Robson pointed out that the fine was $100, but he dismissed the case since the defendant "was laboring under a misapprehension. . . . "

There had been a mild increase in Chinese immigration during the summer of 1880, but it brought no flood of anti-Orientalism. There were, however, frequent references to the Chinese which reminded citizens of the low position of the Oriental in the life of the community. It was noted that two large altars with capacious furnaces had been erected in Victoria's old and new cemeteries for the benefit of the Chinese, moving the *Colonist* to remark, "Heathen altars in a Christian burial ground form a strange spectacle in the 19th century." And the Workingman's Bakery advertised conspicuously in the local newspapers: "Bread for the working class. If you want cheap and good bread, go to John Gerritsen's, Humbolt st., where you will get five loaves for 25 cents. No rice eating animals employed." But the politicians, perhaps overcome with ecstasy generated by railroad construction, were full of brotherly love for the Chinese, though not necessarily for each other. For two days in November 1880, both Arthur Bunster and Premier Walkem could not be found. It was said that they were on San Juan Island fighting a duel over Walkem's appointment of Amor De Cosmos, instead of Arthur, as British Columbia's agent in making arrangements for financing the E. & N. Railway. As it later developed, it was only a rumour, though at the time it seemed to be quite legitimate, since for several months Arthur had been fighting with everyone. During the last session in Ottawa, he had actually come to blows with "a little Frenchman named Monsieur Cheval," who had managed to pull some hair from Arthur's thick black beard. Arthur very nearly killed him; indeed he was advised to slip across the border to New York. Instead, he pulled the remnants of his beard from the hand of the unconscious M.P. from Quebec and announced victoriously, "No Cariboo from Lower Canada can carry my hair" (*British Colonist*, December 29, 1880).

Arthur Bunster was always getting himself into some sort of trouble. In February 1881, while in Ottawa, he was out driving with "a lady friend" whom he left in the cutter while he went into a saloon. In his absence, the horse ran away with the cutter and the lady friend; Arthur sued the Ottawa *Free Press*, for reporting the story. When he returned to Victoria, he appeared in court to protect his son, who was charged under the Militia Act for not attending a parade. But in spite of all this, it was openly admitted that Arthur Bunster was about to become British Columbia's next lieutenant-governor. He received accolade upon accolade from the eastern newspapers. A member of the opposition praised him for some five minutes in the House. His speech during the debate on the syndicate which was about to take over the construction of the railroad was reported in full by an eastern correspondent. It was said to be magnificent. He attacked poor Edward Blake again for saying that British Columbia was an incubus on the Dominion, he twitted Sir John for not visiting his Victoria riding and he concluded his speech by saying "he could not help thinking that the Chinese question would be the next great one before the country."

There was no doubt that Arthur Bunster was to be the next lieutenant-governor of the province—until June 3, 1881. On that day it was announced that Senator Clement Cornwall (who in the Select Committee hearings had expressed his disdain for the lower classes, including politicians) had been appointed.

Arthur Bunster made no public comment on what, to him, must have been a bitter disappointment. In the session ending in the spring of 1881, just prior to the appointment of Cornwall, he had been prominent in a number of debates, two of them involving the Chinese. During the one on the Naturalization Bill, he asked how it would affect the Chinese. Said Mr. Macdonald of Pictou, Nova Scotia, "It does the Heathen Chinee the honor of treating them in the same way as it treats other foreigners."

The Canadian census of 1881 listed 4,350 Chinese in British Columbia, 22 in Ontario, 7 in Quebec, 4 in Manitoba, none in New Brunswick or Prince Edward Island and none in Mr. Macdonald's very own province of Nova Scotia. It must have deeply irritated Arthur to listen to this righteous "Canadian," who was not required to live amongst the Orientals, who was not required to face white labourers, who was not required to present his constituents' anti-

Their fathers came to dig for gold at Barkerville.

The Joss House and Chinese shops on Fisgard Street, Victoria, c. 1892

The triumphal arch on Store Street honouring the visit of the Marquis of Lorne in 1882 annoyed Arthur Bunster.

The elaborate interior of the Joss House on Government Street, Victoria.

Chinese interest in Christian missions always pleased Victorians.

Chinese servants were both a necessity and a source of pleasure to the ladies of Victoria.

A Chinese work crew during construction of the C.P.R.

Some work gangs lived in tents, others in log cabins such as these, north of Yale.

A Chinese funeral passing the corner of Main and Pender Streets in Vancouver in 1893.

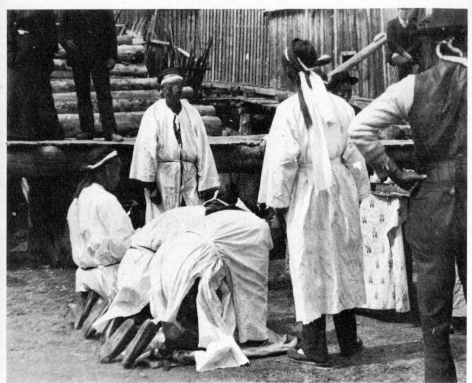

Orthodox Chinese funerals were also held in Barkerville.

Chinatown in the coal mining town of Cumberland, 1910.

The Chinese continued to wash for gold near North Bend in 1891.

(City Archives, Vancouver)

Looking west on Hastings at Carrall Street about 1900 with the Salvation Army Band entertaining.

(City Archives, Vancouver)

Dupont Street, now Pender, c. 1898.

Oriental sentiments. He turned his wrath upon Sir John A. Macdonald. He was surprised, he said, that the leader of the government, whose constituency was totally opposed to the Mongolian race, should support a bill giving to the Chinese equal rights with Anglo-Saxons. Arthur certainly had a point, but Sir John had the seat—after requesting Arthur to "secure" it for him—and perhaps Victorians had their just deserts for humbly electing him. Sir John, as was his habit, chose to brush aside the remark with a joke. "The Hon. gentleman would not prevent Dutchmen holding land, would he?" the Premier asked.

"No," answered Arthur.

"Well, the one comes from China, the other from Delft," said Macdonald.

The Chinese, to Sir John, summoned up visions of porcelain. He probably had never seen a Chinese. But his Victoria constituents did not have mere visions. They saw human flesh which was different from theirs; they saw flesh which they believed to be immoral and flesh which they believed was siphoning their wealth to heathen China. Perhaps it was racial bigotry, but it was also a matter which was 3,000 miles removed from Ottawa. It was no doubt frustrating to British Columbia M.P.s to listen to the pious "Canadians" moralize on racial discrimination when, just a few short years before they had engulfed themselves in the depravity of the Pacific Scandal.

In 1881, British Columbia was still basking in the sunshine of her tardy railroad. It had been under construction for almost a year now, and Chinese labour was being tolerated. The *Colonist* weakly pointed out that Orientals were not preferred, though it did not appear to care whether the rails were laid by whites or Chinese. During the winter Onderdonk had advertised for 3,000 white men in California, and at the end of March the first shipload of labourers appeared. "The 238 San Francisco railway roughs who came up on the *Victoria*," reported the *Colonist*'s Yale correspondent, "were landed at Yale and nearly all were reeling through the town, whooping and hallooing at the tops of their voices. They were penniless, but they got hold of liquor (did you ever notice that when poverty-stricken men can't get anything else, he can get drunk) and made Yale howl. The first night on shore was signalized by three or four fights and twelve of the rowdies were sent to gaol. On the second night, twenty more were locked up. On Tuesday night free liquor gave out and the boys went to bed with their boots on. Black is the fashionable color for eyes at Yale now."

It was a godless spot. "There is no such thing as Sunday in this railroad town," said the *Guardian*'s correspondent. "Every place of business is open and customers go to and fro as on week days. There are quite a number of Chinese stores and wash-houses; in fact Chinatown here would far eclipse the one of your city (New Westminster)—the Swamp included. John does a roaring business, seemingly with his countrymen, in all manners of traps, both civilized and uncivilized."

The population of Yale and Emory had swollen to 3,000 by May with the arrival of whites from California and a constant trickle of Chinese from Victoria. Indeed, there was a shortage of cooks in the capital city and those who had remained behind were considering a strike. To some, the Chinese were becoming too bold. They refused to answer questions during the Yale census and, in the same district, 2,000 of them (or so it was said) went on strike. The Chinese labourers had contracted with the firm of Lee Chuck to supply them with rice, for which the firm deducted two per cent from their wages. The labourers objected to this deduction. They also argued that the supplies were deficient in weight and quality. The incident culminated in 200 Chinese labourers storming into Yale, where they virtually destroyed the warehouse in which their rice was stored. The lone constable and his deputy arrested some of the ringleaders, but were attacked by the mob with sticks and stones.

There would be other incidents similar to this in the future. The Chinese were always under contract to a Chinese boss or "Tyhee" who received from the white contractor a lump payment from which he paid his men. He also managed their affairs. Occasionally when the labourers felt they had been deceived, they rebelled. An incident of this sort had occurred in Victoria when a Chinese boss was attacked over failure to pay his men during the construction of the Grand Trunk Road to Hope in 1874.

Yale was hardly a genteel little town, what with "Chinese barbarians" and "a number of individuals from California and elsewhere of a class for which police were first invented" (*British Colonist*, May 20, 1881). The school had burned down some months before; the government had not replaced it, and 70 children were not attending classes. In spite of numerous construction accidents and illnesses, there was no hospital other than a makeshift "Accident Hospital" built by Onderdonk. And Dr. Mclean was never heard of again.

In mid-April 1881 Andrew Onderdonk was in San Francisco recruiting labourers, but even before this—perhaps during the winter—he must have placed an order for more Chinese workers. The American bark *Herbert Black* arrived in Victoria on April 29 with 300 Chinese from Hong Kong. Shortly after, the *Henry Buck* arrived with 250—and a case of smallpox, requiring her to be quarantined in Royal Roads for three weeks. In May it was reported that the Chinese steamship *Nee Foo* was en route with 600 labourers; in June, 500 were en route on the *Chong.* The *Quinta* arrived in July and the *Xenia* in September, all with Chinese labourers for the Canadian Pacific Railroad, and yet there was no voice of protest; indeed the *Colonist* complimented the 200 on the *Xenia.* "They are a clean, respectable looking lot, much more so than those brought by former vessels during the year. Many of them are old Victorians who have been on visits home to the Celestial Empire."

In spite of his assurance that Chinese would be used only as a last resort, Onderdonk must have spent much of the winter of 1880-1881 requisitioning Chinese labour. In the five years between 1876 and 1880, Chinese arrivals in Victoria totalled 3,326. In 1881 alone, six vessels from China brought 1,739; in addition 387 arrived from Puget Sound and 813 from San Francisco for a total of 2,939.

Despite this great influx there was a labour shortage in Victoria. "Never in the history of the province," said the *Colonist*, "has labor, both white and Chinese, been so difficult to procure as at the present. Railroad contractors at Yale, canning establishments on the Fraser, the drydock at Esquimalt, to say nothing of farmer's wants, are all calling out for labor. That the Chinese in town are busy, numerous as they are, no greater indication is required than the great number of woodpiles of all sizes in every part of the city that are waiting for the buck saw and axe. Until lately, John was on the lookout for a cordwood team and would follow the load to its destination on the chance of getting the job of cutting it. Now, however, it is quite different, and the Celestials act as though they were conferring a favor by sawing wood under any circumstances. The labor shortage, especially the Chinese, will probably get easier as soon as the Fraser canneries shut down, and this may be looked for at any time."

There was no doubt that the Chinese recognized their value. There had been a cook's strike in Victoria, a labour strike and riot in Yale, and in June 1881, Chinese labourers at Spence's Bridge went on strike over the failure of the contractor to pay them for the five days they took to travel there from Yale. "Perhaps no country was ever in a worse plight for labor than British Columbia now is," said the New Westminster *Herald*. "Chinese there are in plenty but they demand fifty per cent more than formerly." said the *Colonist*, "John Chinaman is putting on airs."

But they were still being hounded by Noah Shakespeare. When the *Quinta* arrived in Victoria in July, the Chinese had barely touched the dock before Noah descended upon them, demanding the three-dollar school tax. The Chinese refused, Noah seized their goods, and the rising young lawyer, Theodore Davie, was retained to protect their rights. His application to prevent the sale was granted by Judge Crease. A similar case, involving Hung Chow and 17 others who had arrived on the same ship, was heard in December. Henry Pelling Perew Crease, whom Arthur Bunster would classify as a member of the "snob aristocracy," again ruled that the Chinese, at that moment, could not be considered citizens, and, furthermore, Noah had no official authority to collect the tax.

The tax collector was also meeting opposition along the site of the railroad construction. The Chinese were scattered up the line; there were some 32 gangs, about 30 in each group. In mid-July, Yale's lonesome constable walked along the railroad bed to collect the school tax from the Chinese labourers. "On former occasions," said the *Colonist*, "the Johns pleaded ignorance and no explanation could induce them to advance an inch beyond the 'no sabe' stage. On Tuesday, however, they no longer pleaded ignorance, but flocked about the officer and, with picks and shovels and crowbars uplifted, dared him to attempt to enforce the law." The constable judiciously retreated and the *Colonist* expressed its displeasure with the fact that an officer had to "go among a horde of barbarians to take from them money which they prize more highly than their eyeteeth."

At about the same time, a group of Chinese parents in Victoria decided to send their children to city public schools. If they were denied entrance, they were prepared to appeal to the courts of law. The 'Heathen Chinee' were certainly becoming bolder as their value became more apparent.

As far as the increasing Chinese immigration was concerned, however, British Columbians were not noticeably concerned. It is surprising to consider what 127 miles of railway could do to them. Perhaps they felt a sense of importance now; certainly they glowed with pride when Sir Charles Tupper, Minister of Railways, paid them a visit in August 1881. "This province has been a sealed book to the rest of the Dominion," remarked the *Colonist*. "Sir Hector Langevin was here in 1872 but few Canadians have seen the province."

Tupper was ostensibly on a tour of inspection, but he was shown an uncommon amount of attention by the great Wellington coal magnate, Robert Dunsmuir, now 56 years of age. The welcome was magnificent, if somewhat mysterious, until Arthur Bunster addressed the Minister at a reception in the Black Diamond Hotel in Nanaimo. Arthur, as usual, was a trifle indiscreet on this illustrious occasion. "His remarks were both hot and personal . . . ," it was reported. He complained that his district had not been well-treated by Sir Charles' government. He insisted on the Carnarvon Terms, which supported the E. & N. Railway. Islanders, he said, would not be satisfied merely with a mainland railway. Sir Charles was no doubt familiar with Bunsters' indiscretions, but the hosts of the reception were embarrassed, and the Toronto *Telegram*, in great anguish, referred to the Pacific province as "The spoiled child of the Dominion." This, of course, raised the ire of the *Colonist*, which replied, "As many children are spoiled by kicks, cuffs and disappointments as by overindulgence and lollipops. If this province is really a spoiled child, she has been made so by the bad treatment and ill faith of the Dominion."

Tupper's visit was deemed a great success in spite of the Nanaimo incident. Just prior to his departure, he attended a magnificent banquet in his honour in the presence of numerous dignitaries. Arthur Bunster was not one of them.

Railway construction continued at a slow pace during the winter, but even in fine weather there were delays caused by accidents, strikes, the burning of Yale and the loss of supplies with the destruction of Captain John Irving's "floating palace," the *Elizabeth J. Irving*. But Onderdonk continued doggedly on. The railroad, slowly progressing in Ontario and Manitoba as well as in British Columbia, was now owned by The Syndicate, all of them Scots or descended from Scots: George Stephen, Donald A. Smith, Richard B. Angus, John S. Kennedy and James J. Hill. But British Columbians did not care who owned the railroad or, for that matter, how much they would pay for it, then or in the future. By the end of 1881, seven miles of track had been laid and tenders were being called for the 85-mile stretch from Emory to Port Moody—"the lower section," as the people of Yale disdainfully referred to it. And although the route through the Rockies had been moved well to the south (no one knew exactly where) the popular Yellowhead Pass was finally abandoned. The great railroad centre, however, would still be Kamloops, where, it was suggested, the provincial capital should be moved.

The latter portion of 1881 also saw an uneasy stir amongst the anti-Orientalists. "Fisgard street is alive with human vermin," said the *Colonist* in September, "and no decent person now thinks of venturing into that locality. The Chinese cyprians reign supreme in their quarter and solicit customers with an effrontery which cannot have escaped the notice of Superintendent O'Connor and his aides . . . .The neighborhood is a shame and abomination, not only in sight of the Lord, but in sight of all persons who have a spark of morality in their nature."

There were further complaints of Chinese brothels in October, and in November the unhealthy conditions in Chinatown were brought to the eyes of the public. The Chinese lived in ramshackle, unpainted cabins or shanties, thrown roughly together with lumber of all shapes, sizes and lengths. Two or three were piled one upon the other; from the warren of dirty alleys, rotting steps lead to the upper storeys. Inside, there was filth, unbearable odours and extreme crowding. They were "mere cubby holes" where "the Celestials pack themselves at night like herring on a platter." The cubic air by-law, it was said, was going to be enforced, though there was no suggestion as to what might be done with those Chinese evicted.

In November 1881, too, a poetry competition was announced. There were two subjects, "The Spirit of the Age" and "John Chinaman." Contestants were urged to send their contributions to the Mechanic's Literary Institute for judging, and on Christmas Eve the winning poem in the "John Chinaman" category was printed in the *Colonist*:

> They are coming, they are coming,
> Every week a thousand more,
> From the crowded towns of Asia,
> And the great Mongolian shore . . .

It went on, verse after verse. Victorians were in the midst of their annual winter pastime—the persecution of the Chinese. Occasionally a sign of respect was shown to a Chinese merchant, but the labourers who lived in the squalid dens of Cormorant or Fisgard Streets received no quarter. Their greatest persecutor, of course, was Noah Shakespeare. He had fought his way back onto the City Council the previous January. Victoria had a by-law forbidding the employment of Chinese on city works. There was little more the councilmen could do, other than to enforce that by-law, and the man who kept a constant vigil on the city works and the Chinese was Councillor Noah Shakespeare: Noah the Enforcer. In November he had noticed a Chinaman lighting the coal oil street lamp on James Bay and immediately brought the matter to the attention of the council. It was difficult to obtain a white man who would perform such a menial task, he was told; but Noah persisted. He again raised the subject in December, presumably to bring before the eyes of the public the fact that the Chinese lamplighter had been fired and a white had accepted the job for a salary of $7 a month.

In city politics, then as now, late December and early January were most opportune times to have one's name before the eyes of the voting public. The civic elections were to take place on January 12, 1882. Mayor John H. Turner had decided to retire, and Councillors McLean and Shakespeare ran for the vacant post. Noah's advertising consisted of one brief sentence: "Gentlemen—I am a candidate for Mayor in the ensuing municipal election. N. Shakespeare." But it was enough. He won, 347 votes to 323.

His Worship, Mayor Noah Shakespeare? Noah, the Enforcer; Noah, the greatest Chinese Persecutor of them all; Noah, the tax collector; Noah, the pillar of the Methodist Church; Noah, the Sunday School superintendent for 15 years; Noah Shakespeare, the erstwhile president of the Anti-Chinese Society who in 1879 had proudly displayed the severed queue of a Chinese prisoner to the rabid crowd at the W.P.A. meeting and announced that he would keep it as a family heirloom.

Noah Shakespeare, Mayor of Victoria? Arthur Bunster had failed to become lieutenant-governor, but Noah had succeeded in the mayoralty race. Noah, of course, had never been charged with keeping a public bar room without a licence, he had never brawled on the streets with Terence Monaghan, nor had he been charged with driving over the James Bay Bridge at speeds faster than a walk. He had certainly not all but annihilated that little "Cariboo" from Lower Canada, Monsieur Cheval. Noah was much more genteel, and still a handsome man. His black, wavy hair was just beginning to gray when he was elected, two weeks before his 43rd brithday. Like Robert Beaven, he was a Staffordshire man. He had arrived in Victoria by way of Cape Horn in 1864. The Vancouver and Dunsmuir Colleries had employed him for a while; then he became a photographer and finally a real estate agent before his success in city politics. It is said, no doubt on the word of Noah himself, that he was a descendant of the poet. He later named his home "Stratford Villa," though it was a rather unimposing example of Victorian style.

In a sense, it was perhaps fortunate for Victoria's Chinese population that Noah became engrossed in the affairs of the city. He was more dangerous as a freelance persecutor. In 1882, the Chinese New Year began on a particularly windy day. His Worship warned the Orientals that no fireworks should be exploded, and indeed few were. Strangely, this was the only reference Noah made to the Chinese in his one-year term in office.

The Legislative Assembly, too, was in a surprisingly tolerant state in 1882. The members unanimously passed a motion to memorialize the Dominion government and the C.P.R. syndicate to take steps to use white labour only; they also proposed that the government consider the immigration question.

Andrew Onderdonk meanwhile was in the country's capital in January 1882, comfortably ensconced in the plush Russel House where, it was said, he was hiring several hundred men. John Robson's New Westminster *British Columbian* (he had retired as paymaster of the C.P. surveys, purchased the *Herald* and changed its name to that of his old newspaper) announced that Onderdonk was bringing whites from the east. "They will be much more welcome than Chinamen," said the *Columbian*. In an interview, Onderdonk stated that he had 3,000 workers on the line, equally divided between whites and Chinese, that two whites equalled five Chinese and that he had 15 miles of track laid.

And while Onderdonk lolled in the lush, brocaded chairs of the Russel, other important events associated with the railway had been completed. An unknown (to Victorians) gentleman named "C. Van Horn" was appointed general manager of the C.P.R., and Onderdonk's firm won the contract for the Emory-Port Moody section of the railway, though he was the second lowest bidder. Railway contracts were always an enigma.

In 1882, as melting snow swelled the muddy Fraser at Yale and spring flowers bloomed gloriously in Victoria gardens, the important problems of the day resolved themselves clearly into those of the Esquimalt drydock, the E. & N. Railway and the Chinese. The provincial government had been slowly and ineptly constructing the drydock for some time and were now involved in a scandal over the matter. It appeared that the E. & N. would be constructed by private enterprise, in the person of Robert Dunsmuir, the leading proponent of that philosophy. And the Chinese? The newspapers could protest, the provincial House could rant and rave and write a thousand memorials, His Honor Mayor Shakespeare could enforce his puny anti-Chinese by-law and Amor De Cosmos and Arthur Bunster could plead with Sir John, but there was really just one man who would decide whether Chinese would pour into the province:

Andrew Onderdonk. Even before he returned from Ottawa, there were reports of many ships carrying Oriental labourers en route to Victoria.

They began to slip into Royal Roads toward the end of April. The *W.J. Roth* was the first, with an unspecified number of labourers. She was quickly followed by the *Blue Jacket* with 466 Chinese, the *Escambia* with 902 (all in good health, according to Health Officer Jackson) and the *Adam Simpson* with 500. The *Syren* arrived on May 8 with another 325 "coolies" and the next day the *Suez* anchored in Royal Roads with 890. It was reported that 2,500 were expected in the next few days and thousands more were awaiting transportation in Hong Kong.

News of this massive Oriental influx finally leaked back to Canada, where the Toronto *Telegram* printed a long editorial on the matter.

"A dispatch from Victoria, British Columbia, says that Chinese are pouring in there at a rate of 700 a week. This is a serious matter, but next to the sentimental and mistaken religious view, the comic view of the Chinese invasion is what seems to prevail in Canada. We talk about the 'Heathen Chinee', John Chinaman, Sam Ling and his everlasting 'washee, washee'. To make the matter worse, the burden of presenting the Chinese question before parliament is laid before Mr. Bunster; and everyone seems to think it is his bounden duty to laugh at everything that Mr. Bunster says. We may laugh now but the serious and sorrowful part of the business will come afterwards. The estimate has been made that some 9,000 Chinese will arrive in the Pacific province during the summer; but present probabilities are that this will be greatly exceeded . . . .Meantime, through the prevalence of mawkish, silly sentimentality on the subject of Chinese immigration, the hands of our strong men are tied and our most eloquent tongues are silenced into saying nothing against the tremendous mistake we are making, while some extol it as a grand example of the brotherhood of man. From the pulpit and from the tea table, in great part, we have taken on a weak and entirely false view of Christian duty; a view not merely unwarranted by scripture, but opposed to the whole spirit of scripture teaching. And bitterly will our posterity suffer for it if we do not in time quit ourselves of the delusion."

In the House of Commons, Amor De Cosmos announced that 24,000 Chinese were expected before August, which would make the number of Orientals in the province 32,000 greater than the number of whites. This of course, was one of Amor's embellishments, but it at least prompted Sir John A. Macdonald finally to express his sentiments without the usual witticism he frequently resorted to when he wished to dismiss an awkward political problem.

British Columbia needed immigration from Europe and Canada, he said. (Even Sir John did not consider the western province a part of Canada.) Onderdonk had tried to get whites in the east—in fact, he took 50 or 60 white carpenters "over from Canada to work in British Columbia"—but there was a labour shortage and there was no harm in accepting Chinese as long as they later left the country. They were not likely to become permanent settlers, he said. The premier seemed to be naively impressed with the fact that Victorians had Chinese servants. It had been pointed out in the Select Committee that only a small number of Victoria families, and even fewer elsewhere, enjoyed this luxury, and again Amor De Cosmos informed Sir John of this.

But Macdonald, as reported by the *Colonist* in May 1882, went on: "Their presence, he believed, would not be a wholesome thing for the country. They were an alien race, and there could be no assimilation of the race, therefore when the temporary exigencies had been overcome, and when there was a railway stretching across the continent, and there was a means of sending in white settlers, he would be quite ready to join, to a reasonable extent, in preventing the permanent settlement in the country of Mongolians or Chinese immigrants. But at the present it was a question of Chinese labor or no railway. The government had not had its attention especially called to this matter before, but the subject would engage its attention for the future . . . ."

All Sir John need have said was that it was a simple matter of alternatives. Acceptance of the Chinese was not "a grand example of the brotherhood of man." It was not "Christian duty." It was a hard, cold matter of dollars and cents. This attitude was also prevalent in some British Columbians. Those who pleaded for the Chinese did so on the basis that it was economically good for the province or that it was most convenient to have a Chinese servant or a Chinese labourer saw one's wood. They did not plead that all men were born equal or that it would be racial prejudice to exclude them. Sir John's acceptance of the Chinese was not an especially honourable one. He needed them to build the railway, and to satisfy the exasperating impatience of British Columbians; but he would be quite happy to rid himself of them when they were of no more use to him. Sir John was no better than anyone else; indeed, he was perhaps worse than some. There was at least no deceit in brawling Arthur Bunster. One never had to worry about what he was thinking or what trick he had up his sleeve. Arthur always spoke his mind.

But Bunster must very nearly have fallen from his parliamentary seat when Sir John said that the government had not had its attention drawn to the Chinese question before. Arthur, who had obligingly secured the Victoria seat for the premier, was a noted anti-Orientalist in the east even before he made his maiden speech in the House. He and Amor De Cosmos raised the subject frequently in Sir John's presence and Sir John himself had appointed a Select Committee to investigate the matter. Did he not read Amor's report? And had he forgotten all the memorials and petitions sent to his government? To say, as he did, that he had never had his attention brought to the matter before was more than unacceptable to British Columbian representatives; it also demonstrated the apathetic attitude towards the west.

From late May until late June, barks and steamships poured into Victoria. In this period 3,454 Chinese arrived in seven ships, each with 137 to 750 aboard. Two others arrived in June with 700 Chinese bound for Portland, but since both ships were liable to seizure in the United States, the Chinese disembarked in Victoria and filled Chinatown to overflowing. "The locality is slopping over," said the *Colonist*, pleased with its play upon the frequently used expression, "Chinese slop."

The Orientals were camping on vacant lots and crowding into shanties "like herring on a plate." The *Princess Louise* and the *R.P. Rithet* were loaded to the gunwales with Chinese en route to New Westminster and Yale. There was a near riot when a group of almost 900 were kept overnight on a dock in New Westminster. They split into two factions, chattering wildly at each other and raised their bamboo sticks threateningly. "They were all penned up on the Pioneer wharf overnight, like so many cattle," it was reported. "On Saturday morning they were run on board the steamer *William Irving* and taken up to Emory."

The same group was seen in Yale. "On Sunday morning the cars passed through Yale with 500 more Chinese," according to the *Sentinel*, "so that the line is now swarming with the late arrivals. We learn that 400 of the same importation were scattered along the line down the river where work, we learn, has fairly commenced." The reporter then travelled along the line to see for himself. "Mile after mile along the course of the winding Fraser, enclosed in the narrow dale beneath the clad mountains, are seen clusters of tents and hordes of Chinese who seem to owe their existence to the work of the railway construction more than the wealth of the land."

There seemed to be thousands upon thousands now, crammed tightly into Victoria's Chinatown, strung in a never-ending series of camps from Savona's Ferry to Emory and below and sprinkled in numerous little towns and mining claims over all the province. To mid-June 1882, arrivals from Hong Kong totalled 6,676, out of which 5,297 were consigned to Stahlschmidt and Ward, 929 to Tai Chong and 450 to Welch and Rithet. But they did not all come from China. Later figures for 1882 showed that 295 arrived from San Francisco and 280 from Puget Sound ports, while 7,508 came directly from Hong Kong. The total for 1882 was 8,083; in contrast, the number of white immigrants totalled 6,679.

On only one occasion was there any report of Orientals returning to their native land. On November 1, a "large number" came down the Fraser to await the arrival of the *Volmer*. Said the *Colonist*, "the gentry who arrived yesterday will remain about a month, during which period chickens should be advised to roost high." The *Volmer* arrived two weeks later with 224 Chinese who had been on board for 50 days. They had lived on a pound and a half of rice, a half-pound of meat and a half-pound of vegetables per man per day, with an allowance of fruit or lime juice, and were in good health. The ship sailed again with 360 Chinese bound for "the Flowery Kingdom."

Generally, there were no reports on the numbers who departed or who died, but the 8,083 arrivals for 1882 were far in excess of the 2,326 who entered the country between 1876 and 1880 and almost three times more than the 2,939 who entered in 1881.

For the Chinese, the year passed with little trouble. There were a few incidents in which the Orientals were the targets for stones thrown by school boys, and on one occasion a Chinese was found tied to a telephone post on Pandora Street. On the whole, though, they were tolerated because they were necessary for railroad construction. Only time would tell what would become of them when the last spike was driven home.

In the meantime, political life in the province was changing. In March, Premier Walkem was saved from defeat by the vote of the Speaker, and in June he resigned to become a judge of the Supreme Court. Robert Beaven became the new Premier. He did not do well in the provincial election in July, but he managed to survive; and when he opened the new Assembly he saw an interesting mixture of old and new faces. John Robson, returning to political life after an absence of seven years, had won by a large margin in New Westminster. A.E.B. Davie, William Smithe and William Semlin were back; Theodore Davie, at the age of 30 years, was one of the new faces. Another, but older in years, was the wealthy coal magnate Robert Dunsmuir, now 57. He did not even bother to campaign and was elected while he was on a visit to Scotland. Of interest to the ornithological set were the two members from Victoria: Simeon Duck and Montague William Tyrwhitt Drake.

There was also action in the Dominion arena: Sir John A. Macdonald called an election. This time he accepted the nomination for Lennox, Ontario. He could always fall back on Victoria, should one of those unforeseen calamities occur; they worshipped him there. Victorians did not feel slighted by his desertion—indeed, he was on their side now in regard to the Chinese question. In a speech in Yorkton he was quoted as saying that he was opposed to the importation of Chinese labour into Canada in any form and that if he was kept as a family physician he would see that Canadian labourers would not be obliged to compete with semi-barbarians who had only one shirt to a man and whose backs were so fertile that potatoes could be sewn thereon. His policy was "Canadians for Canadians," and for immigrants from the Old World part of the Great British Empire.

He had won handily long before the election on the west coast was held. Blake, Mackenzie and that rising star in the Liberal firmament, Wilfrid Laurier, managed to survive the Conservative onslaught. In the west, it was reported that Arthur Bunster would not run again, but he soon scotched that rumour. He had spent a most successful spring session in the House badgering Sir John, Sir Charles Tupper and the Minister of Marine. He had also had another tiff with evil Edward Blake. A motion had been placed before the House concerning the duty of the North West police in regard to the control of liquor in that region. Blake, the intellectual, dry-as-dust leader of the opposition, moved an amendment which proposed that alcohol in the north-west be limited to sacramental and medical uses. Arthur, the brewer of Bunster's best, immediately sprang to his feet and announced grandly that "the people of the North West should have as good an opportunity to enjoy themselves as the people of the other parts of the Dominion." Edward Blake withdrew his amendment.

Arthur Bunster also had continued to get a great deal of publicity from eastern newspapers. The Toronto *World*, for instance, praised him for his efforts against the Chinese, and the Ottawa *Herald* credited him with persuading the governor-general, the Marquis of Lorne, to visit British Columbia. When Arthur arrived back in Victoria in June 1882 to start his campaign, he must have known he would again be successful.

So also Amor De Cosmos. A resident since 1858, he had represented the people of Victoria since 1863. Amor, however, had gotten himself into a little trouble with his constituents during the last session by stating that Canada should become an independent state. If one had to make such a statement, the best constituency not to represent was Victoria. Its citizens were rabid Anglophiles. When Arthur Bunster sent a telegram to Mayor Shakespeare announcing that the Marquis of Lorne and his wife, Princess Louise (Queen Victoria's daughter), would visit the Province, the *Colonist* bubbled over with true British patriotism. "It is the first time a Princess of Blood Royal has set foot on the Pacific coast," it said. "Nowhere in the British realm are there found people more loyal and devoted to British Connection than those of the Pacific province."

Soon after the announcement of the coming general election, a strangely familiar notice had appeared in the *Colonist*: "To the Electors of Victoria District," it said. "Gentlemen—I shall be a candidate for the Commons at the coming Dominion election. N. Shakespeare." Success must have gone to Noah's head. Surely he could not succeed again—and yet, when the votes were counted in July, E.C. Baker had 377, Mayor Shakespeare 340 and Amor De Cosmos 235, with three others trailing in the two-seat riding. After 19 years as a representative of the people, Amor had been unceremoniously thrown out of office. Some said it was over his statement on Canadian independence. It would be most fitting if this were so. He was always several years in advance of public thinking.

But there was still Arthur Bunster. No one was more loyal to British Columbia, no one fought harder for its recognition, albeit in a rough Irish fashion. When the ballots were counted in Nanaimo, he had 155 fewer than D.W. Gordon. He slipped silently away to drown his sorrows in San Francisco.

The province's two most fascinating and energetic personalities had been defeated in the same election. Things could never be the same without Amor and Arthur, and without little George Walkem to fight and probe and complain. The new members seemed like such ordinary people, as did the new premier of the province, Robert Beaven—though perhaps Noah Shakespeare would add a little colour. It was a summer of changes. Even the last landmark, the old fort, was being demolished.

But there was no time to become sentimental over change. The governor-general and Princess Louise were due in September (ironically, Arthur Bunster had arranged the visit) and there were a thousand details to arrange: receptions, tours, addresses, drawing rooms, banquets, dinners, balls. Miss Shakespeare and Miss Beaven could surely be prevailed upon to present floral offerings to Her Highness. There were the usual arches to be built, too—a civic arch, a Fireman's arch and of course a Chinese arch. The latter, from the very beginning, was the greatest eye-catcher. It had been designed from a photograph of a similar arch in Philadelphia. The central arch was to tower 45 feet over Store Street, in the form of a Chinese temple. There were two lower side arches with pagoda roofs striped in green and white. It was decorated with flag poles on which the Chinese standard flew and there were Chinese lanterns, pictures, miniature theatrical scenes and the usual mottoes: "God Save the Queen" and "The Orient Greets the Occident."

The construction of the Chinese arch irritated Arthur Bunster almost beyond endurance. He returned from San Francisco in time to attend the final meeting of the Reception Committee in mid-September. "Mr. Bunster wished to know what authorization the Chinese had for erecting an arch on Store street," reported the *Colonist*, "and he was informed that they had obtained permission from the committee in due form. He then denounced the action of the committee and stated that, as he had considerable to do with bringing the Governor-general and the Princess Louise out to this province, he should exercise his influence to prevent the vice-regal party from passing under the arch in question. (Laughter.)" Laughter. It still followed Arthur Bunster.

He was at least consistent. Noah Shakespeare, basking in the glories of his new-found image as mayor and M.P., conveniently overlooked the Chinese arch, which was certainly the most attractive sight in the city. The Oriental shops on Store and Johnson Streets were being decorated with evergreens and Cormorant Street, from end to end, was lined with young fir trees. The Chinese were actually outdoing their white persecutors, and Noah raised no objection.

Victoria surely enjoyed vice-regal visits more than any other city in the Dominion. "God Save the Queen" and "other patriotic airs" echoed over the waters of the Straits of Juan de Fuca when the welcoming ship, *Wilson G. Hunt*, met *H.M.S. Comus* just inside Cape

Flattery. The U.S. Revenue Cutter *Oliver Walcot* fired a 21-gun salute, the *Comus* bravely dipping her flag in acceptance. And that evening in Victoria, His Worship Mayor Shakespeare stepped aboard to greet the marquis and the princess. The next day the festivities began and they lasted from September 20 until December 6.

There were numerous formal gatherings, following which the newspaper listed the names of all the guests: Begbie, Crease, Gray, Walkem, Cornwall, Macdonald, McInnes, Trutch, Helmcken, Davie, Shakespeare, Dunsmuir, Homer, Oppenheimer and a thousand others. Nowhere did the name of Amor De Cosmos appear, and only at "the drawing room" was Hon. Arthur Bunster mentioned, along with W. Sing Kee. The once ubiquitous Arthur was all but ignored. Even the Chinese merchants saw more of the Marquis than did Arthur. Later in September, Chin Chong, Tai Chong, Tai Yuen, Kwong Lee, Goon Gun, Wing Kee and Sun Chong waited on the governor-general, presented an address, received his expression of pleasure on their visit, and withdrew.

Arthur did meet Lorne on one other occasion when the vice-regal party made the rounds of various industrial establishments. "The last call of the day," reported the *Colonist*, "was made at Mr. Bunster's brewery on Johnson street. Here the ex-M.P. was found hard at work chopping wood, with the cares of state laid aside, preparations for making the Englishman's beverage actively going on."

The Marquis had seen the remarkable Chinese arch, he had met several Chinese citizens and, if he was exposed to the newspapers, he had read a series of articles in the *Colonist* on "Chinese vs. White Labor." It almost seemed as if they had been printed especially for his benefit. He also met a delegation consisting of E.C. Baker, Mayor Shakespeare and Premier Beaven, who discussed the desirability of restricting Chinese immigration. The governor-general, however, again pointed out that the C.P.R. could not be constructed in a short time without Chinese.

The Marquis and the Princess departed on December 6, and Victorians were forced to contemplate matters more mundane, notably the railroad and the Chinese. The C.P.R. had stretched now as far west as Pile of Bones River near Regina, 18 miles of track had been laid above Yale, and there was great activity in the Port Moody-Emory Section. "Hundreds of Chinamen, like ants in an ant-hill, are engaged with pick, shovel and wheel barrow at Port Moody, grading the line contiguous to the great wharf," said the *Guardian* in November 1882. "The hum arising from the pick, shovel and wheel barrow is supported by a running accompaniment from carpenter's hammers, the whole forming enlivening music of railway construction."

There were some discordant notes in the Port Moody melody. Sea worms, it was said, were eating up the C.P.R. dock, and another remarkably cold winter was beginning to develop. Ice was forming on the Fraser; James Bay in Victoria was frozen solid; Port Moody was completely frozen in by three inches of clear blue ice extending from the dock to a point two and a half miles down the inlet. The *Maude*, loaded with provisions for the community, was unable to reach the dock and was forced to return to Victoria. The Chinese at the tip of Burrard Inlet "are said to be out of rice and consequently the Johns are on short commons," said the *Colonist*. "There is plenty of the celestial staff of life in this city, and they will not be long without a supply." And from Port Moody came a letter from a disillusioned correspondent. "There certainly has been a mistake made in terminating a great railroad here," it said, "when a few miles farther takes it to a better harbor and water that never freezes." Those rare frigid winters had been instrumental in shifting the capital from New Westminster. Perhaps now they would shift the terminus of the railroad down the inlet.

The icy winter may have been the cause of widespread illness amongst the Chinese labourers. Their staple diet was rice, to which was added small amounts of meat and vegetables or occasionally fruit juice. With the freezing of the river and the inlet, rice was in short supply as were, presumably, meat and vegetables. The Chinese, even under normal circumstances, were constantly on the brink of vitamin deficiency. Now, with their lines of supply cut by ice, the signs of these dread diseases began to appear. Early in February 1883, the *Sentinel* noted half a dozen Chinese deaths above Yale from "a sort of scurvy or black leg." There were no facilities for caring for the ill, Onderdonk's hospital being reserved for accident cases only. This was so for both Chinese and whites, but it was the Chinese who suffered most. "The winter season especially is very hard upon the natives of the Celestial empire," the *Sentinel* said. "It is feared the medical attendance bestowed by those whom they depend upon in illness is not what it should be for this climate."

In the middle of February, the *Princess Louise* steamed up the river with 1,200 mats of rice, but it came too late for many of the Chinese labourers. (The rice was prepared in China. It was first boiled; then the crusted portion sticking to the pot was pounded flat and shipped to B.C. as 50-pound mats, each one a labourer's supply for one month.) The *Sentinel* described the local situation: "Along the lines of the railway the Chinese workmen are fast disappearing—under the ground. Within a few weeks no less than six have died out of a gang of 28 employed a few miles below Emory . . . .About a week since, one died from 1½ hours of illness, and on Saturday another dropped off suddenly. There being no medical attendance provided by the Railway Company for the unfortunate Chinese, we are unable to get at the nature of the disease that is creating such a thinning out of the number employed. However, upon enquiry, we are informed that the symptoms are a swelling of the feet and legs, turning as to dropsy, and soon the whole body was affected. This peculiar disease was known some years since at Singapore as 'berrie-berrie' and proved fatal to many of the Chinese at the time. It is thought that food has something to do with it. Want of vegetable nourishment is assigned as one of the causes. Scurvy or 'black leg' is produced among other nationalities by a too free use of salt pork, and is often cured by change of diet to fresh beef and vegetables."

The sudden deaths continued into the spring. The *Colonist*'s Yale correspondent reported in March 1883, "Here in Yale at the temporary hospital opened at Sam Sing's house are a number of sick. Sunday one died, Wednesday two died and others are very low. Upon enquiry we were told the dead and dying all belonged to the railway company. No medical attendance is furnished, nor apparently much interest felt in the unfortunate creatures. We understand that Mr. Onderdonk declines interfering, while the Lee Chuck Company that brought the Chinamen from their native land refuses, through their agent, Lee Soon, who is running the Chinese store at Emory, to become responsible for doctor's bills or medicine. The illness is reported to be 'berrie-berrie' or swelling of the feet, legs and eyes, getting into the body and in a few hours the victims die in great suffering."

Railway construction was certainly slowed by ice and illness in that frigid February and March of 1883. It was also slowed by conflicts between Chinese labourers and their white foremen. At Port Moody, a gang of chattering Chinese chased their foreman with picks and shovels when they were treated "in a somewhat summary fashion." In early February, two Chinese assaulted a foreman at Maple Ridge; they were arrested, and submitted meekly to the officer of the law. As they were being led up the railway bed, other Chinese labourers began chattering amongst themselves, stirred restlessly and then advanced threateningly with picks and shovels raised. The officer, with his prisoners, took refuge in a nearby store, but he was soon "surrounded by a howling mob of Chinamen holding in their hands the implements with which they had been working—axes, shovels etc. They declared that unless the prisoners were released they would tear the house to pieces and rescue them." The officer was forced to set the men free, but later the local magistrate notified the Chinese boss that he must turn over the prisoners, who by then were nowhere to be found. The magistrate hurried down the river to an Indian camp, where he asked the Indians to capture the two prisoners should they appear. Soon he received word that the fugitives had wandered into the camp and were now being held. "Mr. Harris, the magistrate, came down, organised a court and fined each $15." The fines were paid and the two Orientals returned to work.

The most brutal encounter between whites and Chinese occurred on May 10, 1883. The white foreman at Camp 37, near Lytton, had told two Chinese not to return to work, since they were too lazy. The Chinese boss asked that they be given another chance and the foreman agreed to do so, but the following day, after the Chinese had put in two hours of work, the foreman again discharged them and refused to pay them the two hours wages. The Oriental gang then attacked the foreman, a timekeeper, a bridge superintendent and a teamster with rocks and pick handles. The whites were injured and were forced to retreat. That night, a party of 20 whites crept into the Chinese camp, set fire to their log house and, as the Chinese poured out the door in panic, clubbed them brutally. Ye Fook died that unhappy night, and seven or eight other Chinese were severely injured.

The *Colonist* referred to this encounter as "the most unmanly and cowardly affair that has yet occurred in the country." They were even more shocked when they discovered that the white doctors in Lytton would not treat the injured Chinese. An Oriental doctor from Yale had to be sent for. No clue as to the perpetrators of the deed was found, since the white workmen made every effort to shield their guilty comrades, and when an inquest into the death of Ye Fook was held in Lytton, it was impossible to find twelve disinterested men to act on the jury.

"When we labor for the removal of the Chinese evil from our midst," commented the *Colonist*, "we shall never countenance unlawful proceedings to attain that end." But the newspaper had started the wheel of anti-Orientalism rolling and had sustained it, and once the wheel gained momentum, no editorializing could control it. The newspaper was as guilty as the two governments—and the people of the province.

Late in January 1883, the Beaven government was defeated and William Smithe became premier. In his first session, the Chinese question was raised on several occasions, but no one seemed to know exactly what to do. Robert Beaven wished again to request the Dominion to restrict Chinese immigration, but this had already been done twice and on both occasions the request had been completely ignored. Robert Dunsmuir had a more specific proposal in the form of an amendment to the Coal Mines Regulation Act. It was the first of a long series of amendments to the act. Dunsmuir pointed out that if white boys of 14 years were allowed to perform light work in the coal mines (to replace the 16 year minimum age limit) he could discharge a large number of Chinese. He was the largest employer of Orientals—of some 500, he said—but he would replace them immediately if he could find white labour. There was none available (as there was no additional Chinese labour available). It would certainly be an advantage to the Dunsmuir Mines if they could hire 14 year-old boys at low wages—but the great coal magnate failed in his attempt.

In the end, A.E.B. Davie managed to get an amendment to Beaven's original proposal passed. It was little more than an expression of policy; Chinese restriction would be attempted, white immigration would be encouraged and Chinese would be compelled to comply with the revenue laws.

John Robson, at the age of 59 years, must have listened to the endless debates on the Chinese with a great deal of satisfaction. There were some new, fresh, young faces on the floor now, but others, who had referred to his anti-Oriental proposals ten years ago as "pure buncombe", were still there. He reminded them of this when he rose to speak. Ten years ago, he said, " . . . it was throwing chaff against the wind . . . and now the knife could not be applied to this cancer."

In the meantime, Noah Shakespeare was attempting to fill Arthur Bunster's big Irish boots in Ottawa. Although from the very beginning there was no chance of its being passed, he proposed a motion recommending that Chinese entering the province be assessed $50, and that each ship arriving in British Columbia be restricted to one Chinese to every 100 tons. Sir John insisted that there was no point in excluding Chinese until they could be replaced, and again he naively pointed out that they were not settlers; they had no wives and they would ultimately leave the country. It was premature, he said, to pass the motion until the railway was built. When that time came, he would not exclude them, but he would regulate and restrict their admission. He was paraphrased as saying, "When the gates were shut down against their entrance into Canada, they must rapidly disappear, therefore there was no fear of the degradation of the country by a mongrel race."

Anti-Chinese legislation, then, was attempted by both the provincial and Dominion Governments in 1883, and by both unsuccessfully. There was no doubt, however, that sentiment against the Oriental was rising. Many incidents occurred now in Victoria in which boys, probably reflecting the semi-suppressed attitude of their parents and the less suppressed attitude of provincial members and city newspapers, attacked the Chinese. These same newspapers were indignant when, in the autumn of 1883, a public school boy threw a piece of brick at a Chinese who was patiently cutting wood in an empty lot near the school. Ah Lock fell senseless to the ground. He was found some time later and carried into the school, where Mr. John McKenzie, true to Victorian tradition, provided him with a cup of tea. A plaster was placed on his injured head and, after he had fainted once, he was escorted home. Eleven days later, Ah Lock became ill and had to be admitted to the hospital. For several days he was near death, but he recovered, though it was said that his mind was quite "distracted."

"Things have come to a fine pass if the sensibilities of children who are sent to public schools are to be shocked by the spectacle of a murderous assault on an inoffensive Chinaman," said the *Colonist*, "who, although a most undesirable resident, is entitled to protection." In one breath they deplored the act and in the next they spoke disparagingly of the Chinese as being "inoffensive" and "a most undesirable resident." The newspapers and some citizens were capable of differentiating peaceful opposition from violence, but children and railroad workers were not.

A more sinister form of racial discrimination occurred on the *William Irving* as she steamed up the Fraser to Yale in September. At dinner time, the head of one of the most prominent Chinese firms in Victoria quietly took his seat at the table with the rest of the passengers. A steward ordered him to leave, but he refused and sat at the table during the complete dinner hour while all the waiters ignored him.

By the spring and summer of 1883, it was obvious that the peak of Chinese immigration had passed. Onderdonk had secured some

800 white mechanics and 3,000 white labourers "from the parched fields of California, the worked out silver mines of Nevada and the ice bound regions of Manitoba." The *Colonist* was ecstatic. "Goodbye John!" It bubbled. During the entire year, 793 arrived from Puget Sound, 1,874 from San Francisco and 556 from China for a total of 3,223 compared with 2,939 in 1881 and 8,083 in 1882.

One of the more interesting arrivals was the *S.S. Madras*, which had sailed from Hong Kong on March 16. She had been quarantined in Honululu, where 13 cases of smallpox were removed, and did not arrive in Royal Roads until June 29. Here Dr. Jackson found two more cases; they were removed to the pest house on the Indian Reserve and the ship was again placed in quarantine. On July 11, the remaining 136 Chinese passengers were finally allowed to disembark, almost four months after boarding the ship. "They presented a very sorry appearance," reported the *Colonist*, "many of them experiencing great difficulty walking while others were entirely unable to do so and were carried ashore.... They were all suffering from an Oriental disease brought on by contamination of the blood arising mainly from an almost exclusive consumption of decomposed vegetables."

The following day, the Chinese returned to the *Madras* carrying a large roasted pig, roasted ducks, baskets of apples, pots of tea, trays of rice and flour cakes. These were placed on the ship's hatch and the white crew gathered about in happy anticipation of a great feast. The Chinese, however, were in no hurry. Said the *Colonist*, "they went through a number of heathenish dances, waving their arms and bowing while muttering incantations and prayers to their gods." When the thanksgiving service was completed, the Chinese shouldered their succulent morsels and departed, leaving the crew of the *Madras* in an agony of famished disappointment.

Victorians were simultaneously fascinated by and disdainful of these oriental rituals. They gazed upon the colour and noise of the Chinese masonic ritual with interest, yet rarely failed to show their contempt. The conditions in the Chinese burial ground, however, were especially disturbing: "Those whose sense of decency is rather susceptible are cautioned against visiting the old cemetery unless they would turn sick with disgust and horror," said the *Colonist* in November 1883. "It seems astounding that while there is a cemetery committee which presumably takes some interest in this charge, it should be necessary to call the attention of the public to the state of the Chinese portion of the grounds. This race of people, abusing the very civilization of a Christian country which allows them to practise their heathenish rites even within the most sacred of its precincts, turns religious liberty into license and in the prosecution of their ghoulish work of resurrecting the bodies of their dead countrymen, scraping their bones and burning the refuse flesh in their cemetery furnace (or altar), mayhap neglect or deem it unnecessary to re-fill the graves with earth, which consequently expose to view the boxes and coffins from which the bodies have been taken. Worse than this, there can be seen portions of queues and matted hair attached to sundry planks which have been torn off the coffins and are lying strewn about. Several masses of peculiar consistence, looking strangely like calcined bones, lie near an open grave, in the grass, while a little farther away is a bone—probably a portion of a Chinaman—which bears the marks of some animal's teeth . . . ."

It also disturbed Victorians to see the marked growth of the Chinese community, both geographically and economically. "The Chinese are quietly possessing themselves of the northern quarter of the city bounded by Johnson and Government streets, the water front and the gas works," said the *Colonist*. Their plan, it seemed apparent, was to make Victoria their chief Pacific port and control trade to eastern Canada. Gam Lun Tay, a firm with factories in Canton and Hong Kong and a mercantile establishment in San Francisco, opened a large store on Cormorant Street. During the summer, a Chinese restaurant catering to white workingmen was opened; Kwong Lee was constructing a second and third store; and Tai Chong and On Hing were in the process of constructing new buildings. "In every quarter, new brick and frame buildings are going up in Chinatown," said the *Colonist*. "The area of Chinatown is extending. No figure, however high, causes them to hesitate in closing a bargain for real estate."

With the approaching completion of the railway, Chinese merchants saw their opportunity. The same event affected the Chinese labourer differently. "John Chinaman" was no longer "putting on airs."

CHAPTER IV

1883-1886

"No More Chow Chow."
Resident of Chinatown, Victoria, 1886.

It was expected that by the first week of 1884 trains would be able to travel from the terminus at Port Moody to Lytton, 143 miles to the north-east, but as the railroad lengthened, the fortunes of the Chinese ebbed. Construction had originally begun at various points along its planned route, and from each of these sites it had stretched both north and south. When individual sections were joined, employees were discharged. At the peak of activity in 1883, the number of Chinese labourers varied between 6,000 and 7,500. By June of that year, when the lower section was virtually complete, all the Chinese had departed from the Port Moody area for work farther up the line. But there was still an immigration of over 3,000, and even in the first six months of 1884 the number of Chinese entering the country totalled 1,456.

Unemployment was well established by December 1883, when scores of Chinese could be seen strung along the line in the Lower Mainland without any visible means of support. "How are these miserable creatures to exist until spring?" asked the *Columbian*. By January 1884, some indigent Chinese were seen eating decayed vegetables which they had found about the streets of Yale; along the Thompson River they were camped in hundreds; and below Savona, ranchers were complaining of many petty thefts by hungry Chinese. There were said to be 500 such Orientals around Savona and upward of 2,000 in Spence's Bridge. Some had quit their work before being formally discharged, thus losing their share of the 80 mats of rice with which each gang was presented when they were laid off. Some of those who did receive their share were said to have gambled it away and were now completely destitute. John Robson stated that some 3,000 were burrowing caves in the earth near Tilton Creek and eating dead salmon from the stream. The government, he said, should either feed or transport them.

Some Chinese labourers had escaped the rigours of unemployment by being smuggled into the United States, while others had found jobs in Robert Dunsmuir's mines during the strike of August 1883. In that month, 300 white coal miners went on strike for higher wages. The company's ship, *Wellington*, it was reported, received immediate orders to proceed to Hong Kong for Chinese labourers. The miners received their notice to vacate company dwellings, and it appeared that another long strike similar to that of 1877 was about to take place. The militia had been called out on that occasion and the strike had lasted three months. The miners of 1883 were in an almost impossible position. To begin with, they had a formidable opponent in Robert Dunsmuir, but in addition there were Chinese who could take over their jobs at a cheaper wage scale. The white miners were paid by the ton of coal they delivered to the surface. To save valuable time, they had personally hired cheap Chinese labour to load and send boxes of coal to the surface while they, the white miners, blasted holes, fired shots and erected props. Now the Chinese, having learned these techniques by observing the whites, were taking over the blasting and prop jobs. Robert Dunsmuir brought in more Chinese and, in his own paraphrased words, "There was no doubt that they (the Chinese) had broken the strike."

Dunsmuir was surprisingly candid about this. He did not want Chinese in his mines, he said, though he did not hesitate to use them to break the strike. In January 1884, he pointed out that he had cut his Chinese employees to 40 and soon would discharge them all, though later evidence showed that neither of these statements was so. In 1883, however, his miners did not have a chance of winning their increase in wages. They were poorly organized (they had no connection with the rival Vancouver Coal Company), the newspapers were against the strike—the *Colonist* advised them to go back to work to prevent the mines from falling further into "Pagan hands"—and the Chinese were taking over their jobs. The strike dwindled out in the middle of November with the miners returning at the same wage, poorer, hungrier and perhaps wiser.

They should have listened to Noah. He had warned them about the Chinese long ago, or so he said. Noah was the great oracle now.

Everyone listened to Noah. Following his meteoric rise to political success he had made a pilgrimage to the place of his birth, Brierly, in Staffordshire. Here he basked felinely in the admiration of the villagers—who had no doubt never heard of him—and magnanimously "gave a gratuitous tea to 52 aged people, 92 Band of Hope Children and 118 Ragged School Scholars." Noah was most pleased with himself. In his speech before those gathered for the gratuitous tea at Brierly Hill, he pointed out that, since his humble connection with the Ragged School many years ago, he had risen to such heights that he now entertained royalty. "He felt bound to express his thankfulness for the beneficent influence that had been exercised upon his mind there. It gave him great pleasure to see so many present and to have the opportunity of giving them the treat; for, although it had fallen to his lot to entertain the Queen's daughter and son-in-law, he considered this to be a far greater honor."

Noah Shakespeare had a wonderful time. He visited the French Assembly and the British Parliament, and he lectured throughout England on the potentialities of British Columbia. And when he arrived back in Victoria in September 1883, he and Mrs. Shakespeare were serenaded by the Victoria Brass Band, after which he spoke a few words "and regaled them with supper." He was a standard politician now, though he could hardly fill Arthur Bunster's boots. He became a director of the Victoria Agricultural Society, later "the telling spirit" of the Blue Ribbon Club, and still later, its president.

The club, of course, would have been an abomination to Arthur Bunster, since it was a temperance group which sang hymns at its meetings. But Arthur was no longer exposed to it. He had sold his brewery in March 1883 and had moved to Oakland, California, where he was now brewing his favourite ale. Arthur had twice hinted at such a move because of the Chinese inroads into the province, but perhaps this was not the primary cause. He had been disappointed in his ambition to become lieutenant-governor, he had fought with almost everyone, he had been ingloriously defeated politically and he had had another court case over his son. Arthur Bunster had been a great wanderer for most of his life. Now, after 25 years in Victoria, he had departed for California at the age of 56.

When the Legislative Assembly met in late 1883 and early 1884, they were pleased that the Esquimalt drydock construction had been taken over by the Dominion government and that Robert Dunsmuir and Sir Alexander Campbell, Dominion Minister of Justice, had met to sign a memorandum of agreement to construct the E. & N.

Railway. But they lost little time in turning to anti-Chinese legislation. This promised to be nothing more than the usual "memorials"
to Ottawa or the passage of bills which again would be disallowed as
unconstitutional by the Dominion government, but the Davie
brothers were becoming a power in the provincial government now
and their approach to the problem was more intelligent, more
thorough and more organized.

Attorney-general A.E.B. Davie, at the age of 38, was chairman of a
Select Committee on the Chinese question, and Theodore Davie,
aged 32, was its most active member. (One of A.E.B.'s daughters
married F.J. Fulton who was later a provincial cabinet minister.
Their son, E. Davie Fulton was for many years M.P. for Kamloops
and Federal Minister of Justice from 1957 to 1962. A second daughter married A.E. McPhillips, a provincial Member; a son of that
marriage, A. de B. McPhillips, was later an M.P. for Victoria.) In
mid-January 1884 the Davie brothers presented two bills to the
House. The first of these, "The Chinese Regulation Act of 1884,"
was a very detailed document containing 31 clauses. It took into
consideration all the problems and objections raised in the past. The
term "Chinese," for instance, was clearly defined as "any person of
the Chinese race," thus avoiding the problem of whether a native of
Hong Kong was British or Chinese. It was proposed that every
Chinese over the age of 14 years purchase a licence for a sum set at
$100. Collectors for every electoral district were to be appointed,
anyone without a licence was to be fined and every employer had to
supply the names of Chinese liable to pay the tax. In order to put a
stop to the practice of exhumation, it was to be made unlawful to
remove Chinese remains without permission. Furthermore, opium
was to be prohibited and dwelling rooms occupied by Chinese were
to contain at least 384 cubic feet for each person, with a window
capable of being opened, at least two feet square. The act was to
come into effect in one year.

The second bill was "An Act to prevent the immigration of
Chinese 1883-1884." It was much more brief, perhaps because the
Davie brothers realized that there was little likelihood of its being
allowed by the Dominion government which, under the B.N.A. Act,
had complete control over immigration. Essentially the act stated
that it was unlawful for Chinese to enter the province and that a fine
of $50 or six months imprisonment would be levied on law-breakers.
Furthermore, any person assisting a Chinese to enter was liable to a
fine of $100. This act was to take effect on March 31, 1884.

The two acts were discussed endlessly in the legislature. With one exception, every member was in favour of regulating and restricting the Chinese, though the methods of doing so could not be agreed upon. The one voice which argued in favour of the Chinese was that of Robert Dunsmuir. They had filled the gap in the labour market, he said [certainly they had filled the gap left by striking miners], and they had enabled colliers to compete with San Francisco mines [and provide him with a handsome profit]. As a result of Dunsmuir's isolated opposition, he was accused of changing his mind, now that he had a large contract for the E. & N. The other interesting voice to be heard was that of John Robson. The acts might be ruled unconstitutional, he argued, but they must be passed locally to impress upon the Dominion government that Chinese legislation was imperative. They were indeed finally passed by the province, and British Columbia now had a Chinese Immigration Act and a Chinese Regulation Act.

In Ottawa, Noah Shakespeare immediately began to press for acceptance of the British Columbia bill, but the wheels of government ground exceedingly slowly. By March 31, the date on which the Immigration Act was to take effect, the Dominion had still not decided on its acceptability. Premier William Smithe, at this time, was in Ottawa to discuss the fixing of the eastern boundary of British Columbia, which was believed to be east of Calgary. When John Robson wired him that the *Crusader* was approaching Victoria with 500 Chinese immigrants, Smithe telegraphed back that they must not be allowed to land. Sir John A. Macdonald, sensing the political importance of a decision, said the matter would probably go to the Imperial Privy Council. As it developed, however, the *Crusader* never did arrive in Victoria. Her captain had heard of the passing of the Immigration Act and had cancelled the voyage. But on April 11, 1884, two Chinese were arrested under the Immigration Act; and later the same day word reached Victoria that the Dominion government had disallowed it. The fortunate Chinese were immediately released.

To Victorians, this was "The Immigration Hubbub." The act had failed, but the *Colonist* pointed out that it had brought the attention of the Dominion government to "The Chinese Evil;" it had strengthened the hands of the British Columbia members to get a Royal Commission, and the bill would be brought up again and again until the province received satisfaction.

Although British Columbians expressed no bitterness towards their darling, Sir John, he appears to have been somewhat indecisive at this point in history. He said merely that a 100-dollar fine was too great and that something more moderate might have passed. The *Colonist*, in a verbose manner, said that the matter would be referred to "the home government and affairs would be adjusted with China with a view to protecting our province from the evils accompanying an undue influx of Mongolians who, like the locusts of Egypt, will blacken the air and devour everything in their way, if our port is kept open to the thousands who formerly pushed their way into the Golden Gate, until the working men of California cried out against the invaders who were taking the bread from white families by their cheap labor . . . . "

In late 1883 and early 1884, then, there had been two developments of interest: the first signs of Chinese unemployment had appeared and the strongest attempt at anti-Chinese legislation had been made. At this time, too, there was a restless stir in the ranks of labour and there was a tightening of moral standards amongst the more aristocratic citizens of the capital.

One of the first working man's groups was the Knights of Labor of North America, organized in Victoria in March 1884, with offices on Yates Street. The Nanaimo Trades Association was another. They were objecting to a 20-mile-wide strip of railway reserve which had been graciously presented to the E. & N., the president of which was Robert Dunsmuir. And both organizations began to use such unpleasant words as "capitalist" and "monopoly." Old Robert Dunsmuir must have growled in his grizzled Scottish beard at the thought of what these two organizations could do to his mines, his impending railway and his pocket-book.

Then there were the moral standards of the city. Gambling, drinking and opium smoking felt the brunt of the attack. In April, Victoria's police chief, Superintendent Bloomfield, began the assault on gambling establishments. He had no difficulty closing the white dens of iniquity, but "the wily Chinese bunco sharper" was almost impossible to catch in the act. Victoria's aristocrats were no doubt shocked, puzzled and perhaps curious to read about a game called "stud-horse poker"; they held public protest meetings while Bloomfield continued his remoresless attack on "The Knights of the Green Cloth."

Groups of public-spirited citizens, too, were banding together to contest the apparent deterioration in moral standards. In September, "The Free Thinkers" were organized, later changing their name to "The Liberal League." In October, another group discussed the establishment of a Y.M.C.A. and in November, in the presence of those prominent public leaders, John Robson and Noah Shakespeare, the first organizational meeting was held.

The Blue Ribbon Club, preaching the evils of the demon alcohol, had been active over the past year, but blossomed forth anew in 1884. Its members held frequent meetings with addresses, recitations, singing and band music, and the W.C.T.U. was similarly active. On May 24, the Queen's Birthday, the Union picnicked at Foul Bay, accompanied by Hon. John Robson (a good Presbyterian) and Noah Shakespeare (a good Methodist). There were games, amusement and "sober conversation," and the Blue Ribbon Band, led by Professor Haynes, entertained throughout the day. In the evening all participants attended a grand performance at Philharmonic Hall.

The stir in the ranks of labour and the entrenchment of Victoria's moral standards were a fitting prelude to the appearance of the Royal Commission on Chinese Immigration. Noah Shakespeare was given credit for its appointment, but most of the members from the west had contributed, especially Arthur Bunster, who was still languishing in the San Francisco Bay region. Noah just happened to be the most recent proponent of anti-Oriental legislation. He had placed before the House a resolution which Sir John asked to be withdrawn, with the understanding that he would appoint a commission to investigate immigration of Chinese into the western province. Noah was extremely angry about this, since, he said, it implied that information supplied by British Columbia M.P.s was inaccurate or exaggerated.

The Commission (the word "Royal" was not used) was appointed on July 5, 1884 and consisted of two gentlemen: Hon. Joseph A. Chapleau, Secretary of State, and Mr. Justice John Hamilton Gray, Sir John A. Macdonald's first political appointee to British Columbia. The secretary of the Commission was Nicholas Flood Davin, well known in that part of the North-West Territory now called Saskatchewan. He was the editor of the Regina *Leader*—"a gentleman of high literary renown", the *Colonist* said—and later an M.P.

From the very beginning it was an unpopular commission. The Montreal *Witness* stated that any investigation by Chapleau would be "a simple farce" and that "no one would have the slightest confidence in that gentleman's finding." The *Colonist* believed the commission was merely a preliminary group formed to make final arrangements for a more complete commission with the provincial government. Chapleau, they said, was not an adequate man for the job, especially since he would have to return to Ottawa soon to take care of his cabinet post, and Gray was far too busy in the Supreme Court.

When it was realized that this was indeed all the commission that was going to be appointed, the *Colonist* was even more upset with the personnel. "It is not such as this province and its representatives had a right to expect from Ottawa," they said. The *Standard* was satisfied. "But," answered the *Colonist*, "the editor of the *Standard* (referring to Amor De Cosmos) is the largest holder of Chinese tenement property in the city . . . . He favors an overworked judge and one who has never seen a live Chinaman till he started on his journey to the Pacific province." Even Gray was an employer of Chinese, they said. "Although he is a gentleman of honor and experience, he can in no sense be regarded as a representative of anti-Chinese element in the province nor as a representative of public opinion on the Chinese question."

In July, Chapleau and Commission Secretary Davin stopped off in San Francisco on their journey to Victoria and met various officials who were interested in the local Chinese problem. Many present had taken part in the Joint Committee of the Senate and House of Representatives investigation in 1876. It was a reasonable step, since the histories of California and British Columbia had run parallel, separated only by some ten or fifteen years. It was reasonable, too, since in May 1882 President Chester Arthur had signed a bill prohibiting the immigration of Chinese into the United States for a period of ten years. If British Columbia's history was to continue to parallel that of its southern neighbour, should Canada not immediately pass a similar bill? Must British Columbia suffer the agonies of riots and bloodshed to fill the ten-year gap? Was there any reason to believe that now, in 1884, their histories would suddenly diverge? Chapleau and Gray had been appointed to provide the answers, if indeed the questions were not already answered.

The virtues and vices of the Chinese in San Francisco were the virtues and vices complained of in Victoria, except, of course, that they were on a grander scale in the city to the south. Mr. Chapleau was most impressed with the pleasantness of San Francisco's Chinatown by day, but after his night visit he wrote a long and eloquent description of its horrors. "One of our party, a pretty strong man, began to feel seasick, and it was only by an effort of the will that he repressed nature's protest against such scenes and such smells . . . . "

Perhaps Chapleau and Davin were happy to step aboard the

Mexico and sail out the Golden Gate. A few days later when they rounded Cape Flattery to roll across the Straits of Juan de Fuca, did they feel a faint glow of nationalistic pride? They were back in their own country now—their country in name at least. Officially it was Canada, though to British Columbians "Canada" meant Ontario and Quebec, and when easterners departed for British Columbia, they still spoke of going "out of Canada" to "Columbia" or "the Pacific slope." They were still separate, and Chapleau, if not Davin too, probably felt no different in these waters than he did in the Golden Gate.

When they slipped into Victoria's inner harbour, Huang Sic Chen had already been there for more than a week. He was a member of the Chinese consulate in San Francisco, and newspapermen were most curious to know the purpose of his visit. They followed him about, asking questions through an interpreter while Huang had his hair cut; they pursued him to Tai Song's on Cormorant Street, to the Chinese Benevolent Association's rooms in King Tye's building and still later to Quong Chong's restaurant. At first, Huang said only that China was considering the establishment of a consulate in Victoria, but later he admitted that he was in the city to attend the Royal Commission. He no doubt spent most of his time gathering statistics on British Columbia's Orientals. When he stepped out for a walk on the last day of July, however, "he was grossly insulted by a group of boys who threw stones at him."

On August 9, the *Colonist* printed all the complaints against the Chinese, presumably for the benefit of the commissioners, and on the same evening, a public meeting was held in the city hall. Here Noah Shakespeare presented a resolution which stated that the commission was superfluous, that the Dominion government must doubt all information given to it by the representatives of the people and that he, Noah, be instructed not to go before the commission. Robert Beaven seconded the motion and it was carried unanimously, in the presence of several prominent members of the provincial government, notably A.E.B. Davie and M.W.T. Drake—both of whom later presented evidence.

Commissioners Chapleau and Gray had been invited to the meeting, but they gracefully declined. Instead, they spent the evening rambling through Chinatown accompanied by Superintendent Bloomfield, Victoria's Police Chief. They found the brick houses much superior to those of San Francisco, but the opium dens were the exact counterpart of the American city, though less numerous. The greatest difference was that in Victoria they found one or two whites crowded into the opium dens along with the Chinese and "indulging in this powerful narcotic." It was here that they also encountered "a young woman, well dressed and full of intelligence." She lay on a bunk, fixing her pipe with a practised hand and inhaling the smoke. Her name was given as Emily Wharton. After much persuasion she consented to answer questions.

Emily was 22 years of age; she had started smoking opium in San Francisco four years earlier. "Why did you commence to smoke opium?" she was asked.

"Why do people commence to drink?" she answered. "Trouble, I suppose, led me to smoke. I think it is better than drink. People that smoke opium do not kick up rows; they injure no one but themselves, and I do not think they injure themselves very much. I know opium smokers who are 65 and 70 years of age. There is a man over there who has smoked opium for 30 years."

"Have you read De Quincey's *Opium Eater*?"

"I have .... I was an opium smoker before I read his book. I believe he has drawn more on his imagination than on experience .... I believe De Quincey's book is a pack of lies."

"Why do you smoke?"

"Because I must; I could not live without it. I smoke partly because of the quiet enjoyment it gives, but mainly to escape from the horrors which would ensue did I not smoke. To be 24 hours without smoking is to suffer worse tortures than the lost."

"But does not smoking make you wretched, just as drinking would?"

"No; I require about twelve pipes, then I fall into a state of somnolence and complete rest. When I awake, I feel all right, and can attend to fixing up the house. I am brisk, and can work as well as anybody else. I do not feel sick or nervous, neither have I the inclination to smoke more opium."

"Then why do you return to the drug?"

"Ah! that's it; there is a time when my hands fail me; tears fall from my eyes; I am ready to sink; then I come here and for a few bits have a smoke which sets me right. There is too much nonsense talked about opium smoking. Life without it would be unendurable for me. I am in excellent health; but, I suppose, everyone has their own troubles, and I have mine."

"I do not want to be offensive, but are you what is called a fast woman?"

"I am. But you would be greatly mistaken if you imagined that all the women who come here are of that character. In San Francisco I have known some of the first people visit opium houses, and many respectable people do the same here."

"Are women of your class generally addicted to opium smoking?"

"No; they are more addicted to drink, and drink does them far more harm. Drink excites passion, whereas this allays it; and when a fast woman drinks she goes to ruin pretty quick."

"How have you been treated by Chinamen whom you have met in such places?"

"They never interfered with me in the least. Waking or sleeping, one act of rudeness from a Chinaman I have never experienced. In that respect they are far superior to white men. Unless you speak to them they will not even speak to you; and, indeed, after the first whiff of the opium you have no desire to speak. You rather resent having to speak or being spoken to; and when you want the smoke the desire to get your pipe ready is far too earnest a business to allow of any desire for idle talk. But I have known Chinamen who were not opium smokers, and I believe they are far more certain not to offend or molest a woman than white men, especially white men with a glass in."

"Have you anything else to add?"

"No; I will say this, though: that if opium houses were licensed as drinking saloons are one need not have to come into such holes as this to smoke. There could be nice rooms with nice couches, and the degradation would be mitigated. At all events I think the government that will not license an opium saloon should shut up public houses and hotels where they sell vitriol for whiskey and brandy, and where men kill themselves with a certainty and a rapidity beyond the power of opium."[6]

The commissioners and Nicholas Davin were fascinated with Emily.

The hearings were then heard in Victoria and New Westminster, with visits to Nanaimo, Yale and Portland, Oregon. Thirty-one witnesses were examined "viva voce," while 39 answered printed questions. Many did not reply to the questionnaire but, as the commissioners put it, "persons of all classes" were heard—from Victoria's aristocracy to Wellington's mine labourers.

They met in the legislative hall with Noah Shakespeare an interested but silent spectator. A notable witness, Dr. J.S. Helmcken, was now aged 61 years, 34 of which he had spent on Vancouver Island; in fact he had been around for so long that he had forgotten when the Chinese first appeared, as did several others. Dr.

Helmcken had nothing unpleasant to say about the Chinese. His evidence was full of pithy little philosophical observations. One of the difficulties, he said, was that they could not speak our language. "No one likes a foreigner who can speak only his mother tongue." Their immorality was no worse than that of white men. "Wickedness is the natural tendancy of everyone." Englishmen could not replace them as servants. "They (the English) seem fit for gigantic things; Chinese favor little things." The Chinese had been beneficial in the past but he could not say whether they would be beneficial in the future. "Rain is beneficial, but some people complain of too much of it."

Mr. Gray had apparently read Arthur Bunster's evidence before the Select Committee of 1879. "It has been alleged . . . that white ladies are scrubbed by Chinese whilst in their baths. Is that true?" he asked Dr. Helmcken. "It is a lie," answered the indignant physician.

Sir Matthew Baillie Begbie, Chief Justice of the Supreme Court, and a resident since 1858, was now 65 years of age. He returned lengthy written answers to the questions and, some time later, recalled other facts which he sent on to the commissioners. "Industry, economy, sobriety and law-abidingness are exactly the four prominent qualities of Chinamen as asserted by their advocates and their adversaries," he said. "Lazy, drunken, extravagant and turbulent; this is, by the voices of their friends and foes, exactly what a Chinaman is not. This, on the whole, I think, the real cause of their unpopularity."

Sir Matthew, still a tall, powerful bachelor, had nothing but praise for the Chinese though, as he said, he had never had one in his house. He had, however, employed them, "for there are things that white people simply refuse to do at all, for example, wash and hew stove-wood."

Henry Pelling Perew Crease, Judge of the Supreme Court, had also been a resident since 1858 and was now 59 years of age. He presented a fascinating, though somewhat melodramatic, account of the difficult life colonists led when first he arrived. Ladies had had to do their own cooking and cleaning, men to chop their own wood. The Chinese had met "a want that had become almost intolerable." If they were excluded, he said, "The wail of the housewife would sweep through the land, and find a very decided expression in every husband's vote at the polls."

It is unfortunate that Arthur Bunster was in California. Henry Crease was just the person Arthur would refer to as "the snob aristocracy." He had said, "There are a few would-be aristocrats who like to put on frills, and they are fond of having Chinese servants. They think it is something grand, and something way up."

Crease certainly liked his Chinese servants—as much, perhaps, as he disliked the labourer. His pen spat venom when it considered the lowly workingman. The Chinese had some evils, he said, opium and gambling, but what of the whites? "If enquiry were made of the railway servants and engineers on the permanent railway cuttings, what an account they can give of white, as well as Chinese, abominations that abound there. Who that has seen a leading mainland town on the railway line on pay-days can ever forget the disgusting sights that everywhere met his eyes? Furious drunken men in the streets, saloons and corners at all hours of the day and night, week days and Sundays alike, the fights, the uproar, the gambling, that made day and night hideous, besotted drunken whites kicked out of the houses, prostrate in the morning in the places where they fell over night, sleeping off the previous debauch, only to stagger up and engage again the same round of vice. These are the sights which one would fain forget with other things about which the pen blushes to write." Henry Crease was a sensitive gentleman. Such scenes would pass unnoticed by Arthur Bunster.

Robert Dunsmuir was another aristocrat, though he had risen from humble origins. He was 60 years of age now, had come to the Island in 1852 and was without a doubt the richest man in the province. Indeed he was richer than he knew; the value of the timber on the railway belt recently presented to him was astounding, though at that time unrecognized. He had, by his own admission, used the Chinese to break a strike of white miners and, just a few months earlier, had stated that he had only 40 Chinese working for him and he would soon rid himself of these. Now he stated that he had 700 to 800 working in his mines; that they were as good as whites; that they were industrious, hardy, temperate, peaceable, frugal and faithful. Their only fault was gambling. Dunsmuir stated that the agitation was merely political, that no regulations were necessary. "Most of those who are worthy of a notation on their occupation [presumably on the list of witnesses]," he said, "are in favor of the Chinese. Those who have no occupation noted, usually are violently against them." [Snob aristocracy? Where are you, Arthur Bunster?]

Samuel M. Robbins had the honour of having his occupation noted: Superintendent of the Vancouver Coal Mining and Land

Company. The employer of 400 white labourers at "not less than $2 a day," he praised the 150 Chinese whom he paid $1 to $1.25 a day. "At the time of their coming here," he said, "my company had been suffering from a strike of white laborers, and we accepted the Chinese as a weapon with which to settle the dispute."

After such statements, there is little wonder that the labourer —whose occupation was not worthy of listing—would be opposed to the Chinese. The motivations of the industrialist and the working-man were quite clear, but those of the politicians were less so. A.E.B. Davie, Charles Wilson, John Robson, R.F. John and M.W.T. Drake, all members of the Legislative Assembly, were also anti-Oriental to a greater or lesser degree. David Gordon, who had defeated Arthur Bunster, was venomous towards the Chinese, and towards the eas-terners who seemed to favour them. When asked whether any more Chinese were necessary, he answered, "Yes, enough to distribute amongst the cities of the eastern provinces, as follows: Ottawa 4,000; Montreal 4,000; St. John, N.B. 2,000; Halifax 2,000; Quebec 2,000; Toronto 2,000; London 1,000; and Hamilton 1,000 and as many more as the inhabitants of those cities petition for after they shall have had some experience of Asiatic enterprise and virtue, and the cost of their distribution to be borne by the Department of Immigra-tion."

And the awesome voice of Andrew Onderdonk was heard —through his pen. The American contractor for the C.P.R., unlike the lawyers Begbie and Crease, could hardly be termed verbose. He wrote only brief answers to the 27 questions offered to him: "Yes," "No," "I do not know,"—and occasionally a line or two. His evidence added little. He had employed as many as 9,000 men at one time—6,000 Chinese and 3,000 whites. The Chinese were necessary for the construction of the railway; they were harmless, faithful, law-abiding, and he would require 2,000 more for the spring of 1885.

Huang Sic Chen of the San Francisco consulate made a statement, pointing out that the Chinese were not slaves as alleged; they paid $70 for their transportation. And though indeed they smoked opium, who was to blame for this vice; the Chinese who used the vile drug or the English who introduced it and forced the trade on the nation? But perhaps the most interesting evidence presented by Huang were the statistics he had collected, presumably through the Chinese underground. Although it was generally believed that there were 15,000 Chinese in the province, Huang's figures showed only

10,550, the difference being made up by deaths or departures. He listed the numbers of Chinese in each location, with their occupations. There were, for instance, 1,767 in Victoria, 380 being listed as new arrivals, 180 as cooks and servants and 130 as bootmakers. In New Westminster there were 1,680, most of them fish-hands and ditch diggers. The largest conglomeration was classified as "Railway Construction," in which there were a total of 3,510. Of these, 2,900 were workmen and 230 were woodcutters. And most towns had their prostitutes. In the little village of Soda Creek, on the Fraser north of Quesnel, there were 27 farm labourers, two washermen and two prostitutes. Burrard Inlet, with its two sawmills, did not fare nearly so well. There was only one prostitute for 114 Chinese, most of whom were sawmill hands.

Two labour organizations were represented. F.L. Tuckfield stated that his Knights of Labor were a secret society and that they were not registered, but that they had 3,200 members in the United States and Canada, 100 to 200 in Victoria. Tuckfield was one of the more violent. "Our children must seek employment in other countries," he said, "to make room for a race of cuckoos, who come to our land to purchase their freedom .... The Chinese are a disgrace to a civilized community."

The Nanaimo Trades Association used a much more moderate and novel approach. They did not attack the Chinese for their filth and immorality; indeed they were quite impersonal. Ever since confederation, they said, the Dominion government had been promoting national sentiment amongst its peoples. Their policy since 1878 had been "Canada for Canadians," in order to secure a monopoly of the Canadian market to Canadian manufacturers and employers of labour. It was successful in eastern Canada, but in British Columbia they had tied up the E. & N. Railway belt for 12 years, a belt which was said to be a solid strip of coal, and finally they had presented it to a company whose principal shareholder (Robert Dunsmuir) "has made a visible fortune of $2 million." His railway company and his coal mines were so wealthy that he was in no hurry to develop the belt. If it had been opened to the public, labourers could have bettered themselves on it. Now they must remain forever in the subordinate position of employees, exposed to the terrible competition of the Chinese.

It was a most eloquent and sensible presentation, but one about which the commission could do very little.

The only other evidence of interest in regard to later accusations that the Chinese were shipped from China under most unhealthy conditions, were the 31 answers to the question, "When they arrive here, do they usually arrive in good health and fit for work?" All but one answered "Yes."

Noah Shakespeare boycotted the tribunal, and similar boycotts occurred in New Westminster and in Victoria, where the Board of Trade refused to give evidence. Nanaimo, on the other hand, was insulted at the failure of the commission to take evidence there. The *Free Press* said it was a farce.

This was perhaps an unfair accusation. They had examined the situation in California, they spent two weeks in British Columbia, they made further inquiries in Portland, Oregon, and they presented a most comprehensive report to the government. In the "sea of sterile mountains" they were accepted with indifference by most and with vigorous opposition by some. It was certainly a pleasant outing for Chapleau and Davin, who especially enjoyed their tours of Chinatown in both San Francisco and Victoria. Indeed the dashing young secretary stored away in his mind many little tidbits with which to regale future enraptured listeners. In Portland he told a reporter he liked Chinese servants. "They put a fellow to bed, you know, and never tell on him." And in Ottawa he delighted a *Sun* journalist with exaggerated tales of Emily Wharton.

It would be almost a year before British Columbians would learn of the Commission report. When Chapleau and Davin departed at the end of August 1884, citizens did not know that they would be classified into three groups:

1. A well-meaning, but strongly prejudiced minority, whom nothing but absolute exclusion will satisfy.

2. An intelligent minority, who conceive that no legislation whatever is necessary—that is, as in all business transactions, the rule of supply and demand will apply and the matter regulate itself in the ordinary course of events. (This intelligent minority, by admission, were those who carried on such "business transactions" as the Wellington and Vancouver mining companies, the salmon canneries and the C.P.R.; they were those of "the snob aristocracy" who had to have their servants.)

3. A large majority, who think there should be a moderate restriction, based on police, financial and sanitary principles, sustained and enforced by stringent local regulations for cleanliness and the preservation of health.

The commission could not avoid noting that the great majority were anti-Oriental, though they did manage to avoid labelling them "intelligent." Was a Royal Commission necessary to discover this?

Noah Shakespeare did not think so. But Chapleau and Gray girded up their loins and decided that the matter of Chinese legislation depended upon whether the material advantages of Chinese immigration were greater than the social and moral disadvantages. The moment they made this decision, it was a lost cause as far as the anti-Orientalists were concerned. Material gains would always win over moral disadvantages.

But what were the material gains? There was little doubt that coal mining, fish canning and market gardening could not have progressed to their current state without Chinese labour, nor could the C.P.R. have been constructed within a reasonable length of time. A further indirect gain was the $1,848,587 revenue the Dominion received from trade with China and Japan. Anti-Chinese laws, it was said, might substantially reduce trade and therefore—if one were prepared to accept the premise—such laws affected all of Canada, not just British Columbia, whose representation in Ottawa was merely six of 250 members. It was perhaps this fact which spurred David Gordon's remark that easterners should be made to live with the Chinese.

In regard to the social and moral aspects, the commissioners found that the Chinese were honest, industrious, sober, peaceable, law-abiding, frugal and clean, and at the same time they pointed out that white labourers, as soon as they became contractors, were the first to employ Chinese "because they have no Blue Mondays."

There was no doubt that they smoked opium; importations into Canada in 1884 totalled 60,700 pounds, of which 56,542 pounds were destined for British Columbia. But it was difficult for the Chinese to understand why their opium habit was so objectionable when it was forced upon them by the British. The Dominion government treated opium as a common article of trade, and the city of Victoria charged a straightforward $500 for an opium license. Henry Crease and Emily Wharton, too, had questioned which was more evil, alcohol or opium, and one resident, when asked the difference between getting drunk on alcohol and getting drunk on opium, indignantly replied that one was a Christian habit, the other a heathen vice.

There was also no doubt that there were Chinese prostitutes in the province, but the commission passed this off lightly. There were 10,500 Chinese, they said, and only 70 prostitutes. If the whites felt that these prostitutes were contributing to white immorality, "it is a reflection upon the people of British Columbia to assume that, as a people, they could be led by such degraded tastes."

The commission also received ample evidence that the Chinese had secret societies. (Such societies served as protective devices in a strange culture. W.E. Willmott[7] states that secret societies were a legitimate part of local social organization in China, especially in Kwantung province. The first society in Canada was formed in 1862 and was known by various names, but ultimately became the Chinese Freemasons.) In addition, the alleged "want of truth" was found to be largely due to their way of thinking and their ignorance of the English language. With typical Victorian delicacy, accusers always referred to their "want of truth," "untruth" or "absence of veracity." This cultural gap posed a danger in the administration of justice, but an allowance had to be made for a difference in moral standards

And so it went, page after page of facts and superfluities, couched in flowery but eloquent Victorian language. Three suggestions for legislation were made: firstly, that a Chinese consul be appointed to Victoria; secondly, that a duty of perhaps $10 "for every Chinaman, or Chinawoman, every Chinese boy or girl" landing in the province be imposed; and thirdly, that the sum so raised be used for administration of the Chinese population. The commissioners listed 23 means of spending this duty money, such as for a health inspector, a joint tribunal and interpreters.

Andrew Onderdonk had told the commission that he required 2,000 more Chinese. By August, when he made this statement, arrivals from China had already totalled 1,456 since the beginning of the year. The *Colonist* was somewhat surprised when 300 arrived in June. "As there is no particular demand for Chinese labor at the present time," they commented, "it is a wonderment why more arrive . . . . They are seen passing through the city with their odd baggage into Chinatown where they disappear and are never more distinguishable from those already there." A Chinese informant said there were more than enough six months earlier, but misrepresentations by Chinese merchants lured poor Chinese, who bound themselves to a certain wage from which they paid their passage gradually at a rate of 50 to 75 cents a day. With a further deduction for board, it took four to ten years to pay off their agreement!

They were not only increasing in numbers, but also consolidating their position in Victoria. The building boom in Chinatown continued, with new shops for merchants, new theatres, a bank and a new establishment on Cormorant Street for the Chinese Benevolent Society. The Chinese assumed that Victoria would be the great port of western Canada, but even as the large brick buildings mushroomed up over the expanding boundaries of Chinatown, rumours of the extension of the C.P.R. into Coal Harbour or English Bay spread over the province.

The railroad, though it no longer provided spectacular headlines, was still the hinge upon which life hung, particularly in the south of the province. In January 1884, the first train from Yale arrived in Port Moody and with each passing month, freight could be carried farther and farther past Yale from Burrard Inlet. By June, the old cry of "through to Yale," referring to steamboat navigation from Victoria, had changed to "through to Lytton," referring to railroad transportation from Port Moody. The head of river navigation had dropped from Yale to Port Hammond. And by the end of the year, the trains had reached Savona.

In the meantime, the first survey since the abortive attempt in 1875 for the E. & N. (or Island) Railway had begun; the rails from the east had reached the Kicking Horse Pass, and Andrew Onderdonk was progressing rapidly on his new 150 mile contract between Savona and Eagle Pass, just west of the Columbia River. When M.J. Haney, C.P.R. superintendent for British Columbia, visited Victoria in October 1884, he stated that Onderdonk had 9,000 men working on this new contract, 7,500 of them being Chinese. He reported that there had been no disturbances, that the Chinese were all healthy and that the mortality in the past year had been only 30 in a Chinese working force of 6,000. They stretched all along the right-of-way, dressed, like the whites, in shirt and dungarees and broad-brimmed felt hats, their queues hanging straight down their backs or sometimes over their shoulders and down their chests or wound about their head beneath their hat. They slept in large, sagging grey tents placed in groups, invariably with a gambling tent nearby. Inveterate gamblers they were. And so the railway sped on, usually at the rate of one mile a day. It was hoped that east would meet west by November 1885.

A number of well-known railway men visited Victoria that fall of 1884. Besides Haney, there were J.H. Strawbridge and Charles Crocker for the E. & N. and Collingwood Schreiber for the C.P.R. But the visitor who would affect more lives than all the rest put together, who would affect the lives of millions still thousands of miles away, was a gentleman named William Cornelius Van Horne, the general manager of the C.P.R.

It was not so much his visit to Victoria that would affect many lives, as the trip he took across the gulf in August 1884 to inspect various sites which might be suitable as a terminus for the railway. Following this, he announced it would be either in Coal Harbour, inside Burrard Inlet, or just outside, in either English Bay or False Creek. By December, daily auctions of Coal Harbour lots were being held in Victoria. Rand and Lipsett even referred to the area as "Vancouver," much to the disgust of the Islanders, who felt that even their name was being usurped. There was indeed great activity on Burrard Inlet. Henry Beatty and L.A. Hamilton were about to leave Montreal to settle matters in the Coal Harbour area, Major A.B. Rogers was surveying the route from Port Moody, and David Oppenheimer had let a contract for the clearing of Lot 85 on the inlet. If the Oppenheimers had moved into Coal Harbour, the railroad could not be far behind.

Before the end of 1884, construction of the E. & N. had finally begun. It probably saved some Chinese from starvation. Graham and Busk, the contractors for the upper section, could not find sufficient white labour and were "reluctantly compelled to arrange with the Tai Chong Company for a supply of Chinese labor." Early in January 1885, 120 were set to work and it was reported that 600 more were due to arrive, all apparently from the mainland.

The citizens of Victoria raised no objections to this Oriental labour; indeed there was a new development which rather pleased their puritan hearts. In February 1885, a Chinese Mission School was opened in Cormorant Street under the direction of John E. Vrooman, a former American missionary in China. At the first meeting on February 3, 25 Chinese attended, but by the next Sunday, 200 assembled to hear Mr. Vrooman preach in Chinese, assisted by the Reverend Dong Gong of Portland and Mr. Sam Lee of Victoria. "This is the first religious service exclusively in the Chinese language ever held in the city," said the *Colonist* with obvious pleasure.

It was perhaps at this time that a strange ambivalence towards the Chinese became apparent in the sentiments of Victorians. Certainly the majority did not want them in their midst, and their elected representatives were constantly persecuting them verbally in both the provincial and Dominion Houses, yet Victorians treated the Chinese quite graciously, albeit with some condescension.

With a few exceptions, Chinese New Year was a time enjoyed by most whites almost as much as by the Chinese. In 1885, it happened to occur on February 14, St. Valentine's Day to Christians of varying intensity. The *Colonist* printed a long description of the event. "Kung hae fat tsoi," it said: "Happy New Year." The wealthier class of

Chinese were hurrying from door to door, dressed in their richest silk gowns with red buttons to match. On every Chinese door was the inscription, printed on red paper, "Hoi mun tai kat," meaning, "Only good luck attend you as you open this door." Homes were elaborately decorated with flowers, and on the walls hung huge scrolls of the richest colour, each with an appropriate expression on it. There was a great deal of bowing, handshaking and tea. All in all, said the *Colonist*, it was the happiest season of the year. "Therefore in hearty sympathy with these people of Sinim [China]," they concluded, "we wish them and our readers a very happy Kung hae fat tsoi."

Victorians were really a most remarkable people. Even as they were expressing their pleasure with the Chinese Mission and spreading abroad the good will of the Chinese New Year, there was an ever-growing force, one more determined than ever to restrict further immigration and to regulate those Orientals already in the province. In the Legislative Assembly, Simeon Duck was cursing the Dominion government for disallowing the provincial Immigration Act of 1884 and presenting a resolution which would send another petition to Ottawa. In it, "the Chinese coolies" were described as "leprous in blood and unclean in habits."

And on February 12, Theodore Davie, who had frequently defended Chinese in court, presented virtually the same immigration act that had been disallowed the previous year. The assembly was still furious about this, with one exception.

"When does the act come into force?" asked Robert Dunsmuir, perhaps contemplating whether he should send a rush order to Hong Kong.

"Immediately," answered a bitter Theodore Davie.

"You can't do it. It must go to Ottawa first," stated Dunsmuir.

"We won't give them a chance to disallow it," countered Davie.

His statement reflected the sentiment of the legislature and most of the people of the province. The act was passed on February 27, 1885. Just three days earlier, fragmentary reports on the Royal commission had reached Victoria. Chapleau and Gray had apparently said that the development of the resources of the province depended on the Chinese, and that they favoured continuance of Chinese immigration. "They want all the Chinese they can get," shouted the *Colonist* angrily: "Gray is pro-Chinese, Chapleau is unacquainted with them." In the legislature the next day, Duck's immigration report for Ottawa was read. It used the usual parliamentary term "pray" (that restrictions be made). Mr. Helgesen of New

Westminster rose to say that "we have been praying for ten years." He wanted the word "demand" to replace it. On the advice of John Robson, the more moderate word "request" was inserted.

In their bitterness, they passed once again the immigration act which had been disallowed the previous year, as well as an act to prevent Chinese from giving evidence against whites and an amendment to the Restriction Act of 1884. And they were still not finished. In mid-February they had received a petition from the Knights of Labor describing again the evils of the Chinese and requesting that no Chinese be employed on the extension of the C.P.R. from Port Moody to Coal Harbour. A week later, Premier Smithe announced that he had made such an agreement with the C.P.R. "The stipulation will delay the completion of the work for about a twelvemonth," remarked the *Colonist*, "but better that than the monies paid for labor should go to China." The C.P.R. directors were no doubt only too happy to make this apparent concession. They were on rather shaky financial ground at the time.

There continued to be public meetings and editorials protesting the Royal Commission Report, but on March 9, the provincial House was prorogued, and the act to prevent the immigration of Chinese came into force. On March 10, Captain Wilson, with certain misgivings, brought the *North Pacific* into Victoria with some Chinese passengers, but the necessary arrangements to stop them were not yet organized. On March 11, however, the *George E. Starr* arrived to find Superintendent Bloomfield and a posse of officers awaiting them. The *Starr*'s 20 Chinese passengers were not allowed to land and were returned to Port Townsend in Washington Territory. Three days later, 240 Chinese arrived in San Francisco from Hong Kong. They were bound for British Columbia, but since no one would carry them thither, they created quite a problem for the shipping company. They were, of course, not allowed to land in the United States.

Theodore Davie, who had sponsored most of the anti-Chinese legislation, must have felt a considerable degree of satisfaction. He at least had kept some Chinese out, though he must have known that the greater powers in Ottawa would soon overtake him. Before the end of March, Sir John A. Macdonald stated that the bill would be declared *ultra vires* by the court, and in April the act was disallowed by the Governor-general-in-Council.

There was little comment; it was inevitable. Besides, the country had its weary mind on other matters of importance. In the North-West Territories, Lieutenant-governor Edgar Dewdney was having problems with Louis Riel and was soon facing open rebellion. In the House of Commons, Noah Shakespeare began his attack by asking if the government intended to raise the duty on rice. He received a curt "No," and then inquired into discrimination in the British Columbia penitentiary where, he said, white prisoners were forced to have their hair cut short, while Chinese were allowed to wear their pigtails. The cropping was done for the sake of cleanliness, but, said Noah, "the Chinese need it more than whites or Indians, because they are dirtier." Joseph Chapleau answered that the Chinese queue was not cut "because of the infamy and humiliation which they are subjected to." Noah pointed out that it was also a degrading experience for some whites. Sir John, surprisingly, agreed with him, but the matter was set aside, at least for the moment.

The first Dominion anti-Chinese legislation which appeared to have any chance of acceptance was introduced in April 1885 by an easterner: one Joseph Chapleau who, after his nine-day visit to Victoria, was apparently considered an expert on Chinese matters. His restriction act provided for a system of registration and control and it placed a tax of $5 on the head of each Chinese entering the country. Five dollars? It was a mere gesture, perhaps introduced in the hope of soothing those bothersome British Columbians. If so, the government never showed poorer judgement. The bill, not yet passed, merely fed the flames of bitterness. A public meeting was again held, the act was termed "farcical," and Theodore Davie expressed his acrimonious chargin at the actions of the Dominion government.

Following the passing of Chapleau's restriction act, the provincial tax collector rode forth with renewed vigour. In one incident he took 30 Chinese by surprise in Kwong Lee's Alley. They gave the usual replies to his request for money—"by and by" and "no money now"—and the collector proceeded to fill a large cart with their goods which were trundled away to the police barracks. "Hundreds of Chinamen in our city arranged in goodly costume and apparently well fed," remarked the *Colonist*, "promenade our streets, who have never paid this tax and who manage to elude payment from the difficulty the collector experiences in finding their homes and effects."

At this time, too, there was a concerted attack on Chinese who had not paid the $10 peddler's license, and the provincial government suddenly decided to enforce its Chinese Restriction Act of 1884. This Act had been due to take effect on February 18, one year after it had been passed. That date had slid by, but in May the province found reason to enforce it. Every Chinese who could not present a receipt for the $10 head tax was liable to a fine of $40; employers of Chinese had to present a list of Chinese employees; opium was banned, and the cubic air law was to be enforced.

Those gracious Victorians were really a remarkable people. On May 21, "the workingmen" planned a meeting "underneath the electric light" on Blanshard Avenue. They assembled before 8 p.m. at Campbell's Corner, from which the Blue Ribbon Band led 1,000 of them, "playing a stirring air," down Government and up Fort Street to Douglas. They carried torches and transparencies containing such mottoes as "Boycott the Chinese Employers"; "They that are not with us are against us"; "No yellow slave shall eat our children's bread"; "Cut out the Chinese cancer"; "Down with the dragon flag"; "Let B.C. be a home for men only" and "Let no Chinese leper cross our threshold." One picture transparency showed a Chinese stabbing a white in the back.

Underneath the electric light, the committee climbed upon a wagon and, one by one, harangued the crowd, now swollen to 2,000. It was decided that a notice describing the Chinese evil would be sent to workingmen in the east and that the government must be forced to make restrictions. There were cries of approval and applause at appropriate moments, and when the band agreed to march them back to Frank Campbell's Corner, a few cries of "Through Chinatown" were heard. In any other city it would have been an explosive situation. In Victoria, as the *Colonist* put it, "the noisy and depraved element which sometimes gathers on the skirts of a great public gathering was not there. In its place were well-dressed, sincere, thoughtful-looking men." The cry "Through Chinatown" was hushed by a few timely words.

At their meeting two weeks later, Theodore Davie gave a stirring speech and M.W.T. Drake was condemned for supporting the Chinese Regulation Act in the legislature, then defending in court the Chinese who refused to pay the tax which the act imposed. Later, Mr. Dougherty climbed upon the wagon and announced proudly that he was a hod-carrier and that he was prepared to take up his gun and bayonet "to drive out the Chinese." He would shed his heart's blood willingly, he said amidst roars of laughter and applause, for if he fell, future generations would point to the place and say, "There's where one of our forefathers fell, there's where Dougherty, the hero—the hod-carrier—fell fighting for the rights of the white workingman!"

At one of their gatherings, they decided to name themselves the

Anti-Chinese Union. Regular meetings continued to be held in which many bitter words were spoken, but there was also a great deal of good humour, exhibited and the real possibilities of violence were never taken seriously.

The House of Commons at this time was in the midst of a very long session. The main delay was over the Franchise Bill, which proposed to make property the basis of the vote. It was designed, amongst other things, to allow Indians to vote. One of the energetic debates it stimulated was over "the question as to whether John Chinaman should have the franchise." Sir John himself moved that the phrase "and excluding a Chinaman" be inserted. One member maintained that a Chinaman was as good as an Indian; another said that Chinese compared favourably with those Christian people, the whites of British Columbia. ("There was a lot more trash of this description," remarked the *Colonist*.) Another member pointed out the difficulty of defining "Chinaman," and Sir John then changed his phrase to "and excluding a person of Mongolian or Chinese race." His amendment was adopted.

Indeed, a strange mixture of events was occurring in the country at this time. British Columbians were frantically adopting anti-Oriental legislation, yet treating the Chinese, at worst, with tolerance. The Dominion government was disallowing British Columbia's anti-Oriental legislation, yet passing its own to disenfranchise the "Mongolian or Chinese." At the same time, in the vast region between Manitoba and the Rockies, the government was waging a full-scale war with the Indians and Métis who were fighting for their rights as owners of the land. And when Louis Riel was finally captured, the news "was received with satisfaction by every lover of peace and order." There was no protest when they hanged him in November of the same year.

In June 1885, Police Magistrate Edwin Johnson heard the case of Chong Yuen and Wing Chong, who had refused to pay the $10 fee under the provincial Chinese Regulation Act of 1884. The determination of the government was reflected by the presence of Attorney-general A.E.B. Davie. A former lieutenant-governor, A.N. Richards, defended the Chinese on the grounds of unconstitutionality, but the unfortunate police magistrate had no choice. The government of the province had passed the bill and the lieutenant-governor had given his assent. The two Chinese were fined $20 each and A.E.B. Davie no doubt strode from the courthouse with a great deal of satisfaction. If so, his pleasure was short-lived. In August, one man—Henry Pelling Perew Crease—declared the act unconstitutional.

British Columbia's restriction and regulation acts, then, were both null and void. That summer, over 1,000 Chinese entered the province at Victoria. When the *Queen of the Pacific* arrived with 150 Orientals from San Francisco, the *Colonist* muttered "If the people of Montreal saw all this in their harbor and streets, a cry would soon be raised sufficient to compel any government to grant the restriction that British Columbia has so long prayed for." The barks *Alden Besse* and *W.H. Besse* then disembarked 802 Chinese from Hong Kong, the steamer *Martha* brought another 35 from the same city, and the *Queen of the Pacific* discharged yet another 80 from San Francisco. It was believed that the Tai Chong Company had ordered them, but what they were to do was a mystery. The C.P.R. would be finished in a few months and the E. & N. was expected to be completed in nine months. But they disembarked, the police holding back crowds of curious onlookers. "They were a motley looking crowd dressed in a great variety of costumes, though cleanly in appearance," said the *Colonist*. "They all made tracks for Chinatown, which seems always to have room for more."

In June 1885, however, the House of Commons finally passed a Chinese restriction bill, to take effect on August 3, 1885. It had been strengthened since Chapleau had first introduced it. The tax on each Chinese was now $50, each ship could carry only one Chinese per 50 tons, and arrangements were made for controllers and interpreters. Remarked the *Colonist*, "Constant dripping, it is said, will wear a stone, and constant agitation at Victoria and Ottawa by earnest British Columbians has caused the Dominion people and government to take an intelligent view of this most important matter."

There was no doubt now that anti-Chinese sentiment was growing. It was accelerated by the failure of several businesses and by increasing unemployment. By September 1885 there were 500 to 600 unemployed whites in the city of some 12,000, and the anti-Chinese Union members became more active. They sent letters to Chinese merchants who imported "Celestial slaves," they threatened boycotts, and they condemned Crease's decision as a flagrant injustice to the working classes. They also passed a resolution to start a white labour shirt factory and announced that they were "opposed to all forms of violence and force other than legal and moral, at the same time recognizing . . ." and they proceeded to list all the oft-repeated evils of a Chinese society.

The individual workingman also decided to do something about his unemployment. In the first week of September, 40 of these whites gathered at Campbell's Corner and marched to various construction sites asking for work and demanding the discharge of Chinese labourers. Generally they were told to mind their own business. When they demanded the same at the various factories in the city, the usual answer was that Chinese would be discharged when other industries discharged them. Noah Shakespeare recognized that this was a futile method of approaching the problem and organized a Labor Association. To all those desiring work who signed their names, occupations and addresses in a book and paid 25 cents, the association promised to contact all employers of Chinese and inform them of the availability of whites.

Whether this achieved any success is not known, but it was an interesting development from two points of view: Noah was doing something constructive, and the frustrated workingman was staying within the bounds of the law. The situation just a mile or two across the border was quite different. In Washington Territory and Wyoming there were bloody Oriental riots, and in California, the powerful Tong societies were at their murderous peak. In more peaceful British Columbia, the Chinese faced only legal restrictions—at least for the time being.

The backlash of Noah Shakespeare's debate with Chapleau and Sir John over the cropping of hair in prisons was also quite legal. At the end of September, the provincial government, "having become satisfied that the Chinese custom of wearing queues involves no religious principle or superstition . . . issued instructions to all gaolers to rigidly apply the hair-cutting regulation to convicts." Perhaps it was a vindictive action. In every anti-Oriental move it had attempted, the Province had been frustrated by the Dominion government and by its own Supreme Court. Unlike the Queue Ordinance of San Francisco, hair cutting in British Columbia prisons does not appear to have been aimed directly at the Chinese. White prisoners continued to have their locks lopped, even when the Chinese were allowed to keep theirs. It was a health measure. Hair was "a lodgement for insect life." But now, perhaps in their frustration, the government intended to attack the Chinese by every possible means.

On September 26, two burly white convicts dragged a screaming Chinese, trembling with fear, to a chair and held him firmly while Gaoler Hutcheson cut his hair. The remaining six prisoners were impassive when their turn came. The seven pigtails were rolled in seven sheets of paper marked on the outside with their owner's name, to be returned when his sentence was completed. In November, however, the government discovered that the Chinese did not mind having their hair shorn, provided they got it back, "and so an edict has gone forth that the hair of the Mongol and the Caucasian shall, mingling in a common funeral pyre, be burned before the shorn one's eyes." This was indeed vindictiveness.

British Columbia's Chinese in 1885 at least had a little to be thankful for. There was no violence (other than a small altercation between a foreman and a gang of Orientals on the E. & N. in July); the provincial restriction and regulation acts were null and void, and the Dominion Restriction Act could be considered a moderate one. They also received some surprising support from the people of Lillooet. On June 12, before Crease's decision on the Regulation Act, a public meeting passed a resolution in the presence of A.E.B. Davie, asking that the act be repealed on the grounds that it was "unjust and injurious to the best interests of Lillooet District." The *Kamloops Sentinel* explained this strange request. "The Chinese are numerous along the creeks near Lillooet," they said. "So long as 25 or 50 cents a day can be had, they persevere and occasionally get a rich stake. To these miners, the whites of the neighborhood sell their surplus produce, hogs, chickens and such like. This being their only available market at present, hence the desire to have John for a customer."

The steady decline in the fortunes of the Chinese was also reflected in the financial ruin of two well-established businesses in Victoria. Tai Chong Yuen was arrested for not paying the provincial tax on a number of Chinese he sent to work on the E. & N., he was fined $700, and in August his company went bankrupt.

The second business failure was that of the House of Kwong Lee, established, it was said, in 1858. The ownership of the business was somewhat obscure; indeed it was so obscure that two brothers, Loo Chuck Fan and Loo Chou Fan, fought a prolonged battle in the courts, finally resulting in the failure of the company. An auction sale of goods, including opium, ended the life of the first Chinese merchant company in the Colonies of Vancouver Island and British Columbia.

The economic situation in the province was not at all good. On September 5, 1885 it was reported that 3,000 whites and Chinese had been released by the C.P.R.; on September 30 a similar number of discharges was reported. The railway was nearing completion, and machine shops and saw mills (in which timber for bridges and trestles were cut) were being closed. Early in October 1,000 whites and 1,200 Chinese arrived at Yale. The Chinese were sent on to winter quarters at Port Hammond, but the whites remained behind to carouse and transform the town from a state of decaying death to a hellish nightmare of drunkenness and destruction. When they ran out of money, they threatened to tear down Andrew Onderdonk's house—in which, at that moment, sat Andrew and the Marquis of Lansdowne, the Governor-general—claiming rightly that they had not been paid.

The railway, which had caused so much anguish before its construction and so much anguish during its construction, was still creating anguish as it neared its completion. It stretched now the 350 miles from Port Moody to Sicamous Narrows. For months, travellers from the east had been arriving at the end of the rails to walk or ride over the ever-shortening gap between the east and west sections. Sir Charles Tupper arrived by that route late in September, and in the first week of October the Governor-general, the Marquis of Lansdowne, rode over the 47-mile gap on horseback.

Victoria had not been given sufficient notice of the vice-regal visit to prepare for the celebrations they loved so much. Plans for triumphal arches had to be abandoned, but they did their best with fir tree decorations. It was a very short and informal stay, but Lansdowne at least managed to find the time to chug seven miles up the E. & N., at which point the train was put in reverse, to back its way down to Victoria. "The party will return to Canada by the Canadian Pacific Railway," reported the *Colonist*. Still the east was "Canada."

By October 16, the rails were only 29 miles apart, and on November 7, 1885, the crew at Craigellachie actually had to wait a few hours for the Hon. Donald Smith to arrive and drive the last spike. "Finished!" cried the *Colonist*. "1871-1885. Fourteen years patience rewarded." British Columbia and Canada were at last physically joined, although it was a contrived confederation, created by two tenuous bands of steel 3,000 miles in length.

But the Columbians still had their Chinese problem; indeed, as the last rails were being laid, the *Colonist* noted an ever-increasing anti-Chinese agitation, in spite of the fact that Chinese were now actually leaving the country. Those people who wandered down to Welch and Rithet's dock on October 9, 1885 observed "a curious scene." There, before their very eyes, were three to four hundred "Chinese emigrants" climbing aboard the *Alden Besse*, bound for Hong Kong. "Below decks," as the *Colonist* put it, "they were squeezing and pushing against one another and the barrels of water and bags of rice and flour were to form part of their sustenance, the partial gloom but slightly dispelled by a few candles. They jabbered away at a rate that gave the notion of what Babel must have been.... They were apparently all in good spirits and anxious to start and there is little fear that anyone will endeavour to foil them in their intention." Ten days later, the bark *Spartan* was towed out to Cape Flattery by the tug *Pilot* "with her load of coolies" (320 of them) bound for Hong Kong.

By the last week of October, the *Colonist* noted, "only about 70 of this obnoxious race had entered the province while 700 - 800 had departed," since September 1. By mid-November, 95 Chinese had landed while 1,000 had departed, and it was ardently hoped that a great many more would take advantage of the 15- to 20-dollar sailing vessel fare. It was also noted that, although Onderdonk had employed as many as 8,000 Chinese at his peak period, an estimated 1,500 had died over the five-year period "and a great many, gently and beautifully, had glided over the line."

These were certainly encouraging signs to most Victorians, but the Anti-Chinese Union was still holding weekly meetings, the Knights of Labor were still promoting anti-Chinese legislation, and the Dominion Restriction Act was not being enforced. Customs officers had been given the task of collecting the 50-dollar head tax on Chinese immigrants, but, it was said, they were too busy and too disinterested to do it efficiently. Furthermore, it was charged that Chinese were purchasing re-entry certificates which were then sent to China. (Residents were given certificates which allowed them to leave the country and re-enter without being liable to the tax, providing they could show a certificate.) The illicit traffic in re-entry certificates made a mockery of the Dominion Restriction Act. To make matters even more ridiculous, an Englishman, C.F. Moore, arrived in Victoria with his Chinese wife and children. The Chinese government had declared them non-Chinese, but the Dominion government, in its wisdom, decreed that the wife and children were of "Mongolian or Chinese race" and would be required to pay the tax of $50 each. Perhaps the Dominion authorities, harassed for 14 years by British Columbians, had hoped to please the recalcitrant westerners. The decision served only to irritate them more, as, perhaps, would have any other decision.

For their last complaint of the year, however, British Columbians had good reason. Onderdonk had finished his 350 miles of railroad. He had operated it himself during the construction period, presumably at a profit, but now he wished to hand it over to the C.P.R. Syndicate. The problem was that the Syndicate did not want it until the spring of 1886. The Dominion government, seemingly always willing to assist railroad men, agreed to accept the completed railroad, but also decided to close it for the remainder of the winter. All up and down the line, communities had learned to depend upon it for supplies; they were completely unprepared for disruption of services. After the exchange of several telegrams, the government agreed to operate the line with twice weekly service until the following May when the C.P.R., with its massive land grants tucked safely away, was prepared to accept responsibility. Perhaps this foreshadowed things to come.

There was one other incident in 1885 which foreshadowed the future history of the province. The Restriction Act had provided for the appointment of an interpreter. In July, Mr. William Cumyow, the manager of the King Tye Company, had applied for the position. "There is no one better qualified," said the *Colonist*, and a petition requesting his appointment was circularized. What was so special about William Cumyow? After all, he was Chinese—or, perhaps more accurately, of Chinese ancestry. The thing that was so special about William was that he was born in British Columbia; he had had his school and business education in the province; he was a member of the Episcopalian Church; he could speak perfect English and three Chinese dialects. He even had an anglicized name and wore an occidental overcoat and kid gloves. Many Victorians were proud of him, though others considered him a Heathen Chinee and were in favour of the other applicant, the American missionary, John Vrooman. There were a great many letters to the editor over the advantages and disadvantages of these two gentlemen.

However, the saga of William Cumyow, the bright young Oriental native of British Columbia was destined to end unhappily. William was charged with forgery. From the evidence, it appeared to be merely a rather loose method of practising business, but on December 17, William sat in court, wearing his overcoat and kid gloves. The judge committed him to jail and he was handcuffed. He asked then that his manacles be removed so that he could give his coat to his brother, after which he was led off down the street to the jail. With a mixture of pride and sadness, the *Colonist* again pointed out that William Cumyow was a fine English scholar and a native of British Columbia. Victorians were indeed a remarkable people.

Since the completion of the railway, unemployment had increased by leaps and bounds, and the Chinese labourers suffered more than anyone else. There were almost 3,000 of them in Victoria and environs, 1,435 living on Cormorant Street, 556 on Fisgard, 373 on Government and 219 on Store Street. Most of them were completely destitute—and the wealthier Chinese merchants were said to be indifferent to their plight. Their choice was to beg, steal or starve. Many chose the hen roost. Only a few Chinese were caught in the act, but in general the numerous crimes extending over 1886 were all blamed on the hungry Oriental. It was noted, for example, that the thefts invariably occurred close to Chinatown, and when 12 of Samuel Gray's hens disappeared one night, it was observed that the "impress of Chinese shoes indicate the nationality of the thieves."

The police just could not cope with the crime wave. "The rogues are very sly," said the *Colonist*. A rancher living near New Westminster did manage to catch one Oriental thief in his hen roost, and he dispensed his own form of justice by pulling the man's queue through an auger hole in a fence post and fastening it firmly with a wedge. He then presented the Chinese with a cup of water and a knife and left him to his own devices. It took the poor Oriental 24 hours to decide that his only means of escape was to sever his queue.

Some Chinese certainly survived by raiding hen roosts, but others in Victoria fished for crabs off the Point Ellice Bridge or lined Janion's wharf with hook and line, preserving every minnow they could catch. But the destitution amongst the Chinese was something Victorians had never before witnessed. In January 1886, a reporter accompanied Officer Flewin on a tour of Chinatown's slums. He was shocked to see poorly clad Chinese shivering in their dark hovels. At one point, Flewin kicked in a door, a Chinese voice asked, "What you want?" and the officer did not bother to answer. Another occupant muttered, "No more chow chow." Mayor James Fell found matters even worse in May. Thick green slime oozed from beneath the tenements, while inside, he saw water closets which had not been cleaned for months and which were now overflowing. He came upon a leper—"a horrid repulsive being whose feet had rotted away, leaving only pointed stumps." There was an intolerable stench from the rotting fish, opium and human excrement which was lying in open vessels awaiting transportation to Chinese gardens. The mayor beat a hasty retreat.

Nonetheless James Fell did his utmost for the Orientals. He had been elected mayor in January 1886—a rather surprising event, since he was known to be sympathetic toward the Chinese. In May 1876, he had been hissed from the public meeting in the Theatre Royal for pointing out a few plain truths on the Opium Wars. Shortly after his election, he had a meeting with the Chinese merchants, expressing the hope that they would come to the aid of their countrymen, and on January 30 he again spoke before a public meeting, this one chaired by Noah Shakespeare. He was preceded by J.M. Duval, who said that whites had suffered greatly from cheap Chinese labour and that those who allowed them to be brought into the country should return them. A motion to this effect was made by Duval and seconded by Councillor W.A. Robertson, who then made a most venomous anti-Chinese speech. When William Bond, a Negro, spoke against the motion, he was shouted down with cries of "Hurl him from our midst! Let the slave owners look after the slaves."

James Fell fared no better. Reported the *Colonist*, "Mr. Fell here tried to convince the audience that the Chinese were not a curse, and with almost one accord, they left their seats and with hisses, groans and cries left him alone, the chairman also leaving without asking for an adjournment."

The *Colonist*, however, grudgingly gave its support to the Chinese. "While these people are with us," they said, "we must see that an existence be afforded them." They suggested a soup kitchen, and a week later it was in operation. The Six Companies of San Francisco also attempted to help their unfortunate countrymen. They posted a notice in Chinatown stating that they had hired four steamers which would transport those who wished to return to China, at a reduced rate of $25. Those of 60 years or over would be given free passage and a present of $15 and those younger, if they could prove poverty, could also obtain free passage and a present of $10.

It is not known how many took advantage of this offer. Certainly Victoria's Chinese were not otherwise overwhelmed with kindness at this time. On the contrary, the politicians were planning further anti-Oriental legislation. Theordore Davie was insisting that the cubic air law and the prohibition against removing the dead were still in force, and his brother, Attorney-general A.E.B. Davie, presented a resolution in the Legislative Assembly stating that anti-Chinese clauses be inserted in all private bills. The effect of such clauses would be felt most severely in the mushrooming town of Granville on Burrard Inlet. In early February, a petition had been received by the provincial government asking that the village of Granville be incorporated as a city under the name "Vancouver," and this was followed by many private bills requesting permission to install electric lights, street railways and water systems in the new city. Every one of these bills would contain clauses prohibiting Chinese labour.

A.E.B. Davie's anti-Oriental clauses even found their way into the contract for extending the C.P.R. into New Westminster. W.C. Van Horne had never been very anxious to send a line into the old "City of Stumps," but he was persuaded to do so when New Westminster agreed to subsidize the construction with a $37,000 grant. The province also agreed to a $37,500 subsidy, but they added a Chinese restriction clause to the contract—and William Cornelius Van Horne absolutely refused to build the extension without Chinese labour. This resulted in bitter quarrels between New Westminster-ites, who were now suddenly affected by anti-Oriental legislation and Victorians, who did not particularly care whether New West-minster had a railroad or not. The E. & N. contracts contained no anti-Chinese clauses; the Chinese had formed a large portion of its working force and the railway was almost complete. It was a remark-able demonstration of the utility of the Chinese, the greed of the railway barons and the selfishness and parochialism of the two communities involved. Van Horne, of course, won the battle. Three hundred Chinese and seven whites were hard at work on the exten-sion in May.

They were gloomy days for the Orientals of the province, but a few still trickled into the country. The *Alden Besse* arrived again in May and "Thirty-four Celestials," as the *Colonist* put it, "had the pleasure of presenting the Canadian Government with $50 each for the privilege of viewing our dusty streets and taking up habitation in sweet smelling Chinatown." Matters were no better across the gulf. In April, the Vancouver *Herald* reported, "Mr. Alexander sold a couple of lots to a Chinaman near False Creek but those living nearby were not satisfied so he bought them back."

The C.P.R. was having a great deal of difficulty obtaining the land for its right-of-way into Vancouver, incorporated April 6, 1886, raising once more the hopes of the Islanders. "The objective point of all northern railways is Victoria," said the citizens of the capital, and they released 21 English meadow larks on Beacon Hill to remind them of their distant homes. Even God seemed to be on their side; the new city on Burrard Inlet was consumed by flames in June. "It is a dismal black waste in the woods;" said the *Mainland Guardian*, "the fire eat [sic] up everything."

Until the rail and water transportation problems of the inlet could be settled, Port Moody would be the centre of international trade on the Pacific coast. On July 26, 1886, the first clipper tea ship appeared off Victoria, the *W.B. Flint*, 35 days out of Yokohama, to be towed across the gulf to Port Moody by the steamer *Alexander*. And others were on their way.

The railway was shifting the trade of the province from the old cities of Victoria and New Westminster to Burrard Inlet. It also brought a great influx of visitors in the summer of 1886: politicians, businessmen and tourists. Since there was little to see on the inlet, they proceeded to Victoria, where Noah Shakespeare took great delight in showing them the horrors of Chinatown. Noah had started the tourist industry.

By far, the most outstanding visitor of the year was the darling of loyal Victorians, Sir John A. Macdonald. Their love affair was difficult to understand, especially because Sir John was, perhaps, a somewhat reluctant paramour. He had been most tardy with his railroad which, now that it was finally completed, could do more harm than good for the capital city. He had resisted anti-Oriental legislation in spite of his Victoria constituents' wishes, he had disallowed provincial anti-Oriental legislation, and most certainly the Blue Ribbon Club and the W.C.T.U. would have disowned him had they known of his love for the demon alcohol. Over the years, Sir John had frequently been reported as being "ill" or "indisposed." Less than three months before his arrival it was said that he was very ill and "the end is thought to be approaching." But Sir John always recovered quickly.

The encomiums began to flow well before his arrival and persisted until his departure. At 10 p.m. on July 24, 1886, the *Princess Louise* slipped into Victoria harbour as a band played "See the Conquering Hero Come." There were thousands on the dock, including Noah and Mayor Fell; torch bearers led his carriage through the streets to the Driard, and "the throng pressed closely around . . . cheering ever and anon, with each trying his utmost to gain a glimpse of Sir John and his consort." Consort? Perhaps only Victoria and Albert could have equalled Sir John and his lady. Victorians were a most remarkable people.

Sir John was wined, dined and eulogized. He was "The Chieftain" and "Canada's greatest statesman." Noah did not manage to get him into Chinatown, though it was openly suggested that he visit "to see the evils." He did, however, receive an address from the Knights of Labor in which he was reminded that the Dominion government had disallowed several provincial acts concerning Chinese, that the Dominion Restriction Act was being evaded, and that no Chinese should be employed on public works. The *Colonist*, at the same time, described Chinese immigration as "malific," but when Sir John met a group of workingmen he said that Chinese could not be excluded since it would harm the burgeoning trade with the Orient.

On August 13, Macdonald drove home a golden spike on the E. & N. near Shawnigan Lake, proceeded to Nanaimo and New Westminster and finally departed for Banff Sulphur Springs on August 16.

Victorians turned unhappily to the matter of destitution amongst the Chinese. Mayor Fell held meetings with Oriental merchants, but little was achieved, other than that the merchants agreed to make an attempt to transport a leprous countryman on the *Alden Besse* which was about to sail for Hong Kong. Whether they succeeded is uncertain, but in mid-October the barque departed with a load of lumber and 207 Chinese returning home. This did little to relieve the misery in Chinatown, and Colonel Bee, the Chinese Consul in San Francisco, complicated matters further by announcing that his government would not support soup kitchens since it tended to make Chinese lazy.

Hen roosts continued to suffer nocturnal losses both in New Westminster and Victoria through 1886 and into 1887, and Chinese houses of prostitution were constantly being raided by Superintendent Bloomfield's policemen. Two of these raids received a great deal of publicity since minors were found on the premises on both occasions. One of them, Gook Long, a 12-year-old prostitute, was found bruised and bleeding in the house of Tai Ho, "a hard hearted hag and harlot."

But since the completion of the C.P.R. to Port Moody and the Dominion Restriction Act, there had been no anti-Oriental sentiment of any significance in Victoria, other than from the occasional small boy who preferred to aim his snowballs at Chinese rather than white heads. The Chinese population actually seemed to be decreasing. In November, 110 Chinese were placed upon the barque *Southern Chief* for Hong Kong. "They will never be missed," remarked the *Colonist*. New arrivals had dropped to a trickle. From September 1, 1885, when the Restriction Act came into effect, to the end of the year, 158 Chinese entered the country. Only six entered for the twelve months of 1886. Furthermore, it was believed that about a thousand Chinese had slipped across the border to the United States. Chinese merchants estimated that their population had decreased by some 2,000 in 1886, and would decrease further in the future. "In the course of a few years," said the *Colonist*, "it may safely be assumed it will be greatly reduced and eventually the Mongolians will form a very insignificant element in the British Columbia population."

On Vancouver Island, the era which saw the huge influx of Chinese to the gold mines and to the railroad seemed to be ending on a happy note. On the mainland, the Chinese problem was less clear. The matter would have to be held in abeyance, though certainly the natives of Vancouver were becoming restless. Early in December 1886, the Supreme Court of Canada dissolved the injunctions which Begbie, McCreight and three other British Columbia justices had allowed against the C.P.R. This decision gave the mighty railroad company the right to expropriate land for their railway. It opened the last gate into Vancouver, and with each passing week the 12-mile gap between Port Moody and the new city gradually closed.

On February 4, 1887, a small heading, "Vancouver," appeared in slightly heavier print amongst a pageful of brief items in the *Colonist*. (It had dropped the word "British" from its name on January 1.) It was followed by three short lines: "A number of Chinese left for Vancouver this morning. The first train arrived in Vancouver yesterday afternoon." Possibly no one recognized the significance of those two statements. They marked the end of an era. Times had changed. Eighteen years earlier, the trip from Victoria to Montreal took eight weeks. Seventeen years earlier, the Central and Union Pacific Railways cut the time to 11 days. In 1883, the Northern Pacific cut it to eight days. "But now," said the *Colonist*, "we have a line of railway extending through British territory over which a passenger is whisked from ocean to ocean in five days and seventeen hours. It seems almost incredible that, in a period of time covered by less than half a generation, so great a change in the facilities of traveling has been affected."

The *George Elder*, the *Mexico* and the *Queen of the Pacific* were still laboriously plying the rolling route between Victoria and San Francisco—and their passenger arrivals were still being reported in the newspapers—but there was another list of names now, one headed "Overland Passengers." It would seem that it was only a matter of time before those perilous voyages to California would come to an end—as would the 44-year-neighbourly relationship between Victoria and San Francisco. The *Yosemite* and the *Princess Louise* were making regular trips to Vancouver now, and the great clipper ships laden with tea paused at Victoria only long enough to pull aboard a line from a waiting steam tug before being towed over to Burrard Inlet. They were no longer isolated from the east by "a sea of mountains," and yet Mayor Fell, on returning from a visit to eastern cities in November 1886, stated, "The kindness I received at the East has given me a high opinion of Canada and Canadians." Perhaps now British Columbia would in reality become part of Canada and its citizens would become Canadians. The problem of the railway had been solved. But what of the Chinese? Their numbers in Victoria seemed to be decreasing, but there was a movement across the Gulf of Georgia to Vancouver, where, it would appear, the citizens, were hardly as remarkable as those of Victoria.

CHAPTER V

1886-1887

*"The Chinese Have Came.
Mass Meeting in the City Hall Tonight."*
Vancouver street advertisement, 1887

Soft, sable green mountains hung over the narrow inlet, undisturbed for 20 years while Victoria, Nanaimo and New Westminster grew nearby. Captain George Vancouver had glanced at the inlet in June 1792; Valdez and Galiano a month later. When the Hudson's Bay Company felt it expedient to move northward from the Columbia River, the tip of Vancouver's Island was the logical site for a new fort. The fur trade was still centred there, and the maze of islands between it and the relatively unexplored mainland was an unnecessary hazard for the clumsy sailing ships of the day. And when gold began to tumble past the eyes of awed prospectors, it was the Fraser River, just five miles to the south, which sucked the ships and men and commerce from Victoria—not the inlet. It lay unmolested—peaceful, slender, strictured, almost landlocked—often bathed in fog and mist and rain. On its shores, mighty firs and gentler cedars flourished, and trout and salmon poured through its waters and up the tumbling creeks of the north shore, through deep canyons, into unseen valleys.

But the solitude could not last forever. Colonel R.C. Moody's sappers cut and slashed their way out from New Westminster in all directions, reaching the south arm of the inlet at Port Moody in 1859 and the Second Narrows in 1865. A sawmill had been established on the north shore in 1862, though it was of no consequence until 1865, when modern life on the inlet began. In that year, Sewell Moody's mill on the north shore became a success, and Captain Edward

Stamp built another on the south shore. At the same time, Douglas Road was completed from New Westminster, and the Brighton Hotel was established at its end. A few months later, the region to the east of Stamp's Mill became Hastings and the region to the west became Granville. The City of Vancouver was incorporated in 1886, but its origin was the little cluster of homes which had clung closely to Stamp's Mill 21 years earlier.

A city, it is said, requires a mayor. Vancouver managed to survive without one for a month after its incorporation. When the campaign began, Premier Smithe and John Robson lent their support to R.H. Alexander, a Scotsman who had survived the remarkable trek of the Overlanders in 1862. The Chinese, presumably quite indifferent as to who was mayor, were inadvertantly partially responsible for the election of the other candidate, Malcom McLean. Public notices had been circulated, implying that Alexander was sympathetic toward the Chinese since, as manager of Stamp's Hastings Mill, he employed Orientals. A group of "easterners" faced Alexander with this damning evidence, to which the mayoralty candidate replied, "I do not consider that a Canadian is much superior to a Chinaman. If he can procure a bowl of blackstrap and a piece of fat pork it is all he requires."

It may or may not have been anti-Chinese sentiment which swung the election, but certainly early Vancouverites were most sensitive about their Oriental neighbours. In 1884, the Chinese population of Burrard Inlet had consisted of 5 merchants, 60 sawmill hands, 10 store employees, 30 washermen and cooks, 5 children, 3 married women and one busy prostitute, for a total of 114. There were probably more by 1886. Although the C.P.R. had not yet obtained its right-of-way into Vancouver, the town had grown rapidly to some 2,000 souls. Presumably there had been a corresponding increase in the Chinese population. They had settled largely in wooden shacks around the shore of False Creek, which then extended as far north as Hastings Street. From this point, a heavily wooded area stretched westward to the corner of Dupont (now Pender) and Carrall Streets, where a few more Chinese shacks were clustered. (It is a curious coincidence that the main street of San Francisco's Chinatown was also named Dupont Street.)

Following the great fire of June 1886, there was growing uneasiness over the Oriental influx and the part it would play in the future of the city. It was later said that this was due to "the foreign floating element" from Washington and Oregon, but it might also have been the response of Vancouverites who intended to profit from

Victoria's seemingly unpleasant experience with the Chinese. Whichever it was, by November 1886 the workingmen of the city were well organized.

"The Knights of Labor are still relentlessly pursuing the war against Chinese labor which they inaugurated," reported the Vancouver correspondent of the *Colonist*, "and almond-eyed celestials are finding the terminal city a poor location, and a number of them have taken their departure for better pastures. The knights have instituted a vigorous boycott against all who place themselves under the ban of the order by employing Chinese, selling them food for patronizing them in any way. If a business man creates one of these offences he finds a big black X painted on the sidewalk in front of his store or office when he goes to business in the morning, and the initiated understand that store or office, as the case may be, must be boycotted for supporting Chinese. By this means Vancouver will be ridden of the plague to white labor which threatened to invade the city in great force before the knights made a move in opposition to it. The knights intend to do all in their power to keep the celestials from attaining a foothold in this city and the feeling of the citizens generally is strong in favor of the object. A Westminster company who own real estate here were afraid to send a gang of coolies to clear their property, as in all probability there would have been a collision between them and the representatives of white labor. No Chinaman need apply at Vancouver. They run the risk of a cool reception and a warm send-off."

The Knights had never gone to such lengths in Victoria. They, or organizations similar to them, had frequently recommended anti-Chinese legislation; they had signed anti-Chinese petitions; they had expressed their sentiments directly to such men as Van Horne and Onderdonk, and they had published the names of those citizens who had employed Chinese and those who would not sign their petitions. They had even made attempts to compete fairly with the Chinese by establishing laundries, bakeries and market gardens. They had studiously avoided violence, particularly that night in 1885 when, "underneath the electric light on Blanshard Street," some members wished to march through Chinatown. They had always remained within the narrow confines of the law.

From the very beginning there was something more sinister in the anti-Chinese movement in Vancouver. Even though the C.P.R. extension was being held up, it was a city whose future was assured. Hastings and Granville could boast of old established citizens, but there had also been a great influx of speculators from virtually every province and territory in Canada, from the United States and indeed from almost every corner of the world.

The little settlement at Fort Victoria had seen a similar influx in 1858—the San Francisco *Times* had referred to them as "vermin of the masculine gender"—but most of them had scrambled off to the interior gold fields, leaving a nucleus of respectable British, Canadian, American and European administrators and merchants. In the 1860s, the lure of instant wealth took speculators to the creeks and rivers of Cariboo, Cassiar and Kootenay, where they engaged themselves personally in backbreaking labour. In the 1880s the wealth was on the burned scar on the southern shore of Burrard Inlet, in land speculation and in tea and silk which the new north-west passage to the Orient was about to make possible. It was commerce, not golden nuggets, which established Vancouver as a city, and the workingman had the intuition to foresee that the speculators in real estate and business would be quick to take advantage of cheap Chinese labour.

Mayor McLean was re-elected in mid-December 1886, along with a group of aldermen which included R.H. Alexander and those peripatetic speculators, David and Isaac Oppenheimer. The election was an orderly one, though again the Chinese question was raised. The Vancouver vintners and the Knights of Labor both attempted to press upon all candidates a platform which included an ordinance "to prevent the herding of Chinese and Mongolian prostitution" and an assurance that Chinese laundries would be declared a nuisance.

Whether the candidates considered such matters is not known, but within two weeks of the election it was reported that the Chinese had obtained a sub-contract to clear "the tract of land on the hill." Remarked the blatantly anti-Oriental Vancouver *News*, "Much indignation was expressed by those who heard the rumor and statements were made that the Mongolians would not be permitted to proceed with the work if they once attempted to make a start."

There was an ominous cloud of fear and lawlessness hanging over the money-hungry city on Burrard Inlet as 1887 dawned. Like the tinder-dry slashings in the West End the previous June, it needed only a careless spark to ignite another great conflagration. There was a further threat early in January when all Chinese in the city received a notice which read: "Due notice is hereby given warning all Chinamen to move with all their chattels from within the corporation of the City of Vancouver on or before the 15th day of June 1887, failing which all Chinamen found in the city after the above date shall be forceably expelled therefrom and their goods and household effects shall be consigned to either Coal Harbor or False Creek as convenience may propose. And furthermore, the authorities of the town are kindly cautioned not to risk their lives in trying to rescue the Mongolians, or giving themselves any unnecessary trouble as the undersigned are in terrible earnest." It was signed, "Vancouver Vigilance Committee."

The spark, like that of June 1886, settled in the west end of the city in the area referred to as "the Brighouse estate," pre-empted by Morton, Hailstone and Brighouse in 1862. It stretched from the present Burrard Street to Stanley Park and from Coal Harbour to English Bay. Originally 500 acres, it was now said to be 350 acres. The tale of that strange day in the second week of January 1887 depends upon which witness one believes. The early reports described it as a peaceful, though militant incident.

At a Public meeting in Vancouver on January 8, a committee was appointed "with the power to endeavor to induce employers of Chinese to discharge them." The committee then approached the Chinese who were camping in the Brighouse estate in preparation for clearing the area for John McDougall (who also had the contract for the C.P.R. extension.) "The Committee waited upon twenty Chinamen which Mr. McDougall had brought up from Victoria and politely asked them to depart," reported the *Colonist* quite casually. "No trouble occurred since the Chinamen decided to accept the inevitable and were escorted to the steamer by a large body of white men. Their fare to Victoria was paid and, as the *Louise* left the wharf, cheer after cheer rent the air. The action taken by the citizens of the ambitious little city is one that may breed trouble in the near future and it is stated that Mr. Thornton Fell [for some 40 years clerk of the Provincial legislature] has already taken proceedings against the mayor and those citizens who were prominently connected with the matter."

John McDougall told a much more lurid story; he travelled to Victoria to consult with the attorney-general and, at the same time, presented his account to the *Colonist*. "A large number of the floating population of the city, having no interest in it in any way, incited on by the open approval of Mayor McLean and Alderman D. Oppenheimer and others, hustled the Chinese in every conceivable way. They proceded to the shacks and tents which the Chinese had erected on the land to be cleared, pulled them down and bundled everything to the wharf, including some of the contractor's tools. Mr. McDougall was openly threatened that his life would be taken and that he would be run out of the city with the Chinese. He was abused in a vile manner on the street. Appealing to the chief of police for protection to himself, his workmen and his plant, that worthy officer said he was afraid to give any! Arriving at the dock, the Chinese were surrounded by a gang of roughs and in the presence of the mayor, chief of police and staff, they were kicked, cuffed and pulled about in a shameful manner. Such were the threats against them that they were only too glad to leave. Some Chinese for years have had a vegetable ranche on False Creek, and here their small houses were pulled down. They entered Alderman L.A. Hamilton's house while the family were at dinner, took the two Chinese boys who were servants there and bundled them off to the steamer."

This account of the affair brought a series of protests and accusations. R.D. Pitt was said to be the chairman of the Knights of Labor committee who expelled the Chinese, and was accused of being the same "swashbuckler" who founded a Fenian circle in Portland, Oregon and had organized a plot to blow up British warships and the drydock in Esquimalt. Pitt, on the other hand, answered that McDougall's description of the incident was not worthy of comment; David Oppenheimer had been sick in bed the day of the expulsion, Hamilton's house had not been entered and McDougall was not abused. Moreover, he, Pitt, was a real estate agent and had nothing to do with Fenianism. The people of Vancouver, he insisted, were unconcerned about Chinese, and he protested "Cannot Vancouver go ahead without interference from Victoria?" David Oppenheimer made an official declaration that he was not present at the expulsion, and the *Colonist*, in deep disgust, came to the conclusion that everyone had a different story, though it was without a doubt a deplorable incident.

The citizens of Vancouver did not rest on their laurels. They continued to paint white crosses on the buildings of establishments that dealt with Chinese, and when it was rumoured that Chinese were landing from the Victoria steamer, 300 men hurried to the wharf, only to find that the rumour was false. Shortly after, the *News* announced that Orientals were arriving from New Westminster. "The Chinese tyhees [Chinook for 'big' or 'boss'] are in town and making every arrangement to carry out the contract," they reported. "The citizens have the matter in hand and are on the look out."

A series of meetings caused the adaption of new anti-Chinese measures. In mid-January, 300 citizens signed a memorial "to discourage the location of Chinese within the city limits, to refuse to employ any Chinaman and to discriminate against any party who persists in employing Chinese." At a meeting in the Granville Hotel early in February it was decided that a signed pledge should be placed in the window of every business establishment stating that the owner has "no sympathy with or will not deal with or in any way countenance the residence of Mongolians in the city." Later in February, businessmen were carrying cards which read, "The undersigned pledges himself not to deal directly or indirectly with the Chinese."

In the new city on Burrard Inlet, anti-Chinese sentiment appeared to be unanimous. The Vancouver *News* gave the movement its full support: they pointed out that once the work was begun, it would be useless to withdraw, and the fight must go on. On the other hand, the older cities were appalled, though they never failed to express their dislike for the Oriental. "The country would no doubt be better of being rid of the Chinaman," said the New Westminster *Columbian*, "but it must get rid of them by legal means even if it takes time to do so." Said the Victoria *Colonist*, "While sympathizing with the residents of Vancouver in their desire to become a city free from the Chinese element, yet all well wishers and good citizens of the new town cannot but think that the policy they have pursued in order to attain the end sought, is a far greater evil than the presence of a few Chinese among them."

The last week of February 1887 was one of the more momentous in the history of Vancouver. The C.P.R. had been given 6,000 acres of land in the city, ("The Coal Harbor Give-away," the *Guardian* called it, pointing out that the C.P.R. "would have come anyway.") the right-of-way had been settled by the Dominion Supreme Court and the rails between Port Moody and Coal Harbour were almost all laid. On February 22, Sir John A. Macdonald was gloriously—for most British Columbians—re-elected. On the 23rd, the first train steamed into Vancouver, and on the same day the *Colonist* noted that "Two or three hundred Chinese are preparing to leave for Vancouver for lot clearing." On the 24th, the Chinese stepped ashore on Burrard Inlet. "There was no disturbance at Vancouver yesterday on the arrival of the Chinese passengers by the *Princess Louise*," said the *Colonist* the next day. "Superintendent Roycroft (of the Provincial Police) was on the wharf and no doubt was prepared for any emergency. It is likely that another consignment will be sent on tomorrow morning's steamer."

Everyone breathed a sigh of relief, but on the afternoon of the 24th, a placard was carried about the streets of Vancouver. It read, "The Chinese have came. Mass meeting in the City Hall tonight." At eight o'clock that evening an overflow crowd of some 300 working men and merchants jammed the second-storey room of the hall on Powell Street. A multitude of speeches followed, but nothing could be decided in regard to the proper action to take. The chairman retired and at that point, as reported in the *News Advertiser* of February 25, a member of the audience called out, "Those in favor of decided action being taken tonight say Aye." There was not a single dissent and "Tonight! Tonight!" became the general cry. The audience sprang to its feet, made its way down the stairs and proceeded in a body to the Chinese camp on the Brighouse estate.

The determination and tenacity of the mob was truly remarkable. It was a cold, wet night, there was snow on the ground and the camp was some two miles to the west. Carrying one or two lanterns they tramped through the black streets—along Powell, up Water to Cordova Street and across the Granville Bridge. There was still a mile to go, most of it through a wilderness of half-cleared brush where few Vancouverites at that time had ventured, and where today massive skyscrapers tower above the traffic jams. "The trail was an exceedingly rough one," said a *News Advertiser* reporter, "in many places running down steep ravines, up and down rising ground, over tree stumps and along the edge of chasms many feet deep. One or two lanterns were used by the crowd which trudged its way through the snow with remarkable rapidity, those in front calling frequently to others in the rear to make haste. Within a few hundred yards of the camp a shout was raised and a run made for the spot.... The mob immediately surrounded the shanties and amidst howls and yells commenced the work of seizing the Chinamen. A number got away in spite of their efforts to surround them . . . . " The shanties were then pulled down, bedding and clothing belonging to the Chinese were thrown into a great fire, and the Orientals "were badly kicked and knocked about."

The mob was in the midst of assembling the Chinese in preparation for marching them off to New Westminster when the whistle of Police Chief John Stewart sounded. He appeared from the darkness, his face badly scratched by the brush through which he had scrambled, followed immediately by Superintendent H.B. Roycroft, his clothes torn by the same bushes. The two officers of the law escorted the Orientals to a roofless shed and ordered all present, in the Queen's name, to return peacefully to their homes. No one paid any attention to him. As the *News Advertiser* put it, a loud voice from the crowd then called out, " 'Who says the Chinaman must go? All in favor say Aye.' From 300 throats the answer came as one voice and a tremendous Aye rent the air, the echoes of which reached the mountains across the inlet and reverberated back again. A hush fell on the crowd for one moment and again a voice rang out, 'Who says the police must go home?' Again Aye was shouted but this time the cry was diminished in strength. Again the voice rang out, 'Come on and drive them out.' A general move was then made down the bluff but the people, on getting close to the shed, gradually weakened and finally came to stop, evidently not wishing to attack the law in person. Nothing more was done by the crowd further than to throw snow on the fire or at the Chinamen, and every now and then giving vent to a cheer. Eventually the people left the spot in groups of half a dozen or so and returned to the city."

There had been 24 Chinese at the camp; only 16 remained when Chief Stewart finally managed to count them. Some had escaped into the bush, but others had run into the icy waters of Coal Harbour, to emerge half frozen when the mob departed. They had lost everything, though the police had prevented further indignities. Stewart and Roycroft were resoundingly praised for their courage by the *News Advertiser*.

But it was still not over. At midnight, the city fire alarm sounded. Smoke was found pouring from a number of shanties on Carrall Street from fires set presumably by the returning mob. The occupants had fled. The Chinese shanties on False Creek were also attacked that night, the damage being confined largely to broken glass.

In its 16-year history, the province had never experienced such an event. The strike in the Dunsmuir coal mines in 1877 had resulted in violence, though the Chinese were in no way involved. There had been minor incidents during construction of the C.P.R., the worst being that of May 1883, but these occurred in rough construction camps and the Chinese on each occasion were, at least in part, the intimidated aggressors. Vancouver in February 1887 was a city of over 2,000, it had a mayor and aldermen, it had magistrates and police—and the Chinese played a passive role.

Although the disgraceful action of Vancouverites could not be excused, greedy speculators contributed to the unpleasant scene by taking advantage of cheap Chinese labour. There was no shortage of white labour at the time. It was said that the present owners of the Brighouse estate saved $100 an acre by agreeing to use Orientals. And "Chinese McDougall", as he was then referred to, was also aiming for a handsome profit. He was apparently being paid $150 an acre by the owner, while he paid the Chinese "tyhees" $90 an acre.

On the 350-acre plot, a profit of $21,000 was a stupendous sum for 1887.

But the citizens of Vancouver would not be satisfied until there were no Chinese remaining within their boundaries. On the day following the destruction of the camp, the Chinese living on False Creek were notified to leave. "Shortly afterward," it was reported, "they were busily engaged in packing up all their bedding, clothes, tools and baggage and making hasty preparations to quit. In the afternoon they were seen going away in vehicles along the New Westminster road. A few women were among them. Before leaving, they barred up the doors and windows of their shanties, all the panes of glass having been smashed during the previous night. The number that left is eighty-six and there cannot be many remaining in town now. The whole of the Chinese who arrived on the Brighouse estate on Thursday has left camp for New Westminster. It is reported that the Chinese laundrymen will leave in a day or two. The Pacific laundry on Dupont street is deserted." The best that can be said for the city authorities during this unlawful event was that they prevented bloodshed, yet they appear to have accepted the action of the mob passively. The provincial legislature, meanwhile, had been in session since January 24. On February 28, four days after the battle of the Brighouse estate, Attorney-general A.E.B. Davie asked that the house suspend regular business in order to permit the introduction of a bill "for the preservation of the peace at Vancouver" (The New Westminster *Guardian* referred to it as a bill for "the civilization of Vancouver"). Davie described the incident in detail, blaming it on "outcasts from Tacoma and Seattle," but he also said that he had reason to fear that the municipal authorities were in sympathy with the agitators. He had considered calling out the militia, but thought it best to exhaust the civil power first. His plan was to send 35 or so provincial constables to Vancouver, accompanied by a stipendiary magistrate. The functions of the local magistrates were to be suspended since, he said, they were not to be trusted. The usual discussion followed, the bill was read three times with only two dissentions, the lieutenant-governor came down to the house to give his assent, and the bill became law.

Vancouverites were furious. The legislation was ill-advised and rash. "The city is law abiding and quite capable to cope with disturbances," they said. The bill, however, deprived their mayor and magistrates of the privilege of maintaining peace. The keys of the city jail were to be handed over to the provincial police, muncipal constables were to obey the orders of the special magistrate and, perhaps most galling of all, Vancouver would be handed the bill for the legislation its residents abhorred.

Ever since Vancouver had been chosen as the terminus of the C.P.R., Victorians had treated the young upstart on Burrard Inlet with sneering condescension and Vancouverites had responded with expressions of supreme confidence in their future. The bitterness between the two cities flared forth now, a bitterness which would last for many years.

The Victoria "specials" and Stipendiary Magistrate A.E. Vowell were met at the wharf on March 2 by a large crowd, with no untoward incident. A boat load of Chinese arrived from Victoria on March 4 and those who had fled to New Westminster gradually returned to Vancouver. All appeared to be peaceful on Burrard Inlet now. The *News Advertiser* pointed out that the specials had nothing to do and were enjoying their holiday. They were furious when the *Colonist* charged that the specials were being boycotted. It was said that they were being charged 25 cents a pound for beef with prospects of it being raised to 30 cents and that all other provisions were correspondingly heavier. This, said the *Advertiser,* was an out and out lie, and day after day they attacked the press and people of Victoria.

Perhaps it was the presence of the Victoria specials, perhaps "the floating foreign element" disappeared, or perhaps Vancouverites realized that they could not win the battle against the relentless onslaught of the Chinese. Whatever the reasons, peace reigned in the city. There was now more bitterness towards Victorians than towards the Orientals.

On March 19, the *Princess Louise* returned to Victoria with Judge Vowell, Superintendent Roycroft and most of the specials. "The city [of Vancouver] is now affording ample protection and there is little fear of law breakers,' said the *Colonist*. "A large crowd assembled at the wharf and gave them [the specials] a good send-off, a kind of 'sorry to meet, glad to part and hope we don't see you again.' " Victorians could act unbearably superior at times.

CHAPTER VI

1887-1890

"It is Not Advantageous to the Country that the Chinese Should Come and Settle in Canada, Producing a Mongrel Race . . . "
Sir John A. MacDonald 1887.

The Brighouse estate continued to be an anathema to Vancouverites. Chinese labourers, now grudgingly accepted, were clearing the area and by June they had built up huge piles of brush ready for burning. There had been no rain for several weeks. Each pile of brush was the fuse of an unlit bomb sitting at the back door of every home in the city. The great fire of 1886 had started there and in May 1887 another in the same area had caused great consternation until it was thoroughly demolished by the fire-conscious citizens. New fire ordinances were adopted but "some legal gentlemen from Victoria", as the newspapers put it, stated that the Chinese must not be interfered with. "It is a strange thing if this whole city has to live in dread for some months owing to the presence of a few Chinamen on the Brighouse estate," growled Alderman Humphries.

It was said that there were 300 Chinese there now, though "300" was a very popular number for the scribes of the day. One afternoon in mid-June a *News Advertiser* reporter walked over to the estate and found sixty piles of tinder-dry slashings, a little less than 300 Chinese labourers and an Oriental tyhee who was most annoyed at the fire restrictions placed upon him. Some of the labourers were taking a day off and were sitting about in their shanties playing cards, gambling and smoking opium.

The summer and fall, however, passed without any serious conflagrations, though the presence of Chinese was a constant thorn in the sides of Vancouverites. When an overseas ship arrived with twelve Chinese immigrants they were processed in the customs house. To prevent confusion, a label was attached to the clothing of each. "From the manner they are billed," commented the *News Advertiser*, "one would think it was animals or merchandise instead of human beings." This group contributed $600 to the Dominion treasury, but, said the newspaper, "it is like catching a penny and losing a pound." And when Hugh Keefer was forced to hire Chinese to load his gravel scows, since whites would not perform such a menial task, he found it necessary to inform the City Council that he had not purposefully broken his contract.

Lawlessness seemed to have disappeared, though the Chinese were accepted only as inferior human beings. In 1888, the *News Advertiser* did show a flash of interest in the Orientals' greatest holiday. "Yesterday was New Year's Day for Chinatown," said the newspaper, "and right royally was it celebrated. At all the leading stores and washouses, refreshments in the shape of cakes, wine, nuts, sweatmeats, fruits etc. were provided and visitors were entertained most hospitably. The Celestials amused themselves in their own quiet way and but for some young white hoodlums, the day would have passed off without incident. But these graceless young scamps, after partaking of Chinese hospitality, proceeded to amuse themselves by throwing stones through windows. When remonstrated with, one of them struck a Chinamen with a fist in the mouth, making it bleed profusely. The fellow was chased by the infuriated Chinaman but managed to escape. The police were notified and after an investigation had been held, warrants were issued for the arrest of some of the offenders."

And in June of the same year, citizens were rather pleased to hear that a Chinese school had been in operation for some months. "The Chinese who have enrolled," it was reported, "are desirous of learning to read, spell, write and sing in English and thus far do themselves and their teachers credit by their docility and studiousness."

There certainly had been an improvement in Chinese relations over the year. Perhaps it was because the city was so busy. By the end of April 1887, the last rail was laid on the C.P.R. dock which stretched 500 feet along Coal Harbour; the first train from Montreal arrived on May 23, and on June 13 the C.P.R. steamship *Abyssinia* made her first appearance on Burrard Inlet. And soon the *Parthia*, *Batavia* and *Zambesi* were appearing regularly, carrying all the riches of the Orient to Vancouver: bales of silk, chests of tea, cigars, curios, oranges, opium and, alas, a varying number of Chinese passengers.

The tinkle of the cash register could easily drown the cries of those who complained of Oriental immigrants. The *News Advertiser* recognized this in October 1888 when the editor expressed his continued dislike of the city's Chinese population. But he cautioned forbearance, since any ill-considered action might injure their commerce with the Orient. "Our meaning," he said, "will be well understood by anyone here when we instance the trade between this place and China, which although as yet in its infancy, has contributed in no small degree to the progress and prosperity of Vancouver."

Cordova and Carrall Streets were the hub of the business community, but Granville Street was now lined with shops, and the Hotel Vancouver was perched at its highest point. The Brighouse estate was sprinkled with many fine residences and across the calm expanse of False Creek, the white fronts of pretty villas and snug cottages could be seen amongst the dark setting of giant trees. But it was a company town, virtually owned and operated by the Canadian Pacific. C.P.R. ships carried precious cargoes to and from China and Japan, Vancouver and San Francisco. The railroad carried equally precious cargoes to and from Vancouver, Montreal, New York and all the other great cities of the eastern seaboard. As long as the C.P.R. landlords poured trade and commerce through the city, Vancouverites could suffer "the wily Chinee" or "the simple heathens," as they referred to them. The Oriental lived in a somewhat uncomfortable and degrading state of peace in the community.

Those same C.P.R. steamers upon which Vancouver depended, were all but destroying Victoria. When the *Abyssinia* slipped past the capital city in June 1887, the *News Advertiser* could not resist the opportunity of reminding the older city that its day was past. "Victoria is weeping for her steamers and will not be comforted because they don't call there. It was not until even the smoke of the steamer was no longer in view that they realized Victoria was no longer the only city in the province." Exactly one year later, the egos of all staunch Victorians received another blow when the Dominion government withdrew its subsidy to the line of American ships plying between their city and San Francisco. The railway, for which they had fought for so long, had not only created a monster across the gulf, but was also destroying their 45-year association with San Francisco. C.P.R. ships indeed called at that Californian city on their way to the Orient, but C.P.R. ships were Vancouver ships—and Vancouver was an abomination.

The new city on Burrard Inlet had stolen the commerce of the west coast, as well as all the anti-Oriental headlines, though the feeling against the lowly Chinese still smouldered in Victoria.

George Howe was making an attempt to invade the vegetable business of the capital. "Before long it is hoped he will drive John Chinaman and his typhoid breeding vegetables out of the field," said the *Colonist*. Laundries were being opened to compete with Chinese; the Bricklayer's Union was discharging all Orientals and replacing them with whites; and because the *S.S. Islander* was not keeping up to her schedule, the Chinese stokers were blamed and immediately discharged.

But Victorians expressed their bitterness towards the Oriental in a different manner than did their neighbours across the gulf. They complained, for instance, that their Chinese servants were becoming too ambitious. "Housekeepers bewail their unfortunate fate in not having the benefit of trained servants of a class that are servants by inheritance and have no aspirations to be anything else," they grumbled. When Chinese first arrived from the Orient, it was said, they were meek and docile. They had been a servile race in their own country but "the restraints of despotism removed, they are in one sense at liberty to do as they will, without the mental and moral discipline which, in a measure, trains the passions of a corresponding class of the Caucasian race. It is pretty clear that the average Chinaman has little or no moral sense. Superstitious fear, yes—but no sense of responsibility . . . . A Chinese boy brought up in an English family and treated with the consideration most English people have for their own servants, does not appear to become attached to the family. He shows none of the devotion of other races in subordinate positions. . . . On the other hand, the murders and robberies that Chinese domestics have planned and executed on their employers and benefactors warrant the conclusion that they are deficient in the qualities of the heart which good servants should possess."

The people of Victoria belonged to an old established society. They were more English, more cultured, more law-abiding and more class conscious than the citizens of Vancouver who were from every corner of the earth, most of them residents for only a year or so. And the same could be said, in part, of the Chinese society. The great mass of them in Victoria were labourers, laundrymen, servants and market gardeners, but there was also a well-to-do merchant class who were graciously accepted in town and who contributed their share to the community. They annually subscribed to the Royal Hospital in amounts seemingly commensurate with their position. In 1885, for example, 13 Chinese merchants contributed amounts ranging from $2.50 to $5 each. Compared with subscriptions from the white community, this seems to be quite adequate. Judge Begbie contributed $20, Lieutenant-governor Cornwall $10, R.P. Rithet $10, Henry Crease $5 and the Oppenheimer brothers $5. The merchant class in Vancouver were not yet firmly established.

The Chinese were trickling into the country in much smaller numbers than during the days of railroad construction. In the 15-month period beginning in January 1886, for example, 797 arrived by ship from the Orient, though only 127 were classified as immigrants. The remainder were returning to the United States or were classified as students or travellers. It became apparent in 1887, however, that there were loopholes in the Immigration Act, particularly in regard to re-entry certificates, which apparently were being purchased by Chinese and sold to customers in China. In that year, Joseph Chapleau modified the Act to block these loopholes. His amendment was of no great significance, but the debate which followed its introduction brought to the eyes of the public the opinions of "the grand old man," Sir John A. Macdonald. He had his railroad now, but he still could not rid himself of the habit of speaking of the two sides of the country as separate entities—and he still could hardly be termed an enlightened emancipator. "The whole policy of this measure," he said, "is to restrict the immigration of Chinese into British Columbia and into Canada. On the whole, it is concluded not advantageous to the country that the Chinese should come and settle in Canada, producing a mongrel race, and interfering very much with white labor in Canada . . . . I do not think it would be to the advantage of Canada or any other country occupied by Aryans for members of the Mongolian race to become permanent inhabitants of the country. I believe it would introduce a conflict between the working class which would result in evil."

The great ocean liners of the day continued to steam into Vancouver carrying their rich cargoes and a varying number of passengers. Those travelling first class enjoyed the distinction of appearing in print the day after arrival in the *Colonist* or *News Advertiser*. There were usually only 10 or 20, all white, with the exception of four or five Japanese. The Chinese were confined to "Asiatic steerage." Their numbers were considerable, though most were destined for San Francisco. In June 1888, for instance, 636 Chinese arrived on the *Zambesi*. Of these, 482 would remain aboard for the California city, 79 were for Portland, 2 for Seattle, 8 for Port Townsend, 4 for Montreal, 6 for New York and 55 for Vancouver and Victoria.

American authorities were becoming quite concerned over this new influx. They had an exclusion act which, like that of Canada, permitted Chinese to leave the country and return if they held a re-entry certificate. However, many Orientals, on obtaining a certificate, promptly mailed it to China for the use of a relative, friend or paying customer, and as early as April 1888 the United States was considering an absolute exclusion act. In July of that year, the American consul in Victoria wrote to his assistant secretary of state, pointing out that, over a two-month period, steamers arriving in Vancouver had carried 3,527 Chinese, of which 2,854 were continuing to San Francisco. And it was generally accepted that the smuggling of Chinese into Washington Territory was occurring with almost daily regularity.

Early in October 1888, President Grover Cleveland suddenly signed an absolute exclusion act, forbidding the entry of all Chinese, whether they held a re-entry certificate or not. It was a disaster of great proportions to many Chinese who had left the country temporarily or who were already en route to the United States, and it had its effects on British Columbia. On October 7, the *Parthia* arrived in Vancouver with 118 Chinese bound for San Francisco. Others were en route from American Alaska to Washington Territory, raising the questions as to whether they should be considered as having moved from one part of the United States to another or whether they should be considered as departures and re-entries. One Chinese, whose life's savings were invested in a laundry and store in Colorado, had been visiting China and was now refused re-entry. Yan Skip of Seattle happened to be on a brief visit to relatives in Victoria and was not allowed to return. Steamer captains plying between Puget Sound ports and Victoria were required to post a $1,600 bond stating that crew members did not step ashore in British Columbia. When the *Duke of Westminster* arrived in San Francisco with 211 Chinese, the citizens of Chinatown collected $2,600 to pay the Canadian head tax for 52 of the travellers, who then sailed on to Vancouver. "They expect to smuggle themselves across the boundary into the United States," said the *News Advertiser*. There was really no way to stop them. The Chinese, it was said, took the train some 20 miles east of Vancouver and walked unmolested across the unprotected boundary. Those who could not pay the head tax returned to China.

The American exclusion act undoubtedly increased the flow of Chinese into British Columbia. The head tax revenue for October 1888 was $10,999, representing some 220 Chinese, almost four times the normal number. The act caused a great deal of inconvenience to the Chinese. Sir John A. Macdonald considered it a blunder, but he had no qualms in taking advantage of it. When the Dominion Trades Congress presented two anti-Chinese resolutions to him he gave several reasons for his disapproval, one of which was that, if the United States persisted in excluding Orientals, China might retaliate, to the benefit of Canada.

No one complained too bitterly over the mild influx of Chinese, though the problem was constantly kept before the eyes of the public. The struggle Australia was having over the exclusion of Chinese was also given a great deal of attention by the newspapers, but the Orientals of British Columbia lived for the moment in a relatively peaceful state. Indeed, in Victoria, two Chinese merchants reversed the usual procedure when they presented their member of parliament with a petition complaining of the Custom House interpreter. Another group of Chinese complained to the city council of the sorry state of Fisgard Street. Whatever was thought of Fisgard Street, however, Victorians in 1888 were slowly coming to realize that their Chinatown was becoming a tourist attraction. Immediately following completion of the railroad they had shown visitors the community with the object of demonstrating its evils, but soon they found that visitors, on returning to their homes, wrote about Chinatown as a quaint attraction of their fair city. When the devil, Edward Blake, visited in October 1888 (he was now a retired devil, having been replaced as leader of the opposition by Wilfrid Laurier) he and his sons "took a two hour tramp through Chinatown" (Vancouver *News Advertiser*).

Vancouver, as yet, had no Chinatown worthy of being termed a tourist attraction, though it had a park, named after Lord Stanley, around which Blake was driven by the city's new mayor, David Oppenheimer. Blake expressed unrestrained admiration and astonishment for British Columbia, "which," as the *News Advertiser* put it, "he now considers is not entirely 'a sea of mountains'." Poor Blake was always remembered in the west for his "sea of sterile mountains" speech. It was said by some, in defense of Blake, that the phrase was first used in 1873 in George Grant's book, "Ocean to Ocean," while others attributed it to Milton and Cheadle in their book, "North-West Passage by Land," published in 1865. Grant actually used the phrase twice in his book.

Another visitor to Vancouver in October 1888 was the evangelist, Dwight L. Moody. He began a remarkable religious revival in the city, a revival which even spread to Dupont Street. Every evening there were services held in the Winters Block, presided over by Ch'an Sing Kai, a native Chinese and Christian missionary. Also present were such luminaries as Mr. Kim, the excluded merchant from San Francisco, Ebenezer Robson, (brother of John) and none other than Won Alexander Cumyow. Many years later it was said that this was the brother of William Cumyow who had his opportunity to become government interpreter destroyed by an unfortunate court case. Won advertised himself in the newspapers as a Chinese translator and accountant.

The provincial legislature, in the meantime, heard and largely defeated a number of anti-Chinese bills presented by the opposition member, Robert Beaven. Premier William Smithe died in 1887, to be replaced by A.E.B. Davie, but by the time the 1888 legislature opened, he too had become seriously ill from "consumption" and was unable to attend. It was a momentous session, since it saw the first of a long series of attempts to amend the Coal Mines Regulation Act of 1887. The amendment added to the Act the words, "and no Chinese shall be allowed to work underground in any mine to which this act applies."

For several years there had been bitterness over the employment of Chinese in the mines. It had been brought to a head by a tremendous explosion in the Vancouver Coal Company's mine in Nanaimo on May 3, 1887. Of some 200 miners underground at the time, including 75 Chinese, only six managed to escape. Inevitably the Orientals were blamed for the castrophe and the miners immediately began procedures to prohibit them.

During the debate on the amendment, an old familiar voice from the past was heard: that of John Robson. He had been one of the first to propose anti-Oriental legislation. In 1872, he knew that his bill for the institution of a 50-dollar head tax on Chinese was unconstitutional, but he presented it just the same. Thirteen years later, the Dominion had imposed the 50-dollar tax. In 1888, however, John Robson stated that the amendment would be legislating against a class and that it was unconstitutional.

There was another reason for defeating the amendment. There was no longer an excess of labour, and the Chinese performed underground work which whites refused to accept. "To vote to exclude Chinese from coal mines when there is no other available help to take their place," said the *Colonist*, "would be a mad action. Business is dull enough without being made worse by persistence in the sentimental policy of refusing to allow the Chinese now in the province to remain and earn a livelihood by doing work that white men cannot or will not do." The amendment was defeated, sixteen votes to seven.

The session of 1889 passed most agreeably, as far as the Chinese were concerned, but soon after, Premier A.E.B. Davie died, at the age of 43 years. John Robson became Premier of the province and in 1890 he received a petition from 1,500 miners requesting that a clause be placed in the Minerals Act prohibiting the employment of Chinese underground. This brought action in the form of an amendment to the Coal Mines Regulation Act.

During the debate on this bill, it was pointed out that for years it was believed that the Chinese helpers underground were the cause of mine accidents. Following the explosion of 1887, the Vancouver Coal Company had voluntarily barred Chinese and there had been virtually no accidents.

Another interesting revelation at this time was the method used in producing coal. It was the white miner's responsibility to produce the mineral at the surface. The task of blasting and cutting through the coal seams required certain knowledge and skills, but the transportation of the coal to the minehead was a simple, menial chore requiring no skills although consuming a great deal of time. It was therefore to his economic advantage for the white miner to hire cheap Chinese labour to perform this work. The white miner actually became an employer of Chinese. In 1890 he decided that, for his own safety, he would replace his Chinese helper, whom he paid $1 a day, with whites, whom he paid a two-dollar daily wage. Premier Robson was pleased to hear that this was not just "the old anti-Chinese cry." He was supported by Attorney-general Theodore Davie, Charles Semlin and J.H. Turner (two future premiers) and Robert Beaven (an ex-premier and present leader of the opposition), and the bill passed unanimously.

The miners had obtained their act to bar Chinese from underground operations. The Vancouver Coal Company obeyed it; the Dunsmuir mines ignored it, knowing full well that the legislation would be challenged and probably ruled *ultra vires*. As usual, they were correct. The British Columbia Supreme Court later declared it valid, but still later, it was ruled "repugnant" to the British North America Act.

The Dunsmuir mines had been a source of labour trouble since the strike of 1877; they employed Chinese and they fought every move of the growing labour unions. Old Robert Dunsmuir was a hard-headed businessman. He was the wealthiest man in the province, with black diamonds tumbling from his mines and with his ocean-going coal ships, his Albion Iron Works and his controlling interest in the E. & N. Railway. But he had his problems. He was accused of favouring annexation of the province by the United States and of helping to keep the price of coal in Victoria too high. He was involved in a court case and in January 1889 he was involved in another strike over wages, all this while he was in the midst of constructing "a $500,000 house" in Victoria ("Craigdarroch", which still stands). He stated that he had been subject to "a great deal of annoyance during the past few months" and he closed his mines rather than accede to the union—until the needy workmen were forced to return. The following month his miners again went on strike, this time over the use of Chinese labour, but, said Dunsmuir later, "Enough men were found to take the places of the dissatisfied miners." In April 1889, however, the 64-year-old coal millionaire was found comatose in his home and a few days later he died "of an accumulation of uric acid which resulted in blood poisoning."

Robert's son James took over control of the Dunsmuir empire and by July 1890 he, too, was involved in a strike, this time over better working conditions. Like his father in 1877, he brought in strike-breakers from San Francisco, and by the end of September the miners, hungry and defeated, were again forced to return to their work. Trade unions were slowly gathering strength, but in the last decade of the century they were still far too weak to fight the giants of industry: coal mining and fish canning.

Over in Vancouver, the anti-Oriental violence of its post-natal days had evolved into a slightly more subtle form of discrimination. Early in January 1890, the City Council received a letter from B.T. Rogers announcing his intention of establishing a sugar refinery on the inlet. The obsequious city fathers immediately offered Rogers a bonus, and tax and water concessions—provided that he employ no Chinese. Perhaps the newspapers could hardly be termed subtle when, on a Chinese feast day, they reported, "The denizens of Chinatown during the day feasted on the best fowl they could select from the chicken coops," suggesting that the coops might well have been white ones. The newspapers claimed that for their part, they were opposed to violence, though they apparently had no objection to disdain, reproach and insult. "While it is generally admitted on all hands that the Chinese must go," remarked the *News Advertiser*, "it is not usually conceded that the individual member of the objectionable race should be maltreated, if on no other principle than cruelty to animals." John Robson was re-elected in 1890, as were many of the old faces. It appeared that nothing was going to change. Robson, the wild reformer of past years, was now a firm member of the establishment. Indeed, there were none of the old fire-eaters remaining—men such as the young Robson, De Cosmos and Bunster. Manitoba had one in the person of Joseph Martin, about whom British Columbians read occasionally in their daily newspapers. He would be heard from later, but in the meantime they had to settle for such solid, though dreary, citizens as Robson, Turner, Theo Davie, Beaven and Semlin.

The Dominion House was not much better. In 1890 John Mara presented the first of a long series of requests to raise the head tax (on this occasion to $100) and David Gordon demanded statistics on Chinese immigration. He was told that, over the preceding period of almost three years, only 1,887 Chinese had entered the country, a far cry from the 8,000 who entered in 1882 alone. Indeed the *News Advertiser* calculated that in 1889 there were 500 more Chinese who left the country than entered it. Certainly Victoria's Chinese population seemed to be decreasing. Tai Yune, the largest dealer in opium in the province, believed that the city's Oriental population had dwindled from 7,000 to 3,000 over the previous four years. This was an economic disaster to Kwong On Tai, another opium manufacturer in Victoria. He was forced to close his business, and Sing Wo Chang and Lung Chong were considering a similar action.

It was a rather dull period in British Columbia history, but perhaps this was a sign of maturity. It showed in the relative paucity of complaints to the Dominion and the rather casual manner —compared with the old days—in which Governor-general Lord Stanley was greeted in 1889. British Columbia was no longer isolated; ships and trains carrying visitors from all parts of the world poured into the province and the journals of the day printed world rather than local news. Sir John's railroad was perhaps doing the job for which it was intended.

CHAPTER VII

1890-1898

No Aliens Need Apply
Richard McBride, 1896.

Since its entry into confederation, British Columbia's greatest problems had been the construction of the railroad and the restriction and regulation of Chinese. Its railroad was now an issue of the past, but the Chinese problem was to persist for another six decades. Between 1890 and 1900, numerous attempts were made to pass legislation, centering mainly around the Coal Mines Regulation Act and the head tax; largely they were unsuccessful. In 1891, for instance, Robert Beaven introduced a resolution which stipulated that a clause prohibiting the employment of Chinese be inserted in all bills granting franchises or rights to private companies. When this was defeated, Beaven drove Premier Robson almost to distraction by proposing an amendment to the same effect every time a private bill was introduced. No one wanted to frighten investors away from the province.

The Chinese amendment to the Coal Mines Regulation Act also failed as the result of a number of variable outside influences. The reason given for proposing the amendment was always that Chinese, since they could not read the mining regulations or the signs posted about the mines, were a danger to white workers. The original amendment of 1888 had been defeated, it was said, because it was unconstitutional, though the real reason seems to have been a shortage of labour. In 1890 the same amendment was passed unanimously but was later declared *ultra vires*. It was again proposed in 1891, this time by Thomas Keith, one of the two labour members in the

House (Thomas Forster was the other). The capitalist majority in the legislature, having no use for the representatives of the working-man, soon defeated it. A year later when Keith again raised the issue, the bill had one notable addition: the Japanese, for the first time, were included.

There were seven "Japs," as the *News Advertiser* referred to them, living in Victoria in 1886, including a photographer, but there had been ten to twenty arriving on almost every ship from the Orient since then. Now that they were in the mines, the problems of the Coal Mines Regulation Act became much more complex, largely because Canada had treaties with Japan which she did not have with China. Relations with the Japanese were much closer than with the Chinese, a situation which would become more prominent in the future. The inclusion of the Japanese in the amendment of 1893 was the main reason for its defeat.

Thomas Keith, however, was back in 1894 with the same anti-Oriental gleam in his eye. He first asked Theodore Davie (who had become premier after John Robson's death in 1892) if the Coal Mines Regulation Act of 1890 was constitutional. There was initial confusion on this point, but a few days later Davie ruled that the question was out of order and the speaker, D.W. Higgins, meekly acceded to his superior's interpretation. Keith then asked the question, "Will the government enforce the Act?" Davie answered, "I do not think it is enforceable." Tom Keith was beside himself with anger, and the following day, for the fourth consecutive year, he proposed the Chinese amendment. Davie argued that it was unconstitutional and when Keith asked, "Did you pass it before?" the premier answered, "Yes, but things have changed." The speaker obligingly ruled the amendment out of order.

As Theodore Davie said, things had certainly changed. A Chinese Regulation Act and an Act to Prevent the Immigration of Chinese had been authored and pushed through the legislature by the two Davie brothers in 1884. There could have been no doubt in their minds that the latter was unconstitutional, and the Dominion government later confirmed the fact, but the next year, Theodore had again presented the same act, only to have it disallowed.

Attempts to restrict Chinese immigration had as gloomy a history as the Coal Mines Regulation Act. It was a Dominion responsibility under the B.N.A. Act, but British Columbia could do little to influence the Ottawa House through such procedures as resolutions from the provincial government or private organizations or through its six members—who were outnumbered by the remaining 240-odd members from elsewhere.

The number of Chinese in the country varied considerably, depending on which source one examined, but the census of 1891 listed, 9,129 in Canada, compared with 4,388 in 1881, though still below the level of 10,550 quoted by Huang Sic Chen in 1884. There were 31 Chinese in Manitoba, 97 in Ontario, 36 in Quebec, 8 in New Brunswick, 5 in Nova Scotia, 1 in Prince Edward Island and 41 in the Northwest Territories, for a total of 219, compared with 33 in 1881. The remaining 8,910 Chinese were in British Columbia, almost twice the number of the previous census. The total number of whites in the province was 98,173.

Three of British Columbia's M.P.s, together with a group of labour representatives, met with Sir John A. Macdonald in mid-May 1891, some two months after another Conservative victory at the polls. They asked that the Chinese be totally excluded. The 76-year-old premier was most friendly, but pointed out that the number of Chinese entering the country was so small, exclusion was not warranted. Of those who did enter, he said, most intended to go to the United States, and he reiterated his statement that the American exclusion act had caused strained relations with China, to the advantage of Canada. "If, however, there seemed to be a prospect of the Chinese coming in and swamping the whites," he was quoted as saying, "I should be willing to let the trade go rather than let the interests of the people of British Columbia be ignored."

A week later, in the midst of a magnificent celebration of the queen's birthday, Sir John again became "indisposed." By the end of May it was reported he was on his death bed, and all the following week the same news trickled through to the west. He died on June 6. A strange sense of loneliness and confusion seemed to settle over the country. In British Columbia particularly it was as if they had been orphaned. He had been in the Dominion House for the 23 years of its existence, and even during Mackenzie's five years of premiership he was always there to protect the rights of British Columbia from the demon Blake. With his death, the country seemed to stumble momentarily. The value of C.P.R. stocks dropped to frightening depths, to rise again with the formation of a new cabinet by Senator J.J.C. Abbott. The new premier, for many years, had been the solicitor for the C.P.R. and, until a few days before his appointment, a director of the company. Vancouver was a company town, Canada a company country.

Attempts to restrict Chinese immigration continued into 1892 with Tom Keith presenting a resolution—seconded by his labour friend, Forster—which requested the Dominion to strengthen its act. This failed to pass, but the Trades and Labour Council sent a similar petition to Ottawa, and David Gordon managed to obtain a few minor changes. It was not only the politicians who were expressing their anti-Oriental sentiments. In January 1892, a gentleman named Locksley Lucas called a meeting of "The Canadian National League" in Vancouver's Market Hall. It was crowded to the doors with citizens who apparently all were in favour of Chinese exclusion. "A meeting more unanimous in sentiment there could scarcely be," said the *News Advertiser*. They were regaled by Locksley Lucas, a former resident of Australia—and Locksley knew the Chinese well. They had low morals, he said, they ruined Caucasian girls, spread leprosy and sent their earnings back to China. The tyranny of highbinders was well-known, and no one wanted them but the C.P.R., which was the greatest monopoly in the world and controlled politics in Canada.

The audience gave him a tremendous ovation, following which they passed three motions unanimously, all very much anti-Oriental—one of them requested an increase in the head tax to $500. But that was Locksley Lucas' hour upon the stage. He disappeared, along with the $35.35 collected for the benefit of the association.

On January 26, 1893, the new lieutenant-governor, Edgar Dewdney, opened the Legislative Assembly and shortly after, Tom Keith began his annual attack on the Chinese. His bill was the same as the previous year's, requesting the Dominion to limit the number of Chinese carried by ships and to raise the head tax from $50 to $500. Again Keith failed by one vote, but, said the *News Advertiser*, the government could no longer ignore the general feelings of the public since its near defeat was tantamount to asking for complete exclusion.

The government did not ignore the warning. Within a month, one of their own members, James Punch, moved that the Dominion be asked to raise the tax. There were only two differences from the bill recently proposed by Keith: the first was that Punch suggested an increase to $100 rather than $500, and the second was that Punch was not a labour leader. The bill passed, Edgar Dewdney quietly gave his assent and it was sent off into the limbo of Ottawa.

What happened to provincial resolutions sent to the Dominion government? Some were answered, some misplaced and some simply ignored. Punch's resolution was forgotten until Premier Davie was asked about it in 1894. After a considerable delay, various pieces of correspondence were gathered together. There was a letter to the Secretary of State from Edgar Dewdney, a letter in reply from the Executive Council, a letter from the Under Secretary of State ("These matters will receive consideration," was the grave and frigid answer), and finally "A report of a Committee of the Honorable the Privy Council" to Edgar Dewdney. "The Minister of Trade and Commerce, to whom the matter was referred," the letter read, "states that, having given careful consideration to the subject matter of the Resolution, as well as to the question in general, he is of the opinion that in view of the commercial relations of Canada with China and its possible extension, it is not expedient to change the provisions of 'The Chinese Immigration Act' as it at present exists. . . . " It was, perhaps, a reflection of the times, to have the Minister of Trade and Commerce rule on a matter of immigration, but it was by no means an uncommon ending to a request from British Columbia. And it was by no means uncommon for the provincial House to pass an identical resolution, as they did in 1894, only to have it, too, disintegrate in the labyrinths of Ottawa bureaucracy.

The Chinese labourer was probably unaware of the many attempts to legislate against him. He would know that he was forbidden employment on Victoria City and provincial works, and he perhaps wondered why he was given work in the Dunsmuir mines but not in those of the Vancouver Coal Company. It was only when words were translated into deeds that he was aware of the increasing pressure being placed upon him. The better educated Chinese merchant, on the other hand, could follow the drama in the newspapers. In July 1891, he probably read the *Colonist* headline, "Filthy fertilizers employed by the unclean Mongolians in Victoria vegetable raising." The article stated that there were 20 Chinese market gardens on Queens Avenue and the streets leading into it, as well as on Cedar Hill, each varying from one to 20 acres. Their owners collected human excrement from Victoria's outhouses during the night, "and the foul, ill-smelling stench that has pervaded the neighbourhood had driven residents close to the celestial vegetable patches well nigh to distraction."

It was a most distasteful subject to genteel Victorians, especially to those who bought vegetables from their favourite "Chinaman" who sold his goods from door to door. The first intimation the market gardener had of this, however, occurred when the city health officer put a stop to the nocturnal collections. The solution of this problem unfortunately produced another; the city was faced with the dilemma of what to do with the excrement which the Chinese had previously so admirably disposed of.

The average Chinese citizen of Victoria and Vancouver lived in a state of uneasy peace with the white community, not realizing that he was being accused of being a leper, of having cess pits beneath his living room and of hindering the census takers in 1891. He could not read the protests over the illegal use of re-entry certificates nor of the fact that smuggling 2,000 Chinese a year into the United States was becoming a big business for some whites. He perhaps knew that his white neighbours were suspicious of his secret society, the Chi Gung Tong, which they said was a nidus of highbinders and paid assassins. It was, in fact, a peaceful group of nationalists who hoped to overthrow the ruling Manchu dynasty in China. The Tong had actually adopted the name "Free Masons" because it implied to western civilization a legitimate secret society.

Most of the Chinese did not know what was being said about them. In Victoria, some 200 attended the dedication of a new Methodist Mission Church on Fisgard Street in March 1891. A number were also active in the mission in Vancouver, "doing quiet but effective work." Dr. Lui and his aides could be found, even on a cold January day, at the corner of Carrall and Dupont Streets near the gaming house of Mah Fong, singing hymns to the accompaniment of a harmonium and preaching a sermon in Chinese. Those less religiously inclined spent their free time gambling or playing their drums and cymbals happily and discordantly, much to the annoyance of any whites within hearing distance.

The announcement of the death of Arthur Bunster in October 1891 probably would have meant nothing to the Chinese, had they been able to read it in the newspapers; indeed, the *Colonist*, in a very small item, found it necessary to explain precisely who he was for the benefit of white citizens. He had departed for California nine years earlier. Arthur Bunster died somewhat ingloriously of a stroke while fishing from a dock in San Francisco. The death of John Robson was perhaps closer to home, though it occurred during a visit to England in 1892. Of the three turbulent politicians of earlier days, only Amor De Cosmos remained. At the age of 66, in 1892, he had slid into the abyss of obscurity, re-appearing on occasion to protest Victoria's debt, to appear in court, to write a letter to the editor or to explain a project for a new railroad. In a sense, all three had succumbed several years earlier. The new breed of politician was the well-dressed gentleman of comfortable means who spoke quietly and politely. Reform and fire and brimstone were unseemly to him; his greatest enemies were the new reformers, the socialists, Keith and Forster.

Like the fiery old politicians, the barques and brigs and clipper ships were fast disappearing from the coast, but the old sailing ships were at least replaced by steamers of equal beauty. On April 28, 1891, the first of the great white empresses, the *Empress of India*, swung her graceful prow into Burrard Inlet. Two months later, the *Empress of Japan* sailed through the narrows, and another three months later, the last of the new C.P.R. steamers, the *Empress of China*, put in her appearance. Even Victorians were thrilled with their sleek and graceful beauty. The *Empress of Japan* "sounded her siren and ran up into Royal Roads like a great white bird," reported the *Colonist*, "her beautiful bow cutting the water as she turned swiftly into line with the shore and slowed up off Beacon Hill."

By the following year, however, these ships and others appeared to be carrying more and more Chinese. Actually the influx had begun earlier; in 1890 and the first half of 1891, 2,367 Chinese had entered, paying $131,850 in "head money." The numbers continued to increase with the appearance of 200 to 500 with each ship arrival. Some were re-entries or were passing through to eastern cities, but it was a matter which was noted with uneasy concern.

Of even greater concern was the arrival of the *Empress of Japan* on April 19, 1892. She slid into Royal Roads with 530 Chinese—and one case of smallpox. Health Officer McNaughton Jones transferred all the Chinese to tents on Albert Head, the southern rim of Royal Roads, some six miles from the centre of Victoria. White passengers were "disinfected" and proceeded merrily on to Vancouver, but it was not long before the dread disease began to appear in Victoria, Vancouver, Howe Sound and ultimately in Nanaimo. By the middle of July there were 47 cases in Victoria with four deaths. A hospital was built on Albert Head, against the objections of the local residents. In Vancouver the number of cases was not so great, but there were several deaths, and some houses were burned in order to scourge them of the disease. And in the middle of all this, the *Empress of Japan* arrived again in June with another case—who was promptly transported to the newly constructed pest-house on Deadman's Island in Coal Harbour. There were sporadic cases in Moodyville, Hastings and across False Creek in Mount Pleasant, but it was a mild form of smallpox, affecting only a small section of the population, compared with the cholera epidemic which at the same time was sweeping Europe.

The disease was undoubtedly carried by the China ships, but there was surprisingly little anti-Oriental feeling generated by it. There were, however, some political repercussions in Vancouver, where citizens were indignant at the high-handed methods of Dr. J.C. Davie, the Provincial Health Officer and brother of A.E.B. and Theodore Davie. There were also repercussions in Calgary, North-West Territories, where, after four Chinese were released from quarantine, 300 whites tore apart a laundry in protest. Even distant Toronto was affected. "Almost every day for the past two weeks," said a report from that city, "half a dozen or more Chinamen have arrived here from the west. This has had the bad effect of greatly increasing the Chinese population of the city. As a rule, the Celestials reach here with the intention of not having long to stay and have already made arrangements with some of their fellow countrymen, whereby they can continue their journey to some parts of the States. The only reason advanced here for the large influx is that Chinamen are being scared out of the western cities by smallpox and are fleeing to avoid the ravages of that dread disease."

The smallpox epidemic subsided quietly in September of 1892, but early the following year, a new threat appeared. For several months a business depression had been developing in the United States; banks closed with frightening regularity, the Colorado mines ceased production, and Gatling guns were mounted in the streets of Chicago to battle rioters. In British Columbia, the depression revealed itself in the form of unemployment and with it came further complaints of continuing Chinese immigration and the employment of both Chinese and Japanese as cannery workers and fishermen. The Chinese had been in the industry for years, under the old contract system in which management contracted with a Chinese agent to provide labourers whose life during the season was more or less controlled by the Chinese contractor. It was this type of arrangement which frequently led to the accusation that the Orientals were slaves. When necessary, the head tax for the immigrant labourer was paid by the contractor who then deducted a certain amount on each pay day until the 50-dollar tax was repaid to him. In a sense, during this period the workers were held in bondage.

The Chinese cannery worker was employed soldering cans beginning about March each year and then as a fish cleaner when the season opened in the summer. Soon after the turn of the century, many of these cleaners were replaced by a mechanical device, the

Smith Butchering Machine, which accordingly became known as
"The Iron Chink." Following the fishing season, the worker continued for a few months, lacquering, labelling and boxing cans,
finally disappearing into the Chinatowns of Vancouver and Victoria
for four or five months until the next season began in March.

In the summer of 1893, the Fisherman's Union used the oft-
repeated complaint that the Chinese worked for wages that would
starve a white, and they reacted by going on strike for higher wages.
In spite of their complaint, they would not allow the Chinese or
Japanese to join their union, though the more aggressive Japanese
offered to pay $5 a man to do so or $500 if a separate union was set
up for them. Labour unions were becoming stronger, but the workingman still found no sympathy outside his own ranks. Strikes and
discontent were becoming part of the plodding, clumsy process of
democracy. Thomas Keith preached the concept that the only way
the workingman could gain strength was through the ballot box, but,
to the workers who saw the coal magnates and fish canners waxing
rich, it must have been a frustrating concept. It was the industrialist
who was the winner. The workingman saw him building beautiful
homes, he saw Theodore Davie constructing his new and palatial
parliament buildings on James Bay, he saw the swelling ranks of the
unemployed and he saw 300 Chinese and 100 Japanese arriving
regularly on each of the great white Empresses. C.P.R. receipts were
falling to alarming levels, resulting in the release of 300 labourers
"due to economy and retrenchment." But they still carried their
loads of Chinese and Japanese into Victoria and Vancouver.

In spite of this, there was no concerted effort to persecute the
Oriental. Some were ordered to connect their homes to the sewer
line and some to scrub and whitewash their premises, and one group
in Vancouver was required to gather up "the accumulated filth"
from their dwellings and carry it to a scow on False Creek, following
which the waste would be dropped into deep water.

The dawning of 1894 brought no relief from the depression.
Canada's economy was tied inevitably to that of the United States,
and the price of wheat was falling steadily in Chicago. As a result of
this, farmers in the north-west were holding their grain in the hopes
of a better price and, as a consequence, C.P.R. receipts continued to
drop. Appeals were made in both Vancouver and Victoria to be
generous to the unemployed, the Vancouver Coal Company discharged all its single men, and the Chinese newspaper in Vancouver
had to cut its size from eight to four pages. To add to the miseries of
the province, there were snowslides and washouts on the C.P.R. and

massive flooding of the rich Fraser Valley farm lands. It was a cruel year, too, for Sir Matthew Baillie Begbie. He had become ill in the autumn of 1893 but had insisted on continuing his duties. In mid-May 1894, he was described by the Victoria *Province* as he sat at the Royal Commission on the Nakusp and Slocan Railway: "tall, thin, pale, white hair and iron spectacles." Everyone, including Sir Matthew himself, knew that he did not have long. He died in mid-June of cancer of the stomach, at the age of 75, still a bachelor and still greatly admired.

These were certainly gloomy days, though the railway brought the occasional eastern visitor, who supplied a little interest amidst the dreary days of depression. Sir Charles Hibbert Tupper, Minister of Marine and Fisheries, was, of course, a most popular visitor as far as Conservative British Columbians were concerned. Wilfrid Laurier, the new leader of the opposition since the demon Blake's retirement, was more or less a curiosity piece. He was treated somewhat frigidly, though such uncouth Liberals as Beaven, Semlin and the neophyte Delta farmer, John Oliver, welcomed him with open arms. And the visit of the Governor-general, Lord Aberdeen, was certainly a great event, especially to the loyal British of Victoria, where the Queen's representative addressed the pupils of the Chinese Mission.

Visitors were a pleasant distraction, but one had to face realities. In 1895, the Chinese continued to appear with each arrival of the empresses, in numbers ranging between 250 and 300. Their precise destinations were not always made known, but by no means did all of them remain in British Columbia. Of the 235 arriving on the *Empress of India*, for instance, 50 were destined for Vancouver, New West-minster and Nanaimo, 80 were for Havana and the remainder would distribute themselves over the larger towns of Canada and the United States. Those who arrived in bond for other countries were herded together in a dockside warehouse and fed "50 gallons of tea and a correspondingly large amount of edibles."

On the same ships, there were always some 50 Japanese immigrants. The atmosphere surrounding the arrival of this race, however, was quite different to that of the Chinese. The most obvious contrast was that they always wore European clothes. The *News Advertiser* in March 1894 described them as "wild looking hordes of Japs attired for the first time in European garments." Another difference was that the various Japanese consuls over the years were prominent members of the community with quite a flair for public relations. One never heard of a Chinese consul, and when Chinese arrived, as they did in ever-increasing numbers, they were dressed in their national costume. There appeared to be no control over their numbers and there was an air of mystery and secrecy about them, in the sense that they dressed differently and had no communications through a consul, as the Japanese had. But to the citizen of the province, they were all "Asiatics," and future legislation would largely be directed at both nationalities. Furthermore, on those occasions when one race was singled out for special attention, the effects were felt by the other.

For the moment, however, there was relative peace on the Oriental scene. There were occasional editorials on Chinese labour, and the Vancouver Trades and Labor Council on one occasion protested the use of Chinese firemen, stewards and cooks on the government-subsidized Empresses. On the other hand, the Presbyterian General Assembly went on record as being in support of completely removing the head tax on Chinese, though at the same time they voted against separate schools in Manitoba.

In 1895, however, there were other events in the evolution of the province which were of considerable interest. Henry Pelling Perew Crease, the only surviving judge in Canada appointed by the Imperial Government, retired and was knighted. Shortly before this, one of the saddest events of the year had occurred: Mr. Justice Drake declared Amor De Cosmos of unsound mind and appointed his brother trustee of his estate. It was an unhappy end for the great reformer of the colony's earliest days. There were few of the old pioneers remaining now, yet their passing was a natural process. During the gold rush days, the population had been a young one; now 35 years had passed and new pioneers and new leaders were appearing. One could occasionally catch a glimpse of new names in the newspapers of the day—young men such as W.J. Bowser, Richard McBride and John Oliver.

Theodore Davie resigned in March 1895 to become Chief Justice of the Supreme Court in place of Matthew Baillie Begbie, and John Turner became premier of the province. His first session in the spring of 1896 was a rather dull one—mercifully, perhaps, for the Chinese. The annual amendment to the Coal Mines Regulation Act and the annual resolution asking for an increase in the head tax failed to appear, possibly because Tom Keith had been defeated in the last election.

Dominion politics were in a much more interesting state at this time. Premier Abbott had resigned, his successor, Sir John Thompson, had died suddenly and the present premier, Mackenzie Bowell, was beset with resignations from his cabinet. Early in January 1896 he formed a new cabinet and recalled Sir Charles Tupper from his post as Canadian high commissioner in London.

The great political question of the day was whether Manitoba should be allowed to have separate religious schools. "The Prairie Province" (Alberta and Saskatchewan were still part of the North-West Territories) had voted strongly in favour of severing the tie between religion and education, but the Dominion government was considering the possibility of interfering in what was actually a provincial realm, according to the B.N.A. Act—though, as John Robson had remarked in 1872, "constitutions are very much what people make them."

It was said that Wilfrid Laurier had promised to restore separate schools to the Catholic minority of Manitoba, though the authority for this statement, the Conservative *Colonist* of Victoria, was not an altogether unimpeachable source. Both the ruling Conservative and the opposition Liberals were most cautious over such a sensitive matter as religion and education—though, of course, Joseph Martin could hardly be termed either cautious or sensitive. The former attorney-general of Manitoba had been one of the instigators of separate schools while he was in the provincial legislature. He was now an M.P. for Manitoba and he threatened to break with his chief, Laurier, and join the protestant forces of Dalton McCarthy if Laurier supported denominational schools. Joe had always been an enigma; even his own Liberal party never knew what he would do next. And ever since he had accompanied Laurier to British Columbia in 1894, he had considered himself an expert on that province's affairs. He had interfered on many occasions in British Columbia matters, so much so that the *Colonist* was stimulated to remark, "The Grits are great talkers and Joe Martin is one of the most industrious." The Liberal *Victoria Times*, on the other hand, embraced him as "Victoria's third member."

Late in April 1896, Sir Mackenzie Bowell resigned and Sir Charles Tupper, at the age of 75 years, became the new premier, the fifth in five years. Since the government had been in power for five years, he was forced to call a general election which proved to be the most interesting one since confederation 29 years earlier. The aura of Sir John A. Macdonald had faded, a series of relatively ordinary citizens had succeeded him, Wilfrid Laurier was the new, dynamic leader of the Liberals, the country was now physically united by the C.P.R. and, for the first time, a matter of national interest—separate schools—was the leading political question.

It was assumed that the Conservatives once more would prevail in

British Columbia. In Vancouver, W.J. Bowser was running against the Liberal, Reverend George R. Maxwell, the ebullient minister of the First Presbyterian Church on Hastings Street. (When Theo Davie announced the construction of new parliament buildings in Victoria, Maxwell had denounced it as "a belch in the faces of the majority of citizens of the Province.") In New Westminster, the bright young local barrister, Richard McBride, was expected to demolish the Liberal, Aulay Morrison.

There was little to choose between the platforms of the various candidates, though, indeed, platforms rarely are related to the winning or losing of elections. Everyone was against separate schools, everyone was against the Chinese. "The Mongolians come here as aliens, live as aliens, die as aliens and go to China in boxes as aliens," said a future premier of the province, W.J. Bowser. He pledged that he would introduce legislation to prohibit Chinese and Japanese from entering the country and he complained that Laurier, as usual, was being very indefinite in regard to the Oriental question. Bowser was a little premature with his complaint. Shortly after, Laurier sent a telegram addressed to the electors of British Columbia, one which might be considered either wise, rash or deceitful, depending upon which political party one belonged to. "Chinese immigration restriction not a question in the East," it read. "Views of the Liberals in the West will prevail with me." It was virtually a promise that Chinese immigration would cease. He would be reminded frequently of it in the future.

Over in New Westminster, the 26-year-old native son, Richard McBride, spoke against the interference of the government in Manitoba affairs. He was also vehement against the employment of Chinese and Japanese in the fish canneries of the Fraser. If elected, he said, he would allow only white British subjects to fish. "No aliens need apply" was a plank in his platform.

It was a physical impossibility to dislodge Col. E.G. Prior and Thomas Earle from their Conservative seats in Victoria, but the remainder of the mighty fell before the onslaught of the Liberals. For some it was the end of a political career. Bowser and McBride had long political futures ahead of them, but, for the moment, they were victims of the startling minister of the gospel, G.R. Maxwell, and Aulay Morrison—or, perhaps more accurately, victims of the dynamic leadership of Wilfrid Laurier and the ineffective leadership of the Conservatives. Separate schools and the Chinese question probably played no part in their defeat.

Laurier won handily though, perhaps to his secret pleasure, he lost Joe Martin in Manitoba; British Columbians, for better or for worse, would inherit him. A new era had begun, and it began, as the *News Advertiser* put it morosely, as a racial and religious victory. It was Quebec who had made the difference, according to the Conservative newspaper.

One of the by-products of the election was that it exposed a great deal of anti-Oriental sentiment, largely on the mainland. Just two weeks after Laurier's victory, a mass meeting of the Anti-Mongolian League was held in Vancouver's Market Hall with W.J. Bowser as one of the prominent speakers. The usual references to filth, immorality, polygamy, the opium habit and other evils were heard, and it was pointed out that, since the Coal Mines Regulation Act had not been enforced, the Vancouver Coal Company which had not employed Chinese underground since the explosion in 1887 would soon be forced to do so because of competition from the Dunsmuir Mines. Three motions were passed: firstly, that the head tax be raised to $500; secondly, that a similar imposition be placed on Japanese, and thirdly that a province-wide petition be organized to memorialize the Dominion government on the evils of the Chinese. Many other meetings followed this; the Victoria City Council and the Ottawa Trades and Labor Council sent their approval of the League's actions, and representatives were sent to Nanaimo to organize anti-Chinese groups in that city.

On August 20, 1896, Wilfrid Laurier opened what was to prove a very short session of parliament. If nothing else, it provided the Reverend George Maxwell with the opportunity of presenting a strongly anti-Chinese speech, suggesting finally that the head tax be raised to $500. D.C. Fraser, from the security of his Nova Scotia seat, announced bravely that whites did not fear Chinese competition. This was strictly routine, but the courtly Sir Henri Joly de Lotbiniere, Minister of Internal Revenue, was both horrified and embarrassed that such a subject should 'be raised just as Canada was receiving a visit from Li Hung Chang, variously referred to as the Viceroy of China and Ambassador Extraordinary of the Emperor of China. Parliament was prorogued before any further embarrassment occurred, though not before the Toronto *Globe* had published an insulting commentary on Chinese immigration into Canada.

Li Hung Chang was a very distinguished and world-renowned soldier and statesman. He had fought under "Chinese" Gordon, negotiated the recent peace between China and Japan and was essentially the Minister of Foreign Affairs. Since the defeat of the Chinese armies in Korea, he had been touring the world as a special

The visit of Li Hung Chang was a great event for the Chinese of Vancouver in 1896.

Victorians enjoyed the conviviality and pageantry of the Chinese New Year. . .

(Provincial Archives, Victoria)

. . . but there was always an undercurrent of contempt for the Oriental.

In September 1907, Vancouver's Chinatown was sacked by anti-Oriental rioters.

The citizens of Chinatown.

Eastern and Western costume at the Legislative Buildings, Victoria, 1904.

Three generations of the Kow family in Victoria, 1905.

A labour force of Chinese nationals returned from France to camp at Williams Head in November 1919, prior to re-embarkation.

THE HEATHEN CHINEE IN BRITISH COLUMBIA.

AMOR DE COSMOS, i.e. :—The Love of the World or the Lover of Mankind. HEATHEN CHINEE :— Why you sendee me offee !
A. D. C. :—Because you can't or won't 'assimilate' with us.—HEATHEN CHINEE :—What is datee ? A. D. C. :— You won't drink whiskey, and talk politics and vote like us.

Politicians of the 1860s oppressed the Chinese.

Politicians of the 1960s wooed them.

ambassador. One week after George Maxwell's outburst in the House of Commons, he arrived in Vancouver, to be greeted by a crowd of thousands, many of them Chinese dressed in their finest silk robes. The City Band, and another consisting of Chinese, played stirring airs, and he was transported in a carriage drawn by four white horses through a triumphal arch constructed by the Chinese at a cost of $2,000. At the dock, he was carried up the gang plank of the *Empress of China* in his sedan chair, as *H.M.S. Comus* fired a salute. The ambassador then had his daily nap aboard the white Empress, drove around Stanley Park, and met a delegation of local Chinese, whom, amongst other things, he advised not to smoke opium or gamble. He also let it be known that he hoped the head tax would not be raised to $500.

The brief visit of Li Hung Chang was a magnificent affair. Even white citizens showed a great deal of interest and respect; but it in no way reduced the activities of the unions and the Anti-Mongolian League. Soon after the Chinese ambassador's departure, three Liberal cabinet ministers visited the province, each being lectured on the evils of Oriental immigration. J.L. Tarte, Minister of Public Works, accompanied by the energetic minister of the First Presbyterian Church, was asked to promote the raising of the head tax "on the importation of coolie Chinese labor" to $500 and to enact stringent naturalization laws for the Japanese. The Minister of Marine and Fisheries, H.L. Davies, spent a few peaceful days in Victoria where he toured Chinatown, but in Vancouver he was met by numerous delegations (as well as by the ubiquitous G.R. Maxwell), most of whom pressed him with requests for complete exclusion of Chinese or for laws preventing the Chinese and Japanese from fishing and working in canneries. The Minister answered that he was not favourably impressed with Chinese, and that means must be found to prevent their immigration, but that those who were at present in the country were obviously here to stay.

In 1883, Sir John A. Macdonald had stated that Chinese were not settlers; they had no wives and they would ultimately leave the country. Thirteen years later, a prominent member of the government finally admitted that they were here to stay. In 1885, the Dominion had placed a $50 head tax on the Chinese, but this had done little to stem the flow. Eleven years later, a minister of the crown was admitting that something must be done to prevent Oriental immigration.

The Anti-Mongolian League continued to be active in Vancouver while in Victoria, relations between the Chinese and whites were quite congenial. The City Council gave its Oriental citizens permission to explode their New Year's firecrackers between 5 p.m. and 11 p.m., and on February 4, 1897, young Albert Auld came home from school to tell his mother he was going to Chinatown to watch the celebrations. At 6 p.m. he was still standing on Cormorant Street. A block away, a team of dray horses stood nervously in their halters while their load of coal was being delivered. Suddenly a long string of crackers exploded beside them, in front of Hong Chong's Store, and the animals bolted. Albert Auld's head was crushed beneath their feet. Suddenly there was silence in Chinatown. When news of the disaster reached Victoria's mayor, he immediately cancelled the city's permission for the festivities, but the Chinese, aware they had been responsible for the accident, had already put an end to their celebrations and were meeting to discuss the most appropriate means of expressing their sympathy to the Auld family. Within 24 hours, $281.50 had been collected, largely from the Chinese Benevolent Society, the Chinese Board of Trade and the Tai Yuen Company. A cheque for this amount, together with a most sympathetic note, was sent to the family.

A white carpenter's son had been killed as the result of the Chinese celebrations. Victorians were deeply shocked, but not a word of recrimination towards the Chinese was heard. It was suggested that, in the future, fireworks demonstrations be held in open fields.

It might have been different in Vancouver. On the stump-strewn hills of Mount Pleasant, overlooking False Creek, a 17-year-old boy seriously injured a Chinese by striking him on the head with a rock—"a kind of abuse very common here since the anti-Chinese agitation," it was noted. At the Anti-Mongolian League's February meeting a torrent of abuse flowed from the crowd. There were only two dissenters, one of them the Reverend C.A. Coleman who was given leave to speak for 15 minutes. He said that the Chinese were as good as whites and that he wished he were a Chinaman. According to the Vancouver *News Advertiser*, Dr. W.W. Walkem answered that, "He would to G— that he—Mr. Coleman—would take himself and his Chinamen to China and get out." People were different in Vancouver.

The last session of the provincial legislature to be held in the old buildings on Bird Cage Walk was opened on February 8, 1897. The most active member during this sitting was Harry Dallas Helmcken, the son of Dr. J.S. Helmcken and the grandson of Sir James Douglas. Of the many motions he presented was one to raise the head tax on Chinese. There were nine other motions or questions relating to the

Oriental problem during that session, some passed, some defeated and some ruled out of order. Perhaps the most interesting was the Alien Labor Act which prohibited Chinese and Japanese from being employed on works carried on under franchises granted by private acts. The United States had earlier passed an Alien Labor Act which affected Canadians, and the Dominion, in retaliation, had passed a similar act affecting Americans. In the provincial House there was a long argument as to whether it was constitutional for British Columbia to approve an act affecting Orientals, but it finally passed. A strange thing happened at this point, however; Lieutenant-governor Dewdney declined to give his assent. He said he would pass it on to the governor-general, to whom he was responsible. The bill, of course, was disallowed.

In spite of Laurier's telegram stating that the wishes of the western members in regard to Chinese immigration would be honoured, in spite of lengthy petitions sent to them by the Anti-Mongolian League and in spite of the apparent agreement on the part of visiting cabinet members to British Columbia, the Dominion government did not consider the Oriental question in 1897. It was condemned for this by the Vancouver Trades and Labor Council, by the Trades and Labor Congress meeting in Hamilton and even by the Toronto *Globe*. The Reverend George Maxwell, too, was criticized for not forcing the matter, but, like the true politician he now was, he paid no attention to it. He bustled about attending numerous meetings, accompanied Clifford Sifton, Minister of the Interior, to the Klondike, and reverted occasionally to his ecclesiastical life, performing marriages and preaching somewhat irregularly at the First Congregational Church on Georgia Street. By the end of the year, however, he promised that if the Dominion did not introduce an anti-Chinese bill at its next sitting, he would most certainly do so.

The economy of the province began to improve in 1897 with the growth of the mining industry in Kootenay and the construction of railroads in the interior. The Klondike gold rush, too, brought prosperity. Vancouver and Victoria vied with each other over who could best provide supplies for the far north. Victoria had seen it all before—indeed that is how the city began, 50 years earlier. The men were the same: eager and green, the lust for gold shining in their eyes. But Dr. J.S. Helmcken was the only one who remembered.

Orientals, too, were pouring into the province in greater numbers. The Empresses consistently carried about 500 "Asiatics" on each trip, almost equally divided now between Chinese and Japanese. And when the Legislative Assembly met for the first time in their new buildings in February 1898, there was a rash of anti-Oriental legislation, most of it ineffective. Perhaps the most controversial was Dallas Helmcken's Labor Act, identical to that passed the previous year and ultimately disallowed by the Dominion. They went through the same motions in 1898.

The provincial government could do little to stem the influx. It could erect an endless number of minor obstacles, but those not removed by the Dominion provided merely an inconvenience to the Oriental. Immigration was a Dominion matter and Ottawa steadfastly refused to raise the head tax in spite of motions by western members and in spite of annual requests to do so by the provincial legislature. The new Liberal cabinet members were no less vehement nor verbose than their predecessors in answering such requests. "The Minister of Trade and Commerce, to whom the matter was referred," said the latest answer, "submits that similar representations have, on various occasions, been made by the Legislature of British Columbia, which have been adversely reported upon by his predecessors, and having himself carefully considered the matter, he (the Minister) is not prepared to recommend any change in the present law. . . . "

According to a provincial member, Francis Carter-Cotton, the Dominion relied on the $30,000 brought annually by the head tax. It was, he said, 2.07 per cent of the country's total revenue. If so, the Minister of Trade and Commerce would undoubtedly find exclusion a rather repugnant subject. The Chinese labourer, as an article of trade, was big business.

Once more the two governments prorogued their respective Houses without any effective anti-Oriental measures being taken. Premier Turner, however, had been beset with dissention in the ranks. He called an election for July 1898, the results, being somewhat inconclusive. This led to several protests over voting irregularities and a great deal of bitter correspondence between Turner and the new lieutenant-governor, T.R. McInnes. It was the beginning of one of the most turbulent and acrimonious periods in British Columbia politics. McInnes dismissed a shocked John Turner, and Charles Semlin formed a new government. Perhaps it would not have been quite so shameful a period if it had not been for the election of two new members, James Dunsmuir and Mr. Joseph Martin, late of Manitoba, via Ottawa. Joe had spent two restless years since his defeat in the Dominion election of 1896. He had travelled here and there about the country, remaining long enough in Montreal to have his nomination for membership in the St. James

Club ignominiously blackballed. In March 1897 he was reported as going to British Columbia for a three-month stay, but he remained "to inflict himself on the province," as the *Colonist* put it, and to set up a law practice in Vancouver. Joe was 46 years of age when he was appointed attorney-general of the province by the 62-year-old premier. There were still six months before the next session would be called.

In the meantime, Wilfrid Laurier was knighted; the tumultuous 72-year life of that remarkable man, Amor De Cosmos, ended in Victoria; and Theodore Davie died of valvular heart disease at the age of 46. And in September the old City of Stumps, New Westminster, burned to the ground. Aid in various forms flowed into the ruined city, the most remarkable being a fund from the Chinese of Victoria. As soon as the news of the fire reached the capital, the Chinese Benevolent Association met and immediately telegraphed $500 to their countrymen in the Royal City. The following day they sent another $1,000. For a week, news of the Chinese generosity did not reach the white press, and when it did, they wondered why such a magnificent gift had not received more publicity. "The Oriental, in this case, proved true to his secretive instincts," they said, "and hid his light under a bushel."

But it was not just a matter of unpublicized generosity; it was a reflection of the culture in the two largest cities of the province. The white population of Victoria had always been more tolerant of its Chinese citizens than those of Vancouver—and perhaps this was reflected in the response of the Chinese. Their culture was always in a more advanced stage than that of Vancouver. Their New Year's celebrations were magnificent affairs, enjoyed and respected by whites. Their theatres and joss houses were much more active, as were their Christian missions. Their funerals, strange to western eyes and often looked upon with a peculiar mixture of disdain and interest by Victorians, were elaborate examples of Oriental splendour and culture. The generosity of Victoria's Chinese had been demonstrated for many years by their handsome contributions to such public benefits as the Royal Hospital and the visits of various governors-general. Perhaps all this was only a mark of maturity. Vancouver was young and growing at an unhealthy rate; Victoria had survived that period in her history with more aplomb than the city on Burrard Inlet.

Nonetheless, western civilization was still a source of fear and embarrassment to at least one Victoria Chinese. He was placidly mailing a letter on a rainy September afternoon when bells suddenly began to sound all around him, and in a moment there was a dreadful clattering of horses' hooves on the pavement, and more bells clanging wildly. The Victoria Fire Department found him standing "perplexed, wild-eyed and white" before Fire Box 54, the letter still clutched in his shaking hands.

CHAPTER VIII

1899-1908

"The Dominion Can Get Along
Very Well Without Chinese Labor
And Chinese Parsimony."
Sir Wilfrid Laurier, 1899

In 1899, there were still no political parties as such in the provincial sphere. The new "Government Party" was essentially Liberal, as was Lieutenant-governor McInnes, and was headed by Premier Semlin, though it was said that Joe Martin wielded the greatest power. The New "Opposition Party" was composed largely of Conservatives such as John Turner, James Dunsmuir and the newly-elected Westminsterite, Richard McBride.

The first session, opening in January 1899, was a tumultuous one, mainly through the antics of Joe Martin. In spite of this, and in spite of its being a short session, a large number of anti-Oriental bills was passed. One of these requested that the Dominion raise the head tax to $500. A similar resolution had been passed on several previous occasions, but in 1899 it was done in a much more organized fashion. It was pointed out that in the fiscal year ending the previous June 30th, 2,263 Chinese entered the country through British Columbia ports alone, the average being 2,100 a year for the preceding three years. The estimated Chinese population of the province was 14,000 and this, together with Chinese births, "has already driven working men of British race and blood out of many of the fields of labor." In New Zealand and New South Wales the head tax was £100, or $500, ships were allowed to carry only one Chinese per 100 tons, and the Chinese population of those colonies was dwindling. Seven clearly enunciated points were made, the resolution was accepted on the last day of the session (a "vindictive" Joe Martin voting against it along with three others, since it was an opposition motion) and the assembly rose to sing "God Save the Queen."

When the Dominion House met later that year, three Oriental matters were discussed. The first was G.R. Maxwell's proposal to raise the head tax to $500. This resulted in a Chinese government protest to the Imperial authorities and the matter was quickly dropped. The second was a bill offered by the Liberal, W.W.B. McInnes (son of the lieutenant-governor), prohibiting the entrance into Canada of paupers, idiots, insane persons, those suffering from certain diseases, those with criminal records, prostitutes and those unable to write a European language. The bill was shelved.

The final matter was Ottawa's ruling on all the anti-Oriental bills recently passed by the Provincial government. The crux of this whole problem was that British Columbia had insisted on including Japanese as well as Chinese in all these bills. Such anti-Japanese legislation was hardly in the spirit of the treaties between Great Britain and Japan. It embarrassed both the Imperial and Canadian governments. In attempting to explain his problem to the recalcitrant western province, Sir Wilfrid Laurier said that "there was something more to be done for Britain than singing God Save the Queen and celebrating national holidays." He had previously indicated the futility of coupling the Japanese with Chinese and he had sent a telegram to Premier Semlin suggesting modifications be made, but the premier refused to comply. Sir Wilfrid said he saw no reason to exclude the Japanese "but the Dominion can get along very well without Chinese labor and Chinese parsimony." His government then disallowed all the anti-Chinese legislation passed by the provincial House in its previous session with a promise to attempt to increase the Chinese tax.

This introduced the first of two new complications which provincial legislators had to face—pressure from foreign powers. British Columbia's Alien Exclusion Act of 1899 was aimed primarily at Americans who were invading the new Atlin gold fields. Although the United States had passed a similar act prohibiting Canadians, they protested to the Dominion government, who promptly disallowed the legislation. The Japanese then protested to the Imperial and Dominion governments, the province's Labor Regulation Act of 1898 which prohibited Chinese and Japanese from working on projects granted by provincial franchise. Both London and Ottawa requested the province to repeal the act, but the legislators refused to do so. In 1899, all British Columbia's anti-Oriental bills were disallowed because Britain had signed a trade treaty with Japan. The province now had to contend, not only with the distant government in Ottawa and the more distant government in London, but also with Japan itself, indirectly through the Imperial government. Life in the Colony had been much simpler. British Columbia was now paying the price of progress, of confederation, of a railroad, of shipping and of trade and commerce.

Although anti-Chinese laws had been in existence for many years, it was a rarity to hear a protest from the government of Peking, just as it was a rarity to hear a protest from Washington. It was the Japanese who persistently objected to anti-Oriental legislation. They were different—more aggressive, less secretive, more adaptable to western society and perhaps more crafty. And it was the Japanese who introduced the second new complication which provincial legislators must face. They had discovered that they could escape anti-Oriental laws by becoming naturalized.

In February 1899, it was reported that in the six previous years, from 1863 to the present, 689 Chinese and 1,052 Japanese had become naturalized. Although the Japanese were relatively recent immigrants, they showed a greater tendency to become naturalized than did the Chinese. The frightening thing to British Columbians was that this not only absolved the Japanese from anti-Oriental laws but might persuade the Chinese to abandon their close ties with their homeland by also becoming naturalized citizens. Said the *Colonist* in a somewhat conciliatory mood, "Contact and competition with the Oriental race is one of these thing which British subjects must expect as a price of Imperial Dominion."

The disallowance of provincial bills, the concern over naturalization and the final decision of the Imperial Privy Council that the Coal Mines Regulation Act amendment was unconstitutional, brought strong objections from the western press. Their only suggestion was to continue to pass similar anti-Oriental laws—forever if necessary—until Dominion and Imperial authorities finally came to their senses. But there was another annoying event to face. In mid-October 1899, Vancouverites awoke to find two Dominion cabinet ministers and three ex-ministers in town. There is nothing more despised or useless than an ex-minister of the crown, but the current vintage usually produces some entertainment. Sydney Fisher, Minister of Agriculture, was one of those omnipresent cabinet members with a propensity for creating political blunders by being both ill-informed and verbose. At a meeting in Vancouver he not only spoke favourably of the Chinese but compounded his blunder by innocently stating, "The question as to the Chinese is one

that is very interesting apparently, to the people of this Province."
The Minister of Justice, David Mills, rushed weakly to Fisher's rescue, but the impression left was that easterners were not very
knowledgeable of British Columbia affairs.

Two weeks later, Fisher visited Nelson, one of the few regions in
Kootenay which could boast of a Chinatown. Here he made the
startling statement that he had no idea of the intensity of the anti-
Chinese feeling in the province and that easterners would have to be
educated on this subject. In a great rage, the *News Advertiser* stated
that Fisher had "a penchant for Chinamen, almost as great as that of
his courtly colleague, Sir Henri Joly de Lotbiniere whose pathetic
defense of Li Hung Chang and his countrymen will go down into
Canadian history." The staff of the *Advertiser* did not dream that they
would soon be seeing a great deal of the courtly Sir Henri.

As 1899 drew to a close, politicians of both the provincial and
Dominion genus girded their loins for another attack on the
Chinese, with the exception of George Maxwell who was organizing
a group of ladies to knit socks, woollen caps and jerseys for the boys
off fighting the Boers.

One of the means by which provincial authorities felt they might
solve the persistent complaints of the Japanese, as well as the problem of naturalization, was by presenting an amendment to the Coal
Mines Regulations Act stating that no one who could not read the
mine regulations written in English could work underground. This
was not an entirely new approach but it was one which now became
very popular. It was referred to as a Natal Act, not because it had
anything to do with one's birth (July 1 was often referred to as
"Canada's Natal Day") but rather because it was similar to one passed
by the African Colony of Natal which required immigrants to pass an
educational test. Lengthy arguments followed during which it became apparent that the bill, originally intended for the safety of
miners, then as a weapon against the Orientals, was now a political
weapon aimed at the Dunsmuir empire. The Vancouver Coal Company, it was said, was backing the Semlin government while James
Dunsmuir was on the Opposition side. The former had not employed Chinese underground for years, while the fabulously wealthy
Dunsmuir clan had always done so. The struggle for mine safety,
whether it was justified or not, had become a struggle between two
business rivals, mediated through two political parties.

The bill struggled through its readings followed by the first readings of a bill to regulate the length of hair to six inches and a bill
requesting the Dominion to prohibit Chinese and Japanese from

becoming naturalized. At this point, business in the legislature ceased. The bill had re-awakened the feud between Francis Carter-Cotton and Joe Martin. The trouble probably had started the minute Joe Martin was elected to his Vancouver seat, but it came to a head in October 1899 when Semlin asked for Martin's resignation as attorney-general, apparently on the advice of Carter-Cotton. Joe at first refused, but finally relinquished his post. The continuation of the feud in February 1900 was followed by the defeat of the Semlin government on a redistribution bill. Lieutenant-governor McInnes sent a letter of dismissal to Semlin and asked Joe Martin to form a government. Semlin refused to resign, and complete confusion reigned. Constitutional government completely broke down when, on February 28, McInnes entered the House to prorogue parliament. All members except Premier Joseph Martin left the chamber. McInnes began his speech to the empty House, but there were so many hisses and catcalls from the gallery that he succeeded only on his third attempt.

There never had been such a debacle. It ended with Martin's defeat at the polls, his resignation on June 14 and Laurier's dismissal of McInnes on June 22. James Dunsmuir, the largest employer of Chinese and the richest resident in the province, became premier, and the courtly Sir Henri Joly de Lotbiniere became lieutenant-governor.

The provincial election of May 1900 had demonstrated the unanimity of opinion on the Oriental question. Joe Martin had promised to re-enact all the disallowed anti-Oriental legislation of 1898 and 1899 and to change the Imperial attitude to such legislation. But every platform was similar in this regard. To show any sympathy to the Chinese or Japanese, as the *Colonist* said, was most assuredly to lose one's deposit. "There would be no more certain way of inviting political extinction," it said. And all through the spring of that year, the Japanese poured into the country in huge numbers. In January there were 298, in February 549 and in March 809, and in the first half of April no less than 1,125 "smart little brown men" entered the country.

In spite of the mounting agitation in British Columbia, the Dominion House (which had opened February 1) did nothing but defeat two anti-Oriental bills—until mid-June, when Sir Wilfrid himself introduced a new Immigration Act. He began by stating that there were no more Chinese in the province than there had been in 1885 when the old bill was introduced (certainly an erroneous statement, since in 1884 there were 10,550 while the Dominion census of 1901 listed 17,312). Laurier also promised a Royal Commission to investigate Oriental affairs and stated that the Natal Act proposed by British Columbia was out of the question and that no tax would be placed on Japanese since he could put nothing in the way of an alliance between Japan and England. "The country should be prepared to make that sacrifice in the interest of the Mother Country and the Empire," said Sir Wilfrid. He then raised the head tax from $50 to $100 and he trusted that the people of British Columbia "would be satisfied with the experiment."

They were indeed most dissatisfied with "the experiment"; they had expected an increase to $500. It was referred to as "Sir Wilfrid's half-loaf." It would accomplish nothing. The Chinese companies who recruited immigrants would merely advance a little more cash and, in the long run, would make more profit. "It will not be accepted by the people of the Province," said the *News Advertiser*. Colonel E.G. Prior of Victoria expressed his disappointment in the House, and Aulay Morrison, M.P. for New Westminster, attempted to add a Natal Act during the second reading, but Sir Wilfrid refused to consider it. British Columbians were slowly learning the intrigues of international politics. They were merely a pawn on the Anglo-Japanese chess board—they were still a sea of sterile mountains, 3,000 miles from Ottawa.

Later the same year, the province received another setback in its fight against the Oriental, on this occasion by its own Supreme Court. Chief Justice McColl ruled in favour of an enterprising naturalized Japanese named Tomey Homma. The province had refused to place Tomey's name on the voter's list, Tomey had challenged this and, much to the disgust of white citizens, he had won. "The blow has fallen," exclaimed the *News Advertiser* in horror. They were particularly furious at the Liberal government. Sir John A. Macdonald's Electoral Franchise Act of 1886 had stated that any British person could vote, "person" being defined as "any male person, including an Indian, and excluding a person of Mongolian or Chinese race." This remained in the statutes until 1898 when the Laurier government passed a Franchise Act, repealing that of 1886. The definition of "person" was overlooked in the new act—and now naturalized Japanese or Chinese had the rights of any British subject.

However, British Columbia legislators noted that Joseph Chamberlain, Secretary for the Colonies, had stated that the Natal Act was about as far as one could go in regard to anti-Oriental legislation. Accordingly, James Dunsmuir's first Assembly (after expressing its deep regret at the unsatisfactory new immigration act) spent many days discussing the various bills which ultimately resulted in "An Act to Regulate Immigration to British Columbia." In effect, it was a Natal Act, requiring that immigrants must be able to write a European language. It was passed and was due to take effect on January 1, 1901, as was the new Dominion Immigration Act.

Before this eventful day dawned, two other events of great interest occurred in the province. The first was a general election. Sir Wilfrid Laurier won a comfortable victory well before George Ritchie Maxwell's election in Vancouver. The good reverend was pilloried by the newspapers for failing to clarify the definition of "person" in the Franchise Act, thus allowing thousands of Chinese and Japanese to vote. George nonetheless won the seat. "The majority cast their vote for Mongolian naturalization and Maxwell," growled the disappointed News Advertiser. And there were racial outcries of another sort. For several weeks after the election, bitter westerners claimed that French-Canadian Quebec had elected Laurier. "The majority of the Liberals over the Conservatives," remarked the News Advertiser, "is exactly fifty and it is significant that the Government majority in Quebec is the same—fifty."

The second event of interest was the case of Yip Chuck (or Yip Leck). The story began in April 1900 when Police Chief Alex Main of Steveston, the fishing village at the mouth of the Fraser heavily populated by Chinese and Japanese, set out to search for two Chinese shacks where it was believed stolen goods were hidden. He did not return, but two days later his body was found doubled up in a small, round hole near the Chinese shacks. His legs had been almost chopped off at the knees and his head was very nearly severed from his shoulders. Yip Chuck and Chanyu Chung were arrested. Said the Vancouver Province, "Yip Leck is one of the ugliest looking specimens of a bad Chinaman ever landed in British Columbia. His face is of the blackest of his race, his upper teeth protrude, his eyes are fierce and his hair is like that of a barbarian. . . . " This was the very embodiment of the evil Chinese bogeyman with which disobedient British Columbian children of future years were threatened ("The Chinaman'll get you if you don't watch out").

Yip certainly appeared to be an evil Chinese. He was indifferent to the murder, but Chanyu Chung, "a weak, shrivelled specimen of the race," shook with fear and confessed that he and another Chinese, Kung Wong, were under the power of Yip. They were forced to partake in the murder. Yip had cracked Main's head open with a double bladed axe, cut his throat and slashed him with a brush hook.

After killing a chicken to remove any evil spirit, Chanyu and Kung were forced to bury the body in a small round hole.

Fifty polite Japanese gathered in Steveston and asked that, "if they would be allowed, they would take the Chinese persons out and kill them." They were even willing to start a raid on the Chinese population and drive them into the river. Their offer was politely rejected. Chinese citizens offered a reward of $200 for the escaped Kung Wong, and white citizens searched the unlit streets of Steveston, carrying lanterns, in one hand, revolvers in the other. There was talk of summary justice for those already captured, but Yip and Chanyu were spirited off safely to Vancouver before the mob became violent. Kung Wong was caught a few days later hurrying down the Semiahmoo Trail on his way across the border. For the evil Chinese Yip Chuck, 1900 was eternity—but his frightening image remained for years to come.

On January 1, 1901, the new Dominion Immigration Act came into force. British Coumbians ignored it, realizing that it would be ineffectual in restricting the Chinese. The provincial Act to Regulate Immigration, however (better known as the Natal Act), promised to be a devastating weapon. The humble class of peasant immigrant from China or Japan could not possibly write a European language. In its first issue of the year, the Vancouver *Province* referred to the act as "a very acceptable New Year's gift from the government to the people of the province. Everyone who has had the opportunity of observing the evils wrought by this influx of the coolie hordes and who can appreciate the prospective consequence of their continual inpour, would no doubt be glad to see even more stringent and direct legislation against the entrance of the undesirable class."

Late in January, a ship arrived in Victoria with three Japanese immigrants who could not write a European language. They were refused entry. British Columbians had experienced similar incidents in past years, only to have their most cherished dreams destroyed by provincial, Dominion or Imperial courts, but they always hoped for a miracle. It did not come in 1901. The Natal Act was disallowed. The decision came too late for the legislature to re-enact the bill that year, though they did so in 1902 and 1903, only to have it disallowed again.

And so it went. In 1902, five anti-Oriental bills were passed, three of them being in the form of a Natal Act affecting mines, labour and the franchise. The fourth, presented by Richard McBride, allowed fishing licences to be granted to British subjects only, and a fifth prohibited aliens from voting in municipal elections. That year, the Dominion disallowed a total of 13 British Columbia anti-Oriental bills and in 1903, the frustrated provincial legislators re-enacted all those disallowed by the Dominion.

The plot was becoming repetitious, and to make matters worse, Premier James Dunsmuir was a rather uninterested politician. When asked to carry British Columiba appeals on the Oriental question "to the foot of the throne" during the coronation of Edward VII, he answered only that he did not care whether he went or not. His legislature had become almost as unruly as those of the Semlin-Martin period and he continued to be plagued, like his father, by irresponsible miners who had the absurd notion that they wished to be unionized. In 1900 he had imported over a hundred Scottish coal miners, but most of them soon departed, complaining that they had to work with Chinese, their wages had been illegally garnisheed and Dunsmuir had broken his contract which offered a wage of $3 a day. The premier was accused of paying "Chinaman's wages" and he subsequently closed his mines in Wellington, putting 200 miners out of work. Like his father, he refused to discuss the matter with labour delegates, though he offered to open the mines again if they would accept a 25 to 35 per cent reduction in wages. The miners refused, and by March 1901, Wellington was a deserted town. In December, the employees of the Vancouver Coal Company and the Dunsmuir Mines amalgamated and asked for higher wages, prohibition of Orientals, union labels on manufactured goods, the eight-hour day, the six-day week—and the abolition of the Dominion Senate. Unfortunately, they did not attain all their goals. And Dunsmuir responded by closing the Alexander Mine; no one was more resistant to unions.

Laurier's promised Royal Commission to investigate Chinese and Japanese affairs in British Columbia began it sittings in mid-March 1901, meeting four or five days a week until July. Its members were not as well known as those of the 1884 commission. R.C. Clute, K.C., of Toronto was the chairman and F.J. Deane of Kamloops, Secretary; Christopher Foley, a Rossland labour leader, and D.J. Munn, a Fraser River canner from New Westminster, completed the group. The investigation was by personal interview of citizens over the greater part of the province, largely merchants, labour representatives, boot makers, cigar makers, launderers, police, health officers, miners, fishermen, canners and mill men. The Chinese were also represented.

With two exceptions, the evidence was all very much against the Oriental, though it was by no means as vicious as in the first commission. The main complaint was that the Oriental worked for lower wages and therefore deprived whites of a livelihood. Both the canners and lumber men said they could not compete against Americans without them. It was the fishermen who complained most bitterly about the Japanese, who held 1,759 licences compared with 1,142 for whites. Even the native Indians were bitter toward the Japanese; there would be bloodshed if any more appeared, they said.

Apart from some statistics, there was really nothing in the evidence which British Columbians did not already know. Of interest, however, was the appearance of three old pioneers. When Major L.T. Dupont sat before the Commission, everyone knew the Chinese would have at least one supporter. The Major had been Sir John A. Macdonald's second political appointee to the province, far back in 1873 when he became internal revenue collector. He had given evidence at the first commission; he still praised the Chinese, particularly as servants.

The Chinese found another supporter in the person of old Alex Wilson, who could remember the first boatload of Chinese arriving in 1860. At that time, however, there were already "North American Chinamen" in the colony, he said. These were the Canadians. "They came from a part of the world then called Canada," he said. "These Canadians were as little thought of as were the Chinese, and they had the habit of sending money back to Canada for the sustenance of their families." Alex Wilson and Dr. J.S. Helmcken were two of the few who could remember these days. Wilson's observation, of course, was correct. Many miners returned wealthy to Canada, which, at that time, was as foreign a country as China.

The Royal Commission also caught a fleeting glimpse of the 62-year-old postmaster of Victoria, Noah Shakespeare. He had been an M.P. during the first commission of 1884—which he boycotted. In 1901, he was present to report on the amount of money which Orientals sent out of the province. Since the Chinese used the registered letter system, he said, he could not tell how much they mailed to their homeland, though they had sent 5,010 of these in the past year. The Japanese had the habit of using money orders and he could vouch for $134,000 being sent to Japan in the same period. Noah was so concise, objective and tolerant that he was hardly recognizable. It was nice to see him again.

The Royal Commission, early in 1902, reported adversely on

British Columbia's Orientals. Clute and Foley favoured an increase in the Chinese head tax to $500, while D.J. Munn, the Fraser River canner, suggested a rise to $300 for two years, followed by a rise to $500 thereafter. When the Dominion parliament met in June of the same year, however, the only concession it would make was a promise that soon the province's share of the head tax would be increased from 25 to 50 per cent.

It was obvious that the $100 head tax was no deterrent to Chinese immigration. With each arrival of the Empresses there were 200 to 500 aboard, and the annual income from the tax, reported in 1902, was $1.21 million for the Dominion, $417,000 for the province. In spite of this, there was very little anti-Oriental sentiment expressed publicly; indeed the Chinese Empire Reform Association which appeared at this time in Vancouver was accepted with considerable interest and sympathy. It was one of many groups the world over who were attempting to overthrow the Manchu dynasty and modernize China. In February 1902, its president, Yip Yuen, announced plans for a plush Oriental club at the corner of Hastings and Carrall Streets. In the meantime, the Association held its meetings in the Chinese Opera House, frequently using white guest speakers with W.A. Cumyow acting as interpeter. It was certainly the most western group of Chinese in the province. In March 1902, the Association arranged the funeral of Tai Kee, a leading merchant of New Westminster who was married to W.A. Cumyow's sister. Chinese funerals, especially in Victora, had always been magnificent Oriental displays. Tai Kee's funeral was much more occidental. There were a few joss papers, candles and food for the gods, but much more prominent were the wreaths of flowers strewn about the graveside on 8th Street in New Westminster. Yet another sign of the times was that all the chief mourners wore European dress.

In 1902, the province took a great interest in the coronation of Edward VII. James Dunsmuir and Sir Wilfrid Laurier attended—as did George Maxwell, perhaps to visit his native Scotland for the last time. He knew that he was seriously ill. On his return, he was forced to lie in a Montreal hospital for several weeks with jaundice. His death in November brought a by-election to Vancouver in February 1902, and again all candidates expressed their strong opposition to Oriental immigration. Aulay Morrison, the New Westminster M.P., tried to swing the issue away from the Chinese by stating, "No British Columbia member would dare to have any other view than unqualified opposition to oriental immigration," (Vancouver *News Advertiser*) but each candidate persisted. Perhaps the Liberal representative had the strongest anti-Oriental approach. He won by a close margin.

Laurier apparently felt he could no longer delay the inevitable. On March 17, 1903, he gave notice of a resolution to raise the head tax from $100 to $500. The bill passed its third reading on May 5. British Columbia usually had its wishes granted, but only after an inordinately long wait. After years of threatening and cajoling, it had finally seen the C.P.R. started, six years late; it had finally obtained a mild measure of Chinese restriction with the $50 head tax in 1885; and after 16 more years of waiting, the tax had been increased to $100 in 1901. This "experiment", in Laurier's own words, had failed, and the tax was now raised to the sum for which British Columbians had asked as long ago as 1892.

It was expected that there would be a great influx of Chinese before the tax was raised on January 1, 1904. Until the end of September, 1,538 paid the old tax, followed by a mild increase. When the *Empress of Japan* arrived in Vancouver in October with 500 Chinese, immigration facilities were severely strained. The huge mass of Orientals was herded into the detention sheds which, as the *News Advertiser* put it, "look like abandoned storehouses in their retirement and isolation." All along the sides and down the centre of the cold, empty sheds were tiers of bunks like those of "a military post-house." Guards prevented the Chinese from stepping outside for a breath of fresh air until every detail of the Immigration Act had been completed.

Each immigrant paid his $100, following which his age, height, special marks, birth place, occupation and date of arrival were recorded in a registry. When this was completed, he was given a receipt for his tax and was "free to rove from Halifax to Vancouver." He was allowed to visit China and re-enter without further payment, provided he had a certificate which corresponded with the information in the registry and provided that he was not absent for longer than 12 months.

The province, in the meantime, had been wracked by one labour strike after another: C.P.R. employees, carpenters and the coal miners of Nanaimo, Ladysmith, Cumberland, Comox and Fernie. The situation was so bad that Sir Wilfrid Laurier sent his Deputy Minister of Labor to investigate it. He was a young man of 29 years, referred to in the newspapers only as Mr. W.L. Mackenzie King.

There were two issues at stake in the Island Mines. The first was that James Dunsmuir refused to recognize the Western Federation of Miners and forbade any members to work in his colleries. The second issue was that of Chinese working underground. The legislation forbidding them to do so had been disallowed, but another amendment had been immediately passed, and the miners wanted it enforced. Dunsmuir would have nothing to do with this. He said he would carry it to the Privy Council if necessary. In the meantime, he had two non-union whites working with a number of Chinese and Japanese underground. Dunsmuir was never out of trouble. He had rid himself of one worry by resigning the premiership in November 1902, but now he had a strike on his hands.

He had to wait a little while—he could afford to—but he eventually won. The Western Federation of Mines had no strike fund and the miners were slowly succumbing to starvation. They gave up after four and a half months in Ladysmith and three and a half in Cumberland. Perhaps their decision was accelerated by another explosion in the Cumberland mine, in which 15 Chinese died. James Dunsmuir even won the battle of the amendment to the Coal Mines Regulation Act. The bill had progressed all the way to the Imperial Privy Council which, in July 1905, ruled that the province could not order people to work in different places on company-owned land. In the same year he was involved in another strike which lasted four months (the miners now had strike pay) and in 1906 he even had trouble with his Chinese employees. At Cumberland, his Chinese pushers went on an unsuccessful strike for higher wages, followed by the Chinese labourers at the Union Bay loading dock. In the latter affair, the Chinese were immediately replaced by the most recent arrivals from the Orient, the "Hindoos"; but these were so weak from hunger they could not perform the work satisfactorily and the Chinese had to be re-hired. It was not all unhappy news for James Dunsmuir, however. In 1905 he sold his E. & N. Railway to the C.P.R. for $1.25 million and in May of 1906 he replaced Sir Henri Joly as lieutenant-governor.

Provincial politics in the meantime had seen several changes. E.G. Prior, who had replaced Dunsmuir as premier in November 1902, was defeated in the House in June 1903, and Richard McBride became the first British Columbia-born premier of the province—six months before his 33rd birthday. He announced that the government would be formed along party lines, and in October his Conservatives won by a narrow margin over the Liberals and Socialists in the province's first politically oriented election.

The first few years were easy ones for Richard McBride. The party system brought a certain discipline to the government, and the problem of Chinese immigration seemed to have been taken care of by the head tax. McBride nonetheless began enforcing the Coal Mines Regulation Act against underground Chinese labourers (not yet disallowed by the Privy Council), and in his first legislature he passed another bill to regulate immigration. It was in the form of a Natal Act and was aimed at the Japanese. In 1905 it was disallowed, "since it interfered with Dominion policy." The numerous anti-Oriental bills which had plagued the legislature for so many years were absent in 1905 and 1906, but in their place was heard the old cry of "Better Terms." British Columbia was discriminated against by higher freight rates, higher taxation and higher costs of administration.

The matter which concerned the country as a whole, however, was that of a second transcontinental railway, the Grand Trunk Pacific (G.T.P.). Various routes were being examined by surveyors, there was a great deal of gossip over the possible sites of a western terminus and the usual speculators spread throughout the Land. The greatest arguments, however, were over the subsidies the government planned to present to the private company, and it was this matter over which the general election of November 1904 was fought. The G.T.P., it was said, would be subsidized by either party; it was just a matter of how much each party would give away to the private English company. If the railway was a success, the company would keep it; if it was a failure, the government would accept it.

In February 1903, the by-election in Vancouver had brought a flood of anti-Oriental sentiment. Less than two years later, the Chinese were hardly mentioned. The Vancouver Independent Liberal, James McGeer, the only candidate to enlighten the dull campaign with any wit or wisdom, was the only one who mentioned the Chinese. Referring to the G.T.P., he said, "The people will pay for it, the company will own it, the Chinamen will build it and our descendants will be taxed for it." Sir Wilfrid Laurier increased his majority to 65; Robert Borden, the Conservative leader, was defeated in Halifax, though he later won a seat in Carleton, Ontario. In September 1905, Laurier turned the first sod of the G.T.P. in Fort William—only time would tell the consequences it would have on British Columbia.

The Chinese on the coast in the first five or six years of the 20th century continued to live a relatively unpersecuted existence. In the newer towns of the Interior, however, there were several serious incidents. In April 1905, the Kootenay Shingle Company of Salmo brought 33 Japanese and Chinese from the Coast. When the Orientals arrived in the little town of some 60 residents, they found that workmen, mostly miners from Ymir and other nearby towns, had gathered to turn them away. The Orientals were forced to retreat to Nelson until an escort of provincial police returned them to Salmo. A week later, a forest fire swept the holdings of the Kootenay Shingle Company, in spite of the presence of 50 constables. It was generally assumed that the fire was deliberately set. The company had further problems when they tried to hire a white engineer to run their operation. No one from the Interior dared take the job, although the company later obtained an engineer from the Coast. A similar incident occurred in Penticton in 1906 when Chinese were brought in to clear land. A well attended meeting of the Vigilance Committee threatened to boycott merchants who would not sign a petition against the intrusion of Chinese. Matters got out of hand and a group of whites chased the Chinese out of town. Five residents were found guilty and fined $25 or 30 days in jail. One paid the fine, but the remaining four refused to do so. As they left the courthouse, they were cheered by a crowd of citizens and a collection of $55 was quickly gathered to pay the fines, but the four refused to accept it, preferring to martyr themselves in the village jail.

Anti-Orientalism was always greatest in the towns in which Chinese were first introduced—or rather, in which they were first imported as cheap labour. In Victoria, where the first Chinese had drifted in under their own volition, there was never active physical abuse, but in Nanaimo, Vancouver, Salmo and Penticton, their importation by business enterprises always raised the wrath of the population. Vancouver was the ideal example of this. Agitation reached an early peak when 'Chinese' McDougal brought over Orientals from Victoria to clear the Brighouse Estate in 1887. Within a very short time following this, they were tolerated, if not accepted. By 1904, Vancouverites were fascinated with the pyrotechnic display of the New Year's celebration, though their western tastes were appalled with the "ferocious discords" of an orchestra composed of a gong, a tom-tom and "something that looks like a pair of huge tin trays." By 1906, the Chinese in Vancouver were being described as patient, interesting and hospitable. Said the *News Advertiser* during the New Year Celebration, "The Chinaman is an artist at enjoying himself. He does not plunge into orgies. His New Year is a succession of climaxes carefully graded. . . . "

Perhaps the greater acceptance of the Chinese was the result of the new immigration act—only three entered the country in 1904—or perhaps it was because they were becoming more occidentalized. If the latter was so, the Chinese Empire Reform Association could probably be given most of the credit. Since their meagre beginnings following the visit of the great Chinese reformer, Kang Yu Wei, in 1899, they had grown into a popular body of businessmen, most of whom dressed in western clothes. In December 1903, the Association opened its new three-storey $15,000 building on Hastings Street, and during the New Year celebration of 1904, the public was invited to inspect the premises.

In November 1904, the president of the Association, Charlie Yip Yuen, travelled from Vancouver to Montreal to meet Kang Yu Wei and his Harvard-educated secretary, Cheu Kok Hean, and escort them to the west. There were hundreds of enthusiastic Chinese on the C.P.R. platform when the great reformer arrived, including the corresponding secretary, Won Alexander Cumyow, born in Port Douglas in 1861. Kang was attired in the insignia of a mandarin of the first rank: "a blue jacket ornamented in gold and black braid, closed at the neck, a peculiar nether garment—half skirt, half trousers—made of rich yellow cloth heavily quilted, white stockings surmounted by blue puttees and wearing a black silk cap with yellow tassel." He was driven through the streets of the city to the Association building and was interviewed in the Hotel Vancouver; his secretary, dressed in European attire, interpreted. A few days before his departure, Kang was honoured with a banquet attended by the United States and Japanese consuls, and 11 other whites. The menu was strictly Oriental: bird's nest soup, almond chicken, shark's fins, pickled ginger and "Lai Chee" nuts. This was in sharp contrast to the menu offered Charlie Yip Yuen prior to his departure to take charge of the Chinese Mercantile Bank in Hong Kong. On that occasion there were oysters on the shell, consommé à la Royale, fish, hot-house lettuce, chicken cutlets à la française, loin beef "à la jus" and McLaren's cheese with black coffee.

The Chinese Empire Reform Association, as well as playing its part in the emergence of China from the middle ages, improved the relations between white and Chinese citizens, despite the frequent rumblings of racial and religious sentiment. Of course, not all of these rumblings were directed at the Chinese. French-Canadians were placed in the same class as Chinese by the lumbermen, since they were both willing to perform rough labour at low wages; whites were required for jobs involving "skills and brains." There were objections to the immigration of "promiscuous hordes from all parts of Europe," there was a strong antipathy to the proposal of establishing separate schools in the emerging provinces of Alberta and Saskatchewan and there was increasing concern over the appearance of "brown men from India." The arrival of the "Hindoos" in large numbers late in 1906 resulted in the organization of public meetings to discuss the problem, attempts by M.P.s to reduce the flow and an announcement by the undersecretary for the colonies, Winston Churchill, that steps had been taken to deter further Hindu immigration into British Columbia. It was a serious matter for a time, since these East Indian immigrants were half-starved, penniless and unemployed. They had to be supported by city governments.

For the moment, the problem of East Indian immigration appeared to have been solved, but there followed a series of incidents which culminated in the tumultuous events of the autumn of 1907. The first was a provincial election—an unnecessary one, since there were no serious issues at stake and since McBride had a year remaining on his previous mandate. The Oriental issue was not involved in the campaign; indeed the villains of the day were the unholy easterners in Canada. McBride's slogans were "British Columbia for British Columbians" and "Tolerate no interference from Ottawa." He increased his majority to ten seats and, after supervising the early sessions of the House, set off on one of his many trips to London.

In McBride's absence, the acting premier, W.J. Bowser, presented another British Columbia Immigration Act, which in effect was a Natal Act. In its final form, it prohibited immigration to anyone who could not read or write a European language. The bill passed, but Lieutenant-governor James Dunsmuir refused to give his assent, though at the same time he assented to an amendment to the Provincial Elections Act which disenfranchised "Hindus." Dunsmuir's action would have its later repercussions.

The second in the series of incidents leading to the events of September 1907 was the increasing demand for cheap labour by lumbermen and railway men. There had been a great increase in the forest industry since 1900. All through 1906 the magazine *Lumbermen and Contractor* complained of the lack of cheap labour in mills. Employers insisted that whites, though they were paid $2.25 a day compared with $1.50 for "the much abused heathen Chinee," would not perform such menial tasks as sorting, piling and loading lumber at the sawmills. Furthermore, native Indians were most unreliable, since they frequently departed unexpectedly to attend potlaches. The Chinese worker was willing to perform rough labour and would automatically replace himself with another countryman if he could not come to work. In the words of the lumber magazine, he was "a part of the machinery of the mill, animated with human intelligence." The editors strongly recommended that the $500 head tax be removed.

Robert Marpole, the general superintendent of the C.P.R.'s Pacific Division, made a similar suggestion. The $500 head tax, he said, was a great blunder. The G.T.P. also made it quite clear that unless it obtained Japanese labourers quickly, it could not finish its contract on time.

The private citizen was not aware of what was going on behind the scenes, but he read in the newspapers of the demand for cheap labour and he read of large numbers of Asiatics on each ship arriving from the Orient. It had begun in January 1907, but during a six-week period beginning late in April, 1,447 Asiatics landed on the shores of British Columbia. They were a mixture of Chinese, Japanese and East Indians. Many of the Chinese were returnees or were in transit to other countries, but there was no doubt that an increase in new immigrants had started. Of 574 Chinese arriving on the *Empress of China* in June, only 83 paid the head tax, though this was a marked increase compared with 1905, when there were only 77 for the whole year. Furthermore, there were frequent reports of Chinese being smuggled into the province from Oriental liners and in May 1907, the Intermediate class of the *Empress of Japan* was eliminated "to accommodate the big increase in Asiatic steerage traffic which of late has assumed tremendous proportions." The control of Chinese immigration by the head tax, the voluntary control of Japanese by their government and the promised control of East Indians by Winston Churchill were all unsuccessful. The large increase in immigrants of these nations was the third event which lead to the disaster of September.

Other troubles were brewing. The country was in a mild recession and there were several strikes, again requiring the presence of W.L. Mackenzie King, this time to negotiate with the vice-president of the United Mine Workers of America, John L. Lewis, in the mining town of Fernie. There were also rumours: one, that five Tokyo immigration companies had filled an order for 5,000 Japanese labourers for a Canadian railway company which had contracts in British Columbia; another, that the *Kumeric* had been chartered for $20,000 to bring 1,177 Japanese from Honolulu at a fare of $36 each.

It was actually this new influx of Japanese which concerned the province rather than that of the Chinese. The Dominion government was in a difficult position in this regard. Both the United States and Britain had earlier made treaties with Japan, resulting in increased trade for those countries. In 1905, Canada, wishing to improve her trade, had made a similar treaty at a time when Japan was restricting her immigration. Canada's trade had increased, and the manufacturers of the country had no desire to reduce it by abrogating the treaty because of a few thousand Japanese immigrants to British Columbia. Precisely the same thing had happened in the United States, and anti-Japanese sentiment was running at a very high pitch. The Dominion government insisted that only 80 immigrants a month were arriving from Japan, though it admitted that there were larger numbers arriving from Hawaii.

Two days before the *Kumeric* arrived with its contingent of 1,177 Japanese, the *News Advertiser* announced that 12,000 Japanese were being brought to the province and on the same evening, June 24, 1907, the Vancouver Trades and Labor Council met to form an Asiatic Exclusion League. There was nothing remarkable about the formation of such a group. Many had sprung up over the years, all popular during the waves of anti-Orientalism, all dying early, natural deaths when the feeling had subsided.

It was a quiet summer. The population of Vancouver at the time was said to be 69,850, including 750 East Indians, 1,800 Japanese and 4,500 Chinese, although many other Asiatics lived in the environs, notably at Steveston, which was a community almost entirely made up of Chinese and Japanese. One of the more interesting forms of entertainment that summer was the Dominion Day "Oriental Sports" promoted by Con Jones. Huge throngs crowded into Brockton Point Oval to watch, with great amusement, the confusion of a soccer match between the Red Indians and the East Indians, neither race of which was familiar with the game. To whites it was a circus; to the Japanese, it was a degrading display. "The Japs did not turn out for the Racial Contest," remarked the *News Advertiser* somewhat disgustedly. The same newspaper, about the same time, began using such headlines as "Two years for Chink burglar," "Chink's Death" and "$50 for Beating Chink."

On August 18, the *Indiana* arrived from Honolulu with 300 "little brown men" and on the same day, the *Empress of China* disembarked 123 Chinese in Victoria and 548 in Vancouver. On September 5, Louis D. Taylor's Vancouver *World* ran a large headline announcing that all the "Hindus" in Bellingham, just south of the border, had been herded to the boundary by a number of angry whites and on the 6th, a smaller headline announced a large parade to be held the following day by the Asiatic Exclusion League.

September 7 was just like any other Saturday of the year. Children played, men set off for a half day of work and women did their household chores or perhaps some shopping. They could buy three pounds of creamery butter for a dollar, 20 pounds of sugar for a similar amount, or a full-length winter coat for anywhere between $9.75 and $22.50 at either Spencer's or Woodward's. And if, by any chance, they were in the market for a 16 horse-power Franklin touring car, one could be purchased for $1,850. Perhaps some of them dropped in to the Orpheum or Grand Theatres in the afternoon to watch the vaudeville acts or, if they preferred drama, they could see "Wedded, But No Wife" at the Dominion or "The Moonshiner's Daughter" at the Lyric. Certainly some walked down to Coal Harbour to view the Vancouver Rowing Club's annual regatta, while others watched the Vancouver field lacrosse team play the Maple Leafs. Perhaps some sat at home and read the newspapers: President Teddy Roosevelt, the *Province* said, was planning a boar-hunting expedition, using only javelins, and all three newspapers had articles on the parade to take place that evening. The *Province* said that hundreds of little brown men were pouring into the city from the surrounding districts and were gathering in "Little Yokohama"—east of Westminster Avenue (Main Street) in the neighbourhood of Powell and Cordova—to talk over the problems of racism, particularly in regard to the parade that evening. None of the dailies expected any trouble, but they urged "All trade unions, members of fraternal societies, men who have served the Empire and all others in sympathy with the objects of the League" to take part in the parade. The *News Advertiser* also published a dispatch from Yokohama stating that a fresh outbreak of anti-Asiatic agitation could be expected in the province when the C.P.R. steamship *Monteagle* arrived in Vancouver. She had just left Japan with 900 Sikhs, 1,100 Chinese and a few Japanese.

The vaudevillians in the Orpheum and the Grand, and the thespians in the Dominion and Lyric, had a miserable evening; hardly anybody turned up for their performances. Practically the whole city went to the parade, which assembled on Cambie Street Grounds (the site of the present bus depot). Promptly at 7:30 Major E. Browne the parade marshal, had the first carriage moving up Georgia towards Granville Street to the pleasant clip-clop of horses' hooves. In it were the officers of the Asiatic Exclusion League, guest speakers and "lady sympathisers." Following the carriage was a long line of representatives from various organizations, and two bands. By the time the last man stepped from Cambie Street Grounds, the head of the parade was turning down Granville between the Hotel Vancouver and the Hudson's Bay store, five blocks to the north.

There was an almost festive atmosphere with the bands playing "Rule Britannia" and "The Maple Leaf Forever" and the crowds singing happily along with them. But look at the banners waving unsteadily above their heads: "Asiatic Exclusion League—stand for a white Canada"; "We have fought for the empire and are ready to fight again"; "Steamer *Monteagle* will arrive September 11 with 900 Hindus, 1,100 Chinamen and a bunch of Japs"; "White Canada—patronize your own race and Canada"; "Steamer *Woolich* will arrive in a few days with 500 Japs"; "They failed to do their duty or heed their constituents" (and beneath it, an effigy of James Dunsmuir); "The *S.S. Indiana* with 1,000 Japs due September 18"; "Who will defend Canada in case of attack?"; "A white Canada and no cheap Asiatic labor"; "What shall we do to be saved?" These were certainly intimidating banners, but the citizens of the day were used to this sort of thing and no one seriously considered violence—certainly not with four ministers of the gospel sitting up there in the leading carriage with the rest of the guest speakers.

The parade had started with about 700 to 800 members of various organizations, but the streets were thronged with people all the way down Hastings Street past David Spencers, past Woodward's and the B.C. Electric tram depot, up the little slope to Westminster Avenue and down a few blocks to the City Hall. By that time, thousands had joined the parade until it was estimated that 30,000 were in attendance, completely blocking Westminster Avenue around City Hall—which, alas, was situated virtually at the gates of Chinatown and just two blocks away from Little Yokohama on Powell Street.

The first arrivals entered City Hall where the meeting was to take place, but there were so many citizens left on the streets that arrangements had to be made for the speeches to be given outside. It was later said that the trouble started when the effigy of Lieutenant-governor James Dunsmuir was burned amidst howls and cheers, since he had refused his assent to the Natal Act. When speeches began there were so many people gathered that everyone could not hear; a group of young hoodlums seized some banners and went off into the gathering darkness about 9 p.m. to attack the Japanese quarter. They were largely repulsed, but they retired to the C.P.R. dock where they found half a dozen Japanese and promptly threw them into the waters of Burrard Inlet.

The speeches, in the meantime, went on in a reasonably orderly fashion. The Reverend Dr. H.W. Fraser, from George Maxwell's old church, the First Presbyterian, was one of the most inflammatory. He felt that if the influx were not stopped immediately, his own pulpit would soon be in the hands of a Jap or a Chinaman. There was no such thing as this cheap or common labour that was talked about. It was pure Anglo-Saxon blood that had made the Empire and it would never be made with a mixture of Asiatic blood. There were howls of approbation. Rev. G.H. Wilson of St. Michael's Church of England was sympathetic with the League, but he pleaded that they proceed peacefully. Other speakers, too, were in favour of achieving their aims by democratic means, but as the evening wore on, E.A. Fowler of the Seattle League roused the crowd to a pitch. "There are no Hindus in Bellingham tonight!" he shouted, referring to the recent expulsion of East Indians. J.E. Wilson, a New Zealander, harangued the crowd with the evils of the Chinese throughout the world, pointing out that they had been driven away from practically every country in which they had settled. He was given a great ovation. A resolution requesting the promised restriction of emigration from Japan was voted down because it was too mild, but several others were passed, including one demanding a Natal Act. The meeting then formally adjourned.

This was how it was meant to end. The Reverend Dr. Fraser went home to prepare his sermon for the following morning and much of the crowd drifted away in various directions, but a group of hoodlums, followed by the usual herd of curious, poured into Chinatown, just a block away. It was said that a young boy broke the first window, and after that, glass splintered everywhere. The Chinese put up no resistence. They barricaded themselves in their shops as the mob swept down Dupont to Pender, then up Shanghai and Canton Alleys and back to Pender and Carrall. The streets rang with the sounds of splintering glass and the gongs of ambulances, fire wagons and the police patrol. Every member of the local constabulary had been called out, but they were mere specks in the surging mass of rioters. Fire Chief Carlisle stood at the corner of Pender and Carrall with a hose in his hand, completely helpless. Some rioters climbed telephone poles to urge the crowd on, yelling "A white Canada!" and "Down with the Japs!"

When there were no more windows to break in Chinatown, the mob swept back up to Westminster Avenue and along to the Japanese quarter on Powell. Every window in the area was shattered, with the exception of the Japanese Mission and a few isolated shops owned by whites. The Japanese, unlike the Chinese, were prepared for the attack. Armed with clubs, bottles and boards, they charged the whites, screaming, "Banzai!" and the mob began to break, only to drift to other streets where more windows were broken. Sporadic attacks continued until 3 a.m.

When it was all over, seven whites had been arrested along with one Japanese who had been foolish enough to threaten a member of the press with a knife. There were remarkably few injuries. Several whites had knife and bottle wounds and "an old Jap about 70 years of age," as the *Advertiser* put it, "was badly cut about the face by a stone which went through a window and several of his teeth were knocked out."

On Sunday morning, when they should have been at the First Presbyterian Church listening to Dr. Fraser, crowds poured into the blighted areas, to be quickly dispersed by the police. And in the evening the Japanese patrolled their streets, this time with bowie and butcher knives—one of their countrymen was arrested for carrying a large rock in a woollen sack. The Chinese, too, organized their own policemen, but at no time did the two Oriental nations unite to form a common front.

The following day there was a great rush, mostly of Chinese, to shops which stocked "guns and other offensive weapons." The sidewalk in front of McLennan and McFeely's was completely blocked with customers until every gun was sold, at which time the police forbade their sale. The Japanese went back to work that day, mainly in city sawmills, though they asked permission to attend a meeting in the afternoon, during which Mayor Bethune spoke to them. Chinese cooks, servants and waiters, on the other hand, went on strike, and when the *Comox* and *Cassiar* came into port, all cooks and helpers were called off. Half the restaurants in the city were forced to close, including that of the Hotel Vancouver which lost 60 Chinese employees. The Japanese returned to regular work on Tuesday and the Chinese on Wednesday. Any plans for a further confrontation were firmly dampened by a pleasant Vancouver drizzle; so was an attempt to burn a Japanese schoolhouse on the 12th.

The events of September 7, 1907 were both unexpected and startling. Almost as startling was a telegram the mayor of Vancouver received from Sir Wilfrid Laurier. It read, "His Excellency the Governor-General has learned with deepest regret the indignities and cruelties to which certain subjects of the Emperor of Japan, a friend and ally of His Majesty the King, have been the victims and he hopes that peace will be promptly restored and all offenders punished." There was no mention of similar indignities and cruelties inflicted upon the Chinese.

Sir Wilfrid also sent a cable to the Emperor of Japan. He apologized for "the deplorable disturbances in British Columbia" and added, "Amongst the people of the Pacific Coast there are strong racial prejudices." No mention was made of a cable to the Chinese government. Laurier had a trade treaty with Japan, trade means money. Apologies were certainly in order. There was no trade treaty with China, no profit and no apology. Forty years later—following the Second World War—British Columbians were to feel the shame of their inconsiderate treatment of the Chinese compared with their solicitious consideration of the Japanese.

Although the riot could not thereby be excused, immigration laws were undoubtedly inadequate. This was amply demonstrated when, on September 11, the *Monteagle* steamed through the First Narrows with the largest contingent of Asiatics ever to arrive; 1,165 in all. There were 901 East Indians, 60 Chinese and 65 Japanese, others having been disembarked in Victoria. The East Indian population of the city up to that moment was 750. It was suddenly more than doubled. The new arrivals were said to have money, but no arrangements for housing or employment had been made for them. Mayor Bethune telegraphed to Ottawa asking for permission to use the Drill Hall. If he was refused, he said, he would transport all the East Indians to the Dominion capital. He received no answer. The Chinese had two large vacant buildings in Chinatown, but they, too, refused to allow the immigrants to occupy them. After a great deal of hardship, the 900 were settled in two old houses in the Fairview district and in numerous small tents.

In Ottawa, the Vancouver Liberal M.P., R.G. Macpherson, stated that "British Columbia is to be a white man's country" and that citizens were against flinging wide their gates to Asiatics. He conferred with Sir Wilfrid who, in turn, conferred with Mr. Ishii, the special Japanese commissioner who had been investigating Japanese persecution in the United States and who had arrived in Vancouver on the evening of the riot. Ishii agreed that the spirit of the treaty had been broken by arrivals from Hawaii, and Sir Wilfrid requested that no more than 600 a year be allowed to enter the country.

Soon after this, Laurier spoke to a convention of the Canadian Manufacturers Association in Toronto. He described the treaty arrangements with Japan of two years previous and said that now Canada was beginning to reap the benefits. Amidst the cheers and applause of 400 manufacturers he stated ". . . to denounce it (the treaty) would be simply panic."

It was an old and very simple story: those who profited from the Oriental, loved him; those who lost, hated him. The Canadian Manufacturers Association was more important to Sir Wilfrid than the wishes of the vast majority of British Columbians. He accused the people of the Pacific Coast of racial prejudice. Without a doubt, he was correct, but it was the Pacific coast of British Columbia, Washington, Oregon and California that were forced to accept the Oriental and it was here that serious riots erupted. He implied that neither prejudice nor riots occurred in the east where, of course, there were few Orientals to tempt the prejudices of its citizens. Indeed, his failure to show the slightest concern for the Chinese during the September riots suggested that he considered trade more important than racial bigotry.

The effects of the September riot were felt for the remainder of 1907 and extended well into 1908. Both the British Columbia Liberal Party and the Asiatic Exclusion League requested the Dominion to pass a Natal Act and abrogate the Japanese treaty. At one of the League meetings, the Reverend Dr. Fraser announced that he was not at all repentant for the September riot. "The action of the rioters has done more to impress upon the citizens of Canada the necessity of doing something than all the words spoken at the City Hall." he said. "Words are all right, but there are times in the evolution of things when actions speak louder than words."

Another speaker at the same meeting was the 49-year-old publisher of the Vancouver *World*, Louis D. Taylor. He would later serve as mayor of Vancouver for eight terms and eleven years. His newspaper, he said, was a party organ (Liberal), but he placed British Columbia before his party. He would desert that party if he was forced to support Asiatics. He did not want to see one mile of railroad built by Asiatics nor one salmon caught by Japanese fishermen.

In the last week in October 1907, W.L. Mackenzie King appeared in the troublesome western province for the third time in recent years. He had come to settle the Japanese damage claims amounting to $13,500. King, not yet in politics, was a most thorough, astute and understanding commissioner. He managed to reduce the claims to $9,036, but in doing so some rather disturbing facts came to light which he received permission to investigate.

The results were most startling. King discovered that the Canadian Nippon Supply Company of Vancouver, backed by the C.P.R., had indicated to the Japanese government that labour was needed in British Columbia. There was no malice on the part of the Japanese officials, King hastened diplomatically to point out; they were persuaded by the Canadian Nippon Company. The result was that, in the first ten months of 1907, the number of Japanese entering Canada amounted to 8,125, though only 4,229 remained, and of this total, 2,779 came from Hawaii, 1,641 directly from Japan. Of the latter, 900 were brought by the C.P.R. under contract. The Canadian Nippon Company also had the assurance of a contract from a gentleman named James Dunsmuir of the Wellington Mines, and application had been made to the G.T.P. for a contract but their answer had been non-committal. All the suspicions of a conspiracy to import Orientals, and the aggravating rumours of behind-the-scenes intrigue by big business, were amply confirmed. It was a magnificent scandal—about which nothing could be done.

W.L. Mackenzie King summarized the matter of the riots with a considerable amount of understanding. "The influx of 8,125 Japanese in ten months," he said, as reported in the Vancouver *News Advertiser*, "naturally caused great alarm and if anything more were needed to occasion unrest, it was found in the simultaneous arrival from the Orient of Hindus by the hundreds and Chinese in larger numbers than in preceding years." There indeed had been an increase in Chinese immigration since January 1, 1904, when the head tax was placed at $500. In 1904 there were no entries (though earlier, three had been reported), in 1905 there were none and in 1906 there were 16 entries. For the first three months of 1907, there was not a single new Chinese immigrant, but in April there were 26, in May and June combined 66 and in the following months there were 36, 60, 54 and 96.

The Reverend Dr. Fraser's observation that sometimes actions speak louder than words was an unfortunate truth. The riot had revealed the seriousness of the Oriental influx as well as the conspiracy of James Dunsmuir, the C.P.R. and the G.T.P. And there was more to come. When Lieutenant-governor James Dunsmuir arrived to open the Legislature in mid-January 1908, J.H. Hawthornthwaite, the Socialist member from Nanaimo, refused to stand in his presence. His Excellency, however, proceeded with his speech from the throne, promising the immediate passage of a Natal Act —even though he had refused assent to a similar act the year before. Hawthornthwaite was furious. He proposed a motion of impeachment and removal of the lieutenant-governor on the grounds that he had violated his constitutional rights by refusing to give assent and that he had made contracts for the importation of Japanese. The member from Nanaimo was promptly ruled out of order.

The Natal Act passed quickly through its readings. Dunsmuir, the hard-nosed business man, probably suffered no qualms as he signed the document he had refused to consider the year before. It was now a question as to whether it could be enforced. "Between the haste of the Provincial Government to get it working quickly and the haste of the Dominion Government to dissallow it," remarked the *News Advertiser* wryly, "there will probably be an interesting race." The Dominion parliamentarians, however, did not wish to become involved in a matter which, at best, could be a political embarrassment, since they almost certainly had to disallow it. They hoped that the Act would be challenged in court, in which case the burden would be lifted from their shoulders. Within the week, two Japanese were arrested for entering the country without being able to communicate in a European language and the very next day Chief Justice Hunter ruled that the Natal Act was inoperative against Japanese because of the various Anglo-Canadian-Japanese treaties.

As matters stood, then, the Chinese were somewhat restricted by the high head tax (though in May 1908, 120 paid $60,000) and immigration from Japan would be voluntarily restricted by that government. The loophole through Hawaii was sealed by a new Dominion law stating that all immigrants had to enter directly from their country of origin. This also stopped the East Indians, since there was no shipping directly from their country. They had previously all entered by way of Japan. One had to admit grudgingly that the September riot had met with some success.

But there was one tattered remnant remaining before the shame of the event could be forgotten. Mackenzie King had begun his investigation of the Japanese claims on October 22, 1907. The Chinese, however, were ignored. Since then, King had investigated Japanese and East Indian immigration and had taken a trip to Europe. On May 6, 1908, almost six months after the riot, he was back in Vancouver to settle the Chinese claims. The reason for the delay, he said, was that, unlike the Japanese, the Chinese had no consul in Vancouver. Chinese claims were sent to their attaché in Washington, who sent them on to the Central Government in Peking. From there, the claims travelled to the British Foreign Office in London and finally to Ottawa. By this time, King was on his way to London to discuss Oriental immigration.

The Japanese had received all the attention up to this point, though it was agreed that the Chinese suffered twice as much damage to their property. Indeed, Chinese claims totalled $26,217.12, compared with $13,500 for the Japanese. Mackenzie King was again most polite and considerate. He apologized to the two representatives of the Chinese government sitting with him in Pender Hall and pointed out that the Chinese in 1905 had paid $50,000 in compensation to British subjects during the riots in Shanghai. He would not allow Chinese claims for the purchase of firearms, but he was most liberal. Of the $26,217 claimed, he allowed $25,900. He suggested also that the Dominion government recompense the Chinese for $1,000 in legal fees.

But again, as King put it, "a matter of serious significance was disclosed" during the settlement. A claim for $600 by each of two Vancouver opium manufacturers was made for the loss of six days business. The 34-year-old, god-fearing bachelor was properly shocked. He had no idea that opium was legally manufactured, sold and smoked here in his home and native land. He personally examined the premises of the two firms and discovered that there was an enormous profit in the opium trade, against which there was no legislation. In his report, he recommended that parliament give immediate attention to this nefarious practice, from which the city gained a licence fee of $500 a year.

Islanders and Mainlanders, whether they lived in the colony or the province, had always known of the opium traffic. They had cited the opium habit of the Chinese as a reason for the need for federal anti-Oriental legislation shown in the Report of the Select Committee of 1879, chaired by the late lamented Amor De Cosmos. Secretary of State Joseph Chapleau and Nicholas Davin had been fascinated by the opium dens and Emily Wharton as far back as 1884. It was all in the Royal Commission Report of that year. The Chinese for many years had advertised their rice, tea, sugar and opium on the front page of the *Colonist*. Then there was the Chinese Regulation Act of 1884. It was a very thorough piece of legislation prepared by the Davie brothers—and it included a clause prohibiting the sale and use of opium. The Dominion government had disallowed the Act. British Columbia had joined confederation 37 years earlier. The last spike in the C.P.R. had been driven home 23 years earlier. It had brought wealth to the country as a whole, but easterners were still abysmally ill-informed on matters in the western province. British Columbia was still a sea of sterile mountains.

It is remarkable that the Toronto-Chicago-Harvard-educated

William Lyon Mackenzie King did not know that opium had been imported, manufactured, sold, advertised and smoked extensively and legally in Canada since the day British Columbia joined confederation. It is remarkable, too, with what dispatch legislation can be hurried through the House of Commons when the suggestion comes from the right source. Mackenzie King's report and recommendation on opium was dated June 26. On July 13, the House passed a law prohibiting the importation, manufacture and sale of opium for other than medicinal purposes.

The Vancouver riot was a year past when Sir Wilfrid Laurier called a general election. It was not a particularly fascinating campaign. There were perhaps three matters of interest. The first was that the Asiatic problem was debated thoroughly, though uselessly; it was largely a contest as to who disliked Asiatics most. The second point of interest was the appearance in the Political arena of that frequent visitor to strife-torn British Columbia, W.L. Mackenzie King. And the third matter of interest was the return to the same arena of a gentleman named Joseph Martin. Since his retirement from politics in 1903, Joe had been practising law in Vancouver and travelling about the world. He returned from a trip in August 1908, at which time the Asiatic Exclusion League nominated him as their candidate in the Dominion election. There were 31 clearly enunciated planks in his platform, amongst which were the formation of an Independent Western Party for the four western provinces and the Yukon, the absolute exclusion of "Chinese, Japanese and Hindus and all other undesirable foreigners," abolition of the Senate, and resistance to any change in the B.N.A. Act which would force separate schools on British Columbia.

Sir Wilfrid's relative unconcern over Oriental immigration placed him in an awkward position in British Columbia, and the province returned a predominately Conservative slate. William Lyon Mackenzie King won in North Waterloo, Joe Martin lost his deposit— and the winds of change were sweeping through the couloirs of history.

CHAPTER IX

1909-1923

*"We Licked the Hun,
and This What We Got."
A 25 Cent Meal Ticket.*
Returned men's banner, 1921

Populations had migrated, the New World had exploded into prominence, governments were expanding and with each passing year, life was becoming more complicated. James Watt's tea kettle was still rattling round the world, but toward the end of the first decade of the 20th century, there were other rattles—rattles of new discoveries, of new methods of transportation, of new attitudes, and distantly of swords. Emily Pankhurst and her suffragettes had been agitating for years; in 1909, they kicked and bit and brawled their way into the headlines, horsewhipping a youthful Winston Churchill in the process. In September of the same year, Robert E. Peary "set the world agog" by discovering the North Pole, and in October, Captain Robert F. Scott was organizing an expedition to the South Pole.

The change that affected the world more than any other event since James Watt's steam engine, however, was the development of the aircraft. It was a constantly recurring subject of conversation in 1909. In February, Dr. A.J. Graham Bell, the inventor of the telephone, sent a telegram to a friend in Victoria announcing the first successful flight of his "Silver Dart" in Baddeck, Nova Scotia. In July, Louis Bleriot flew across the English Channel and in the same month, Orville Wright sped ten miles cross-country at the breathtaking speed of 42 m.p.h. at the remarkable height of 500 feet. In October, he reached an unprecedented altitude of 1,600 feet. A month earlier in Germany, the Zeppelin III flew successfully from

Fredrickshafen to Frankfort and John Sebastian Helmcken, who had stepped boldly through the gates of old Fort Victoria for a five-year stay—long, long ago in 1850—must have wondered what greater feats man could perform in his lifetime. He was now 86 years of age.

In British Columbia it was rumoured that New Westminster would soon obtain an airship and that the Gibson aeroplane would be developed in Victoria. But the railroad was still a much more practical means of transportation, a much more practical source of wealth, in the sea of sterile mountains. Unlike the new aircraft, however, trains required rails—and rails, it always seemed, required cheap labour in the form of Chinese. The G.T.P. was not allowed to use them in British Columbia, and it complained bitterly over this fact. The G.T.P. line between the Lakehead and Winnipeg was nearing completion in the autumn of 1909, while the rails between Winnipeg and Edmonton were well and truly laid. But the English president of the Grand Trunk, Sir Charles Rivers Wilson, stated that unless he was given permission to use Asiatics in the western province, the railroad might not reach Prince Rupert for another ten years. His consulting engineer, Collingwood Schreiber, agreed: 35,000 men were required; there were only 2,000 whites available.

Back in London after a visit to Canada, Sir Charles expressed his inability to appreciate the position of the people of British Columbia in their attitude towards Asiatic labour. Three or four thousand Chinese would save three years, he said, and not a single Canadian workman would be displaced. All Asiatics would be returned to the Oriental port from which they had embarked. The situation, however, had changed since the years of C.P.R. construction. A second railway was certainly not as necessary as the first, and though Chinese labour had been tolerated in those palmy days, the Orientals had remained, much to the annoyance of the whites. Labour unions, too, had grown stronger. In September 1909, the Vancouver Trades and Labor Council sent a telegram to Sir Wilfrid Laurier stating "We will not peacefully stand for the proposed further importation of Oriental labor into this Province at the behest of merciless, profit-seeking railway contractors. If the working conditions were made fit for animals, there are lots of available jobless men in Canada. . . . Better no G.T.P. than to add to the huge non-voting Oriental population which already controls the fishing and lumbering resources of the Province. . . . "

Shortly after this, Mackenzie King, now Minister of Labor, found it necessary to inform the Dominion Trades and Labor Congress meeting in Quebec that the G.T.P. had not asked for permission to use Asiatics, but that if they did, there would be ample time for the Congress to make representations opposing it. King pointed out, however, that if Asiatic labour were not allowed, construction of the railroad in British Columbia would cost an enormous sum. The Congress nonetheless presented a resolution pledging its members to do all in their power to protect Canadian workmen from "hordes of coolies." It was passed, along with the usual resolution to abolish the Senate.

The G.T.P., then, was undoubtedly moving towards the importation of Asiatic labour. On October 14, 1909, however, the vice-president of the Canadian Northern Railway, Donald D. Mann, appeared in Vancouver. His company was constructing railroads in the interior of the province, but the purpose of his visit to the coast was somewhat of a mystery. He stated that, in his 30 years of railroading, he had never found it necessary to employ Orientals, and he disappeared into the peaceful English atmosphere of Victoria. On October 20, Premier McBride very unexpectedly called an election for November 25, just two and a half years after he had received a firm mandate from the voting public. The reason he gave was that he required approval for an agreement he had just made with D.D. Mann and the Canadian Northern. The company, with the assistance of the government, was to build a railroad through the Yellowhead Pass, down the North Thompson. It would provide ferry service to Victoria and a line would be built from that city to Barkley Sound as well as branches to Fort George (later Prince George) and through the Kettle Valley. But most delightful of all, the directors had no desire to use Orientals.

"The People's Dick" or "Trickie Dickie"—the nickname depending upon the political party of one's faith—had struck again. How could the people of British Columbia resist such a delicious plum? There was something for everyone. R.G. Tatlow, the Minister of Finance, and F.J. Fulton, Commissioner of Lands, resigned over the generous assistance the government promised the Canadian Northern, but it did not harm McBride. Two Liberals and two Socialists managed to survive the Conservative onslaught. John Oliver, the recently elected leader of the Liberals, lost both the seats for which he ran.

The Canadian Northern's offer to spread railroads indiscriminately over the province without the use of Orientals was a much more attractive proposition than that of the G.T.P., now approaching the Yellowhead Pass. It was highly questionable, however, whether the western provinces were in need of a railway over the southern prairies to Vancouver (the C.P.R.) and two others paralleling each other over the northern prairie, passing through Edmonton and converging on the Yellowhead, from which one line would continue west to Prince Rupert while the other turned south to Vancouver. And if the G.T.P., already in financial difficulties, thought it almost impossible to construct its line without cheap Oriental labour, how could the Canadian Northern hope to do so? One or more of the three railway companies was likely to suffer, and it seemed unlikely that it would be the C.P.R. whose western portion had been built some 25 years earlier, mainly by Chinese labour. Only time would tell who would suffer.

The Chinese citizen all this time was being harried in a variety of ways. There was a constant argument in both Vancouver and Victoria as to whether Chinese should be allowed to attend white schools. During the 1908 celebrations of New Year, Vancouver enforced its ordinance forbidding fireworks, though the friendly spirit of house-to-house visits continued and Chinese shop windows were filled with ginger, candied fruits, nuts and other delicacies, "Chinese youths gazing at them with languishing eyes," as the *News Advertiser* put it. Some Chinese lost their jobs in 1909. In July of that year, Fraser River Lumber Mills brought in its first contingent of 500 French-Canadian families from Quebec. The head of each was given a job, an acre of land and a house, "to be paid in easy payments at 6 per cent interest."

The Chinese of Vancouver, too, were harried by the election in 1910, of a new and very durable mayor, Louis D. Taylor. Three years earlier he had been one of the noisiest members of the Asiatic Exclusion League. Immediately after his election he held a meeting to discuss the cleansing of Chinatown, but he was faced with nothing but discouraging reports from city officials. The Chief of Police said it was impossible to catch Chinese gamblers, the building inspector found it unbearable to examine the filthy premises, and the Health Officer stated that he was continually duped in his efforts to tear down condemned buildings, since the Chinese were always able to obtain injunctions against the action. Mayor Taylor, however, attacked the matter with the vigour of a novice and soon the courts were filled with gamblers and opium dealers.

For a short period, too, it appeared that the mayor's plans for purification would be aided by a move of the Orientals from Chinatown—"that patch of Oriental shabbiness and scene of mystery and squalid romance." The Chinese had lived in their own snug little corner bounded by False Creek, Westminster Avenue, Hastings and Carrall Streets for almost 25 years. In 1910 they were planning to move to the south shore of False Creek near the Westminster Avenue Bridge. The move failed to materialize, as did another in 1911.

There was perhaps some solace in the midst of their adversity to hear in February 1909 that one of their great persecutors, Joe Martin, was departing forever. Or so it seemed at the time. Joe moved to England and by May he was back in politics, running as a Liberal candidate in Stratford. He was defeated, but within the year, the remarkable ex-premier of the province had won a seat in the British House of Commons in the London riding of East Pancras.

There was little the provincial legislature could do at this time to harry the Chinese, though they made several attempts to do so, including one recommendation by the socialist, J.H. Hawthornthwaite, to give school boards the power to prohibit Chinese from attending their schools. The legislature in 1910 was more interested in railroads than in Chinese—though the two, in a sense, were inseparable. The Canadian Northern and Kettle Valley Railway bills were passed without difficulty. They stated that white labour only could be used. The province's side of the agreement was that they guaranteed a payment of $35,000 a mile for 600 miles of railroad, with control over passenger and freight rates.

The scene was set, then, for the Canadian Northern to begin construction in British Columbia. In 1886, it had built 100 miles of railroad in Manitoba. By 1910, it had 4,000 miles stretching from Lake Superior to Edmonton, and in the autumn of that year, railway shops were under construction at Port Mann, a few miles up the southern shore of the Fraser from New Westminster, and grading was taking place at Chilliwack.

The G.T.P. was progressing only slowly. In 1910, 100 miles of rails had been laid east of Prince Rupert and had extended 122 miles west of Edmonton, but its directors were still complaining over their inability to use Oriental labour. They brought 2,000 workmen from Scotland, promising to pay them $2 a day, but on their first night on the prairies a number decamped and at the end of three months, only 500 remained. Collingwood Schreiber reminisced on the good old days when, as director of C.P.R. construction, he had thousands of faithful Chinese at his beck and call. Indeed, as the G.T.P. and Canadian Northern plodded slowly on, it became more and more apparent that the Chinese were a great asset when it came to railroad construction. But there was not a chance in the world that the provincial government would ever allow Chinese labour on the G.T.P. Perhaps the Dominion might have, if it were not for the fact that such a move would be political suicide for the Liberal party in British Columbia.

Sir Wilfrid Laurier was well aware of the situation. In August 1910 he stepped off the transcontinental in Vancouver and that evening he addressed a huge crowd in the Horse Show Building. His hair was white now, his head balding, the lines of his face deeper. Sir Wilfrid was 69 years of age. They referred to him as "Canada's Grand Old Man", in the same way that they had once referred to Sir John A. Macdonald. The *News Advertiser* naturally covered the event.

After expressing his thanks for the great ovation that greeted him, he launched headlong into a matter which was constantly on British Columbian minds. "I tell you my object in coming here was to be informed as to what would be the needs and requirements of the western population," he said in his "suave and polished" manner. "I know that of all the questions which have been agitating the public men in British Columbia for the last 15 or 20 years, the one question that has more than engrossed attention, which has caused the greatest amount of discussion, has been the question of Oriental labor." A wave of applause and cries of, "Hear! Hear!" shook the Horse Show Building. For the next hour, Sir Wilfrid discussed the Oriental problem. He had carried the province and the city of Vancouver in 1896, 1900 and 1904, he said, but he had lost both in 1907—and the most prominent cause for his defeat was the question of Oriental labor. It was said in the last election that he would allow the G.T.P. to use Orientals, but, he pointed out, in the intervening four years not a single Asiatic had been employed. As for his failure to exclude completely the Chinese and Japanese, he had done it out of "Imperial sentiment" and because it was to the commercial benefit of Canada. Sir Wilfrid's speech and his visit to the province appeared to have been most successful.

All was quiet on the western scene until October, when a number of irregularities in Chinese immigration into the port of Vancouver were suspected. It was said that the Immigration Act was frequently ignored and that both Chinese and opium were being smuggled into the country indiscriminately. This resulted in the fourth Royal Commission to investigate Chinese immigration. In addition to the Select Committee under Amor De Cosmos in 1879, there had been commissions under Joseph Chapleau in 1884, under J.C. Clute in

1901 and under W.L. Mackenzie King in 1907. It was said that the commission of 1910 was a political move in preparation for a coming election; if so, it was a disastrous mistake.

The lone commissioner, Mr. Justice Denis Murphy of Vancouver, held the first session on December 15, 1910 in the Detention House, and for over two months he listened to numerous allegations of plots, counterplots, charges, denials and conspiracies.

It was revealed that there were two methods by which Chinese entered the country without paying the $500 head tax. Merchants were officially exempt; Chinese cooks, restaurant keepers, laundrymen, labourers, clerks and sundry others could join a business firm in China by the simple expedient of paying $100, thus becoming a bona fide merchant "within the meaning of the Act." They managed this, in part, through the connivance of Yip On, the government interpreter in Vancouver. The second method was for the Chinese to hide in the holes in the huge coal bunkers of the Oriental steamships. There were guards posted around each ship as it lay at dockside in Vancouver, but these guards had the habit of sitting comfortably in the ship's saloon where "they could not see a large army of Chinese leaving the ship." It was during the discussion of this matter that the collector of customs stated that the guards were appointed from the Patronage List sent from Ottawa. To add further to the intrigue, it was revealed that various officials were referred to in all correspondence by code names. Laurier's alias, for instance, was "Smith."

There were other scandalous revelations, one of them involving T.R.E. McInnes, who at that time held a governmental position in Ottawa. In his testimony, McInnes blurted out the fact that Sir Wilfrid Laurier had said that he would like to abolish the head tax, since it would be good for trade. The prime minster found it necessary to clarify his statement which had been somewhat twisted by McInnes.

The investigation was an unpleasant, sordid affair, until who should arrive in town but the Liberal M.P. for East Pancras, none other than "Fighting Joe" Martin. "His was a meteoric appearance," said the *News Advertiser*. Politics in British Columbia was rotten, shouted Joe. Graft permeated every department of the government. He attacked the Dominion and provincial Liberals in general and Robert Kelly, a local Liberal executive, in particular. (Kelley's code name, for some unknown reason, was "Jew.") Joe did not add anything specific to the investigation, but he certainly enlivened the proceedings.

The Commission hearings ended on February 22, 1911 and Justice Murphy's report appeared in July. The charges against various Liberal officials, he ruled, were unfounded, with the exception of those against T.R.E. McInnes, who was involved in some indefinite intrigue "to serve his personal end." The situation in the Vancouver Immigration Department, however, was disgraceful. Yip On, the Chinese interpeter, was singled out as the king-pin in the fraudulent entrance of an unknown number of so-called "merchants." Criminal charges were recommended, but Yip On (one of the most westernized of Chinese who always dressed in a neatly tailored dark suit, high, stiff collar and loosely knotted tie and wore his hair short and unerringly parted) had long since slipped off to China. Of course it was not just Yip On who had contributed to the smuggling of Chinese. Murphy found the watch on the ships at dockside to be farcical, and the means of identifying Chinese by such methods as names, scars and birthmarks was useless.

There was no doubt that many Chinese entered the country illegally through Vancouver, but, said Justice Murphy, "the Port of Union Bay is practically a free port for the entrance of Chinese and for the smuggling of opium." It was here, at the mid-point of the eastern coast of Vancouver Island, that the great ships from the Orient loaded their coal bunkers and it was here that Chinese and opium were discharged with wreckless abandon. Nanaimo, Ladysmith and Boat Harbor, served largely, by tramp ships were almost as bad. "The quantity of opium coming into Canada," said Justice Murphy, "is regulated simply by the demand for the drug."

The number of illegal entries was unknown, but revised figures showing legal entries had demonstrated a marked increase in Chinese immigration. It was now said that in 1904 there had been four, in 1905 eight and in succeeding years, 50, 745, 893 and 469. Up to mid-December 1910, there had been 1,286, for a total of 3,455 since 1904 when the head tax was imposed. This news, together with the release of the damning Royal Commission, came at a most inopportune moment for British Columbia Liberals. Sir Wilfrid Laurier had called a general election for September 1911. Nationally, the great question of the day was reciprocity with the United States, but locally the great increase in legal Chinese entries and the scandal of the Vancouver Immigration Department, the T.R.E. McInnes affair and the Patronage List was of more immediate concern. Joe Martin did not help matters by rocketing through the west between Winnipeg and Vancouver like a wild tornado, clawing at the heart of the Liberal machine. September 22, 1911 must have been a jubilant day for Joe Martin. Sir Wilfrid Laurier, prime minister for 15 years, had met defeat. A Liberal majority of 43 had been replaced by a Conservative majority of 48, Robert Borden was the new prime minister, and every Liberal in British Columbia had been defeated. Amongst the Conservative victors was the 33-year-old Vancouver alderman, Henry Herbert Stevens.

The defeat of the Liberals was hardly a world-shaking event; there were more important matters developing in Europe and Asia. In September 1911, the German Kaiser was threatening to increase his fleet, and Winston Churchill was appointed First Lord of the Admiralty; in December it was announced that the British fleet was ready for war. The British House of Commons had the benefit of Joe Martin's presence by then. He fiercely attacked the Admiralty over the grounding of the warship *Niobe*, only to be completely and unceremoniously silenced by a biting answer from the First Lord.

In Asia, the Manchu Dynasty which had ruled China for 300 years—considerably more than the Liberals' 15-year rule in Canada—appeared to be tottering. Since the Boxer Rebellion in 1900, there had been a great deal of reform, including an agreement with Britain to reduce and finally stop the opium trade. But for three centuries the Chinese people had resented the occupation of their land by the northern Manchus. In the autumn of 1911, open rebellion at last burst upon the decaying Manchu government. Confusing reports of its defeat were carried by the great Oriental steamers arriving in Vancouver, but it was not until February 1912 that the Manchus finally abdicated. Dr. Sun Yat Sen, who had visited Victoria one year earlier in his 16th year of exile, had returned to China in December 1911 to head a provisional government, but with the abdication of the emperor, he resigned in the hope that the country would be further unified.

The establishment of the Republic of China had its effects on the Chinatowns of British Columbia and also on the importation of a certain article into Canada. The queue had been forced upon the Chinese by the Manchus 300 years earlier. Originally a symbol of subjugation, it had become a badge of honour, serving to remind them of their subjection. It was now being severed by millions upon millions of citizens in the freed country—and it was not wasted. Hair in large quantities was being exported to Canada, where health authorities became quite concerned. A strangely worded Dominion order-in-council was passed to amend the quarantine regulations. It read, "Human or other hair unmanufactured or uncleaned must be unpacked and disinfected by boiling before it is allowed into Canada."

Citizens of British Columbia could read daily of the mounting problems in the Balkans—but it all seemed so far away. Much more real to them were the masses of Chinese, Japanese and East Indians in the province, the increasing power of labour unions and the magnificent skyscrapers rising in Vancouver (many of which still huddle venerably beneath the high rises of the '70s). It was a large, impersonal city of 110,000 now, with all the problems of a growing giant. There were riots by "alien agitators," a remarkable increase in crime, and an invasion by undesirables, vagrants and idlers. The chain-gang was re-established, and everyone was worrying about the possible adverse effects of the Panama Canal on local trade. Premier McBride called yet another election in 1912, the issue again being his chosen favourite, railroads. It was another Conservative landslide. Shortly thereafter, he moulded the Pacific Great Eastern Railway into existence, and in September 1912, at the age of 42 years, he received his knighthood.

H.H. Stevens, in the meantime, had taken it upon himself to fight the invasion of the Asiatics—which any self-respecting Vancouver M.P. was expected to do. The greatest threat now was from the Japanese, though Asiatics were Asiatics, no matter what their country of origin. Stevens discussed the problem in the House of Commons, spread the gospel in public meetings in the east and even wrote an article in Toronto's *Monetary Times* decrying the immigration of East Indians in the west. To his own constituents, he said that Robert Borden would soon deal with the problem. But when was "soon"? If it was not very soon, European war clouds might burst and dampen the little anti-Asiatic conflagration Stevens had lit and nurtured.

There was yet a little time—enough, at least, to allow Vancouver's Chinatown to celebrate its first New Year since the establishment of the Republic of China. By coincidence, it came on January 1, 1913. The final stroke of midnight had not completely faded when the rattle of firecrackers and the flash of bombs echoed through Chinatown's "gay thoroughfare," Pender Street. Flags of the republic blossomed suddenly from every rooftop and every window, barely discernible through the heavy pall of firework smoke hanging over the quarter. Thousands of Chinese scrambled wildly along Pender and down one block to the corner of Hastings and Carrall where, across the road, the interurban station loomed dimly through the acrid smoke, "from which constantly came quick flashes followed by deep, shaking detonations and the loud volley of smaller explosions as bombs and crackers fractured the air and city ordinances."

No one seemed to worry about city ordinances in 1912. The white population, whether it was in Victoria or Vancouver, always enjoyed the Chinese New Year—and in 1913, who could deny the Chinese special joy in their newfound freedom. It would probably produce no material change in their lives, though already the cabinet of the Republic had issued an edict stating that the traditional costume worn for hundreds of years would be changed now to one resembling western dress. The edict, it was said, had been sent to California, where Chinese were expected to change their habit; and all up and down the coast, the queue was fast disappearing.

In California, the Chinese Tong wars had flared up again, and there was a great deal of legislation against the Japanese. In Canada, for the moment, the "sikhs" or East Indians were in the limelight. There were said to be 5,000 in the province; none had entered since the legislation was passed insisting that immigrants come directly from their country of origin, but there were complaints from eastern senators that the wives of East Indians already in the country were not allowed to enter. "Unchristian, un-British and ungrateful," was the cry of one Ontario senator. But even eastern senators, when they discussed "sikhs," went on inevitably to Chinese and Japanese. They were all Asiatics, they were all problems. During the debate it was stated that 7,705 Chinese had immigrated to Canada in 1912, paying $3.45 million in head tax, British Columbia's share being $1.75 million, or half the tax charged to those Chinese remaining in the province.

This, in turn, lead to a series of editorials in the *News Advertiser* which pointed out that there were 25,000 Asiatics in British Columbia—one-tenth of the population—while Ontario, from which most of the complaints emanated, contained only 3,000. "It is obvious that the present system of admitting Chinese cannot go on much longer," said the editorial. It originally was expected that the $500 head tax would be prohibitive to the peasant Chinese, and indeed it was for a few years, but two years previously 5,000 paid the tax, in 1912 there were 7,000, and in 1913 the figure was expected to go over the 10,000 mark. Five hundred dollars was no longer a deterrant. A labourer or servant, the editor said, could save this much in a year or two.

Through the remainder of 1913 and on into 1914, there were

numerous minor incidents aimed at harassing the Oriental. Some of these perhaps were justified. Much of the white community were god-fearing citizens who believed in attending church on Sunday, while the remainder at least refrained from working. It was annoying for them to see the Oriental, with whom they were in competition, treat the Sabbath as any other day. This resulted in Richmond farmers petitioning the Council to pass a by-law prohibiting Orientals from working on Sunday. In two other incidents, Japanese storekeepers were told they could sell only fruit, tobacco, candy and ice cream on Sunday, and two Chinese found weeding their fields were ordered by police to desist from their labours on the Sabbath. But there were many other examples which were purely discriminatory. They were promoted by such groups as the sailors of Vancouver, the Farmers' Institute of Victoria, the Boards of Trade of New Westminster and Vancouver and the British Columbia Federation of Labor. Perhaps the most interesting resolution in this regard was passed by a public meeting at old Fort Langley in the summer of 1914. It stated that the Fraser River should be reserved for whites and native Indians. The original owners of the land and river and the fish therein must have been somewhat amused over their inclusion in the resolution.

And through it all were heard the strong and impressive voices of Sir Richard McBride and Harry Stevens calling for a white British Columbia. The Dominion government responded in 1914 by passing a new naturalization bill. It had been a scandal to westerners to consider that "hundreds of foreigners" could be naturalized without the knowledge of a word of English. The old law had merely required a residence of three years. This was extended to five years residence in the British Empire (the last being in Canada), an educational test was added, and an adequate knowledge of English or French was now necessary.

There were two more matters which would shake the province to its very roots before the greatest disaster of all. The first was the strike of coal miners on the Island over the failure of the companies to recognize their union, the United Mine Workers of America. The Chinese were hardly involved. A few insisted on continuing to work in the mines; a few were run out of various towns. Law and order broke down completely, special police could not cope with the riots, and the militia finally had to be called in. It was a part of the evolution of labour in the province, but a most terrifying one.

The second event occurred in the spring and summer of 1914. The year had started quietly enough. On January 1 the *News*

Advertiser printed a sketch of the new immigration building about to be constructed at the foot of Burrard Street and in the following days the paper carried pleas for peace—not to the Germans, Austrians or Russians, but to the Irish who were demanding home rule. In early spring, Vancouverites, always great baseball fans, were not at all impressed by the unheard-of contract for $18,000 which the Boston Red Sox player, Tris Speaker, had signed. He, said the proud citizens of Burrard Inlet, had to play 154 games while their own hero, Fred "Cyclone" Taylor, had played a mere 20 games in the National Hockey League for $4,000—which made Taylor the highest-paid athlete in existence in terms of dollars per minute.

All these events, however, paled into insignificance when it was learned that the *Komagatu Maru,* carrying 370 East Indian immigrants, was approaching the shores of British Columbia. The law which stated that immigrants had to come directly from their country of origin was being challenged. On May 23, 1914, "the Hindu boat" dropped anchor in Burrard Inlet, and for the next two months the city was tense with excitement. Not one of the passengers was allowed ashore, the East Indians would not allow the Japanese crew to depart, and a police force was repulsed when it tried to climb aboard. *H.M.C.S. Rainbow* then fitted up her great guns in Esquimalt, steamed bravely across the gulf, and trained her armament on the single stack of the *Komagatu Maru.* "After a day of excitement unparalleled in Vancouver's history," as the *News Advertiser* put it, the East Indian passengers decided to relent. On July 23, exactly two months after her arrival, the unfortunate ship steamed out through the First Narrows—and when Vancouverites turned again to their newspapers they discovered that the situation in the Balkans was "of extreme gravity." Twelve days after the *Komagatu Maru* departed, Britain declared war on Germany.

The natural evolution of the history of the Chinese in British Columbia was disrupted by the war, perhaps to their advantage. Over 7,000 entered the country in 1914, but in the latter few months of the year, more and more were returning to their homeland. There was always an exodus to China for the New Year celebration, but in 1914 it came earlier and in larger numbers. Perhaps it was the war; perhaps it was unemployment. War contracts had somehow evaded British Columbia, and the great Oriental ships which brought business, in the form of tea and silk and many other articles, were conscripted for wartime duty. The new *Empress of Asia* and *Empress of Russia* disappeared to the war zone, as did the beautiful old white Empresses. The *China* ran aground in Japan in 1911 and was sold to a Japanese company. The *India* was purchased by an Indian potentate for use as a hospital ship. The *Japan* became a naval auxiliary, later distinguishing herself by capturing German officers escaping from the Cocos Islands after the famous German raider, *Emden*, had been destroyed by the Australian warship *Sydney*.

Harry Stevens successfully accelerated the exodus of Chinese by promoting an order-in-council which allowed them to return to their homeland for the duration of the war, after which they would be allowed to re-enter without paying the head tax. J.H. McVety of the Trades and Labour Council considered this an act of kindness to the Chinese since there were said to be 6,000 unemployed Orientals. That McVety's heart was filled with kindness for the Chinese, however, was at best doubtful. "Any movement to help them, helps whites," he said. It appears that a considerable number of Chinese took advantage of the situation. At the end of 1915, when the *Empress of Japan* returned from her one-and-a-half years of war duty, she transported 500 Orientals back to China, stimulating the *News Advertiser* to note, somewhat happily, that "the exodus is still in full swing," though, less happily, it agreed that most would probably be back.

Those Chinese who chose to remain behind were constantly reminded of their lowly position in the white man's society. The market gardeners were said to be a menace since they refused to cooperate in controlling an epidemic of Powdery Scab in potatoes. Property owners on Sea Island refused to renew leases to Chinese gardeners. Even the women of the province—at this time still fighting for a reasonable semblance of equality with men (of the white variety)—attacked the harried Oriental. The Women's Employment League requested the city licence commissioner to replace all Orientals working in Vancouver hotels with white women. Health authorities continued to attack the violation of building and health by-laws, and the Labour Council continued to protest against those industries who employed Chinese. It would take more than a mere world war to dampen the spirit of anti-Orientalism in British Columbia.

Nonetheless, the Chinese plodded patiently on in the mines, the sawmills, the market gardens and the laundries. Some still scurried out of Chinatown each morning to toil in the great homes of the wealthy, but the majority pursued their mysterious ways in the depths of Victoria's and Vancouver's Chinatowns. For amusement, they read the ten-page *Chinese Times* (the successor of the *Chinese Daily News*) or attended the Kwok Tai Ping Theatre on Columbia

Street. Many satisfied their strange national desire to gamble their meagre savings in games of Fan Tan, while others relaxed in the peace of the poppy, to be rudely awakened, on occasion, by bothersome gambling and opium squads.

By 1916, the unemployment picture had improved; the province had obtained a share of the war contracts and the Empresses had returned to the carry once more the wealth of the Orient into Burrard Inlet. The following year, Harry Stevens formulated plans to expand Vancouver's harbour. On the surface, this was not an important event, but it revealed for the first time that the city was no longer an exclusively C.P.R. town. The Dominion had built a dock on a piece of waterfront property which the C.P.R. had somehow overlooked. The government, said Harry Stevens, must now have its own rail connections. To some, this was rank heresy. They believed that the C.P.R. had established the city and that the city was entirely dependent upon the largesse of the C.P.R. This, said Stevens, was not so. Certainly the company brought a great deal of commerce, but it purchased the bulk of its supplies in the Orient, where they were cheaper, and the crews of its ships were almost wholly Chinese who were not allowed ashore, and therefore spent nothing in the city.

"It should be borne in mind that we are under no particular obligation to the C.P.R.," said Stevens in a Vancouver *News Advertiser* report. "It is time that we realized that the C.P.R. is not a philanthropical institution considering the interests of Vancouver, but a corporation influenced by its board of directors whose interests are almost exclusively centered in the East and which looks to Vancouver as a necessary terminal point to be used only in so far as it will advance its Eastern interests and general transportation; furthermore, this corporation is deliberately committed to a policy of strangling in every conceivable manner any competition which might tend to develop the transportation facilities which Vancouver should possess."

The C.P.R. had to face the fact that it no longer held a stranglehold on the transportation system of the country. In its earliest days, it had been saved time and time again by massive financial aid from the government, it had received enormous land grants, and its British Columbia section, though constructed under contract from the government, had been saved from ruination by cheap Chinese labour. The G.T.P. and the Canadian Northern, too, received financial aid, much to the disgust of the young Calgary M.P., R.B. Bennett, but not a single Chinese had wielded a pick or shovel or wheelbarrow for them. Neither was able to survive. In 1917, the

Dominion government nationalized them and amalgamated them with other railways to form the Canadian National Railway—and the C.P.R. finally had some competition. Up to this point in their history, British Columbians had had an inbred filial respect for the C.P.R. and an inbred disrespect for the Chinese. The former was suddenly dissolving; the latter was much more resistant.

The shortage of labour caused by additional war contracts, the departure of Chinese, and army enlistments was further increased in July 1917 by the Military Services Act. Conscription, as in later years, was a sensitive matter in Canada. The riots in Quebec which followed the passage of the act were not unexpected, but perhaps it was surprising that Sir Wilfrid Laurier, now 76 years of age and a staunch supporter of Empire ties, opposed the act. He said that the legislation was "a blot on justice" and that a referendum should have been held. He refused to join a Union or Coalition government and late in December he led his abbreviated Liberal Party into a Dominion election against the Union Party, composed of both Conservatives and Liberals. The Unionists won handily, though the Liberals took 62 seats in Quebec, only three going Unionist.

Conscription not only reduced the labour force further and split the country into two camps, but also raised the question of what one did with naturalized Orientals. Should they be allowed to wear the king's uniform? China had declared war on Germany in August 1917. Though internal disorders prevented the Chinese from taking an active part in the war, they sent a reported 200,000 "coolies" to work behind the lines in France. in 1916 and 1917, many of these travelled across Canada in bond from Vancouver. A camp was set up for them at Petawawa, where they rested before continuing to France. Japan, too was at war with Germany but, like the Chinese, did not play an active part, other than in the seizure of German-held islands in the Pacific. There is no doubt that naturalized Japanese subjects were conscripted (a memorial in Stanley Park attests to their achievements); the part played by their Chinese counterparts has been obscured by the passage of time. Whereas many Japanese applied to the Tribunal set up in Vancouver for exemption, no Chinese names were listed in the newspapers of the day. Furthermore, the Public Archives of Canada can find no record of the presence of Canadian Chinese in the armed forces, though they admit that it is quite possible that some were conscripted. General George Pearkes, however, recalls that at least one platoon of the 52nd Battalion was composed largely of Chinese Canadians who fought in the Ypres salient in 1917.[8]

Even before conscription further depleted the ranks of labour, there had been a movement by the fruit growers and mine operators either to abolish the head tax or to allow the Chinese to enter the country for the duration, with the provision that they would return to China following the war. This was strongly opposed by the Farmer's Institute of Victoria, the Council of Agriculture, the British Columbia Federation of Labor and by Harry Stevens, who was continuing his chosen task of educating easterners on the evils of introducing more coolie labour.

Before the election of 1917, however, the government of Robert Borden had made it clear that further Chinese immigration was inadvisable. Perhaps they recognized the growing anti-Oriental sentiment of the country or perhaps they had the vision to foresee a postwar problem. By early 1918, it appeared that the war might soon end, in which case there would be a surfeit of labour in the form of returned soldiers. Indeed, some had already returned by early 1918, and they stood for no nonsense. In August they attacked strikers who, it was said, had been exempted from military duty because of jobs in essential industry. And in early November, they seized a Cloverdale "alien" named Peters who had never contributed to a patriotic fund during the four years of the war. The returned men escorted Peters to a wharf and gave him the choice of kissing the Union Jack or being dropped into the icy waters of the Fraser River. "Peters applied his alien lips to the flag," reported the Vancouver *Daily World*, "then was marched off to the Victory Loan headquarters, where he subscribed $500 to Canada's Victory Loan." If this was any indication of how the mass of veterans would act when they returned, the future indeed was not bright for the Chinese of the province.

Before this matter had to be faced, though, a minor but fascinating incident occurred in Vancouver which caused strange recollections of the past to be raised in the minds of those few who had lived in Victoria since 1885. Did they remember? Someone did. In March 1918, a complaint was made against the newly appointed court interpreter, Won Alexander Cumyow. It was said that he had "served time." The chief of police categorically denied the rumour, stating that the sentenced man was Cumyow's brother. The truth of the denial does not matter. The interesting fact was that some anonymous individual had recalled that little incident of 33 years earlier when William Cumyow had been jailed for a questionable misdemeanor in Victoria. Whether or not William and Won were the same person, the new interpreter had led a colourful and useful life in the Chinese-Canadian community. He was now 57 years of age and still had 37 years of useful life to lead.

It was a new British Columbia to which the soldiers returned. When they departed, Richard McBride was premier. He had resigned in December 1915 to become agent-general for the province in London, where he died in 1917. His successor as premier, H.C. Brewster, had also died suddenly in 1918, and the old Delta farmer, John Oliver, was now premier. Robert Borden had been prime minister when the troops sailed overseas—and he still was—but in February 1919, before many had returned, Sir Wilfrid Laurier died. It was the age of "the exquisite art of Maggie Teyte," of Madame Melba, Pearl White, George M. Cohan, Harry Lauder —and a young Boston Red Sox pitcher named Babe Ruth; in spite of his feat of hitting four home runs in four games, his batting average had slumped to .371, though he still led the league. Joe Martin was still drifting back and forth across the Atlantic, and short skirts and open blouses were in fashion—a mode which Vancouver's medical health officer, Dr. J.F. Underhill, heartily condemned, if not for the sake of modesty, for the sake of health. The Spanish grippe was killing thousands who had survived the war.

Armistice Day had hardly drifted into history when a great new wave of anti-Orientalism swept the province, strengthened by veterans' organizations and the ever-growing power of labour unions. Gambling, it was said, was rampant in Vancouver's Chinatown, and officers of the law did little to control it. City detectives Sinclair and Ricci could hardly agree. They were making nightly raids on the well-guarded dens of Chinatown. On one occasion, they crashed through a flimsy door on Main Street to find a group of Orientals playing "a Chinese game" under filthy conditions. When they nudged a figure lying on a bunk, he did not respond. The Chinese gamblers coolly pointed out that he had recently died of influenza. Sinclair and Ricci were kept very busy, but the attorney-general continued to grant licences to Chinese "clubs," over the protest of the Methodist Church Oriental Mission. The solution to the problem, said a Chinese resident in a letter to the City Council, was to build a moving picture house in Chinatown and lure the gamblers from their dens of iniquity.

There was also some concern when it was learned that 45,000 Chinese coolies who had worked behind the lines in France would be returned through west coast ports. Shortly before the celebration of the first Armistice Day, 1,450 of these coolies arrived by train, heavily guarded by Imperial and Canadian troops. They were transferred to the *Princess Charlotte* and taken to William Head, the quarantine station on Vancouver Island, to await the next ship to the Orient. Two months later, another 3,500 arrived, bringing the total at William Head to a reported 8,000. In March 1919, they began rioting, and 2,000 broke out of their enclosure. Most of them were "rounded up and herded back" at bayonet point, but an indeterminate number slipped away to melt into Victoria's Chinatown.

And when the bulk of the servicemen returned in 1919, they did not like what they saw, in spite of the efforts of Vincent Massey (for the Dominion) and G.G. McGeer, the provincial member from Richmond, to re-settle them. The objects for their disapproval were enemy aliens, strikers and Chinese. There was an excess of each. The Great War Veterans' Association went on record as favouring the complete cessation of Oriental immigration for 20 years. The conditions under which the non-whites lived, the Association said, were a detriment to the country. Furthermore, there were 700 Orientals working on Pacific ships, all of whom could be replaced by whites. When Association members discovered that the steel freighter, *The War Column*, built for the British government by Coughlan Shipyards of Vancouver, was to have a Chinese crew, they announced that they would cable their English fellow workers that the cargo of Hastings Mill lumber was "hot."

The cry was taken up by the newspapers, by the Vancouver City Council and by provincial politicians. Attorney-general J.W. deB. Farris travelled to Ottawa to discuss the Oriental problem, but all he got was an amendment to the Immigration Act preventing enemy aliens interned in allied countries from entering Canada. The provincial government amended the Factories Act, making it illegal for laundries to operate between 7 p.m. and 7 a.m., and the Retail Merchants Association pointed out that while Canadian boys were fighting in Flanders, Orientals stepped in to take over much of the commerce of the province. "Today our country is flooded with Orientals and southern Europeans," said the president of the Retail Merchants; "They form a large part of the commercial community and their standards of living and their character of trading is un-British and therefore their immigration must be limited."

Through this not uncommon marriage of patriotism and bigotry, these groups met with some success. The Retail Merchants lobbied for a 50-dollar licence for the Oriental hawkers who travelled about in wagons or old Model T Fords to sell vegetables and fruit house to house. "Cabbagee? Plotlatoe? Lettucee? Velly nice clucumber? Plenty good evelything!" quoted the *World* with unflattering accuracy in March 1919. "The familiar greeting of the itinerant Chinese merchant to the housewife in Vancouver when she responds to the timid tinkle of the door bell will no longer be heard if an effort set on foot by the local branch of the Retail Merchants Association meets with success." The Vancouver City Council dutifully imposed the tax and the Chinese protested, but soon they were back, timidly tinkling city door bells.

The Chinese made their presence felt on more than one occasion. In 1919 they set their quota in the Victory Loan campaign at $50,000. This was soon subscribed and a second goal of $100,000 was easily achieved. A few weeks later, in protest over Japan's imperialistic policy in Asia, the Chinese refused to sell Japanese oranges, a luxury to which British Columbians had become accustomed during the Christmas season. Since the Chinese controlled the greater part of the fruit business of the province, Japanese importers were left with a mass of rotting oranges.

It was only rarely, however, that the Chinese took the initiative in attacking their tormentors. Perhaps they had been suppressed too long by Manchu, Japanese and European invaders of their homeland, and by whites in their adopted land. The Japanese were much more aggressive, more ambitious and more energetic than the Chinese who, in order to maintain the even tenor of their ways, seemed to be willing to accept the white man's insults. The Chinese had certainly made gains during the war in that they had taken greater control of the fruit and vegetable business and they had acquired more land in the Interior, but these were quiet, unspectacular gains. The Japanese, on the other hand, were less patient. In 1920, they were reported to be purchasing the orchards of Kelowna, Maple Ridge and South Vancouver, and it was even rumoured that the old Coldstream Ranch near Vernon was about to pass into Japanese hands. The Provincial Board of Trade suddenly saw the Japanese as land owners and employers, and immediately began a campaign to halt Oriental immigration. Unorganized labour had been promoting this for years without success, and although unions were more powerful, there was still a great deal of resistance to their requests. Boards of Trade and Retail Merchants Associations, however, have easier access to governmental ears, and it appeared in 1920 that exclusion might at last be accepted in the near future.

Unemployment and the presence of a militant group of returned men brought further pressure upon the various governments involved. In January 1921, the Vancouver City Council gave permission for a tag day for the benefit of famine-stricken China. It was organized by the pastors of those Anglican, Methodist and Presbyterian Churches with missions in Chinatown. Bright and early on the last Saturday in January, Chinese and white girls appeared at every street corner in the city. They were soon joined by unemployed veterans bearing signs, in some instances, one standing on each side of the collector. The signs read, "Canada first—China last," "We licked the Hun, and this is what we got." A 25-cent meal ticket was attached to the sign.

The veterans were bitter. It seemed strange to them that money should be collected for a country that had played no part in the war, and they became even more incensed when they read in the newspapers that eggs were being imported from China. If Chinese were starving, why did they export eggs? They were told that Chinese had always given generously to local relief and patriotic funds. When the Reverend S.S. Osterhout of the Methodist Mission tried to remonstrate with the picketers by telling them their actions were "un-British"—a popular epithet of the postwar period—loud voices were raised, the police were called, and the good reverend was followed down Granville Street by a howling mob of veterans.

On the same day, the Right Reverend Bishop A.U. de Pencier of the Anglican diocese was driving down Georgia Street with his two sons when he espied a Chinese girl closely flanked by two returned men bearing a sign which read "Why not take care of our own homeless, starving, and unemployed?" The indignant bishop wheeled over to the side of the road and used "severe language" to reprimand the men. Loud words were passed back and forth; but it all ended in laughter when a very small veteran strode up to the six-foot bishop and threatened that he would "lay him out—if he was not a reverend gentleman."

In the postwar period, then, the Chinese were faced with new problems: unfriendly business organizations, unemployment, organized trade unions, militant returned men and anti-Japanese sentiment (since antipathy to one Asian nation always affected the others). Politicians had always been present. Attorney-general and Minister of Labor Farris was in the process of testing various provincial orders-in-council, his successor as attorney-general, Alexander Malcom Manson, was investigating the number of Chinese who could be replaced by whites in the industries of the province, and

Minister of Agriculture E.D. Barrow was collecting statistics on the Oriental inroads. Barrow stated that 90 per cent of the produce supplied to the Vancouver market was grown by Chinese, that more than 55 per cent of the potatoes grown in the province were grown by Chinese, and that Chinese owned 2,500 acres of land in the Ashcroft and Lillooet District and leased another 1,905 acres. Around Victoria, he said, all greenhouses but two were owned by Chinese, who swamped the market with early tomatoes, lettuce and flowers. Speculators were purchasing land owned by whites and selling it to Chinese, who worked harder and lived more cheaply than whites. Fifty-three acres in South Vancouver had recently been bought in this way. The minister also revealed that of 4,500 acres planted in small fruit in the province, 2,341 acres were controlled by Japanese. As far as his portfolio was concerned, the dairy industry was the only one to escape the onslaught of the Oriental.

These statistics were not hidden away in some obscure government document: they were printed boldly in the newspapers of the day where every citizen could read them. The Vancouver *Daily World* went even farther. It sent J.S. Cowper, a former member of the local House, on a tour of the province. From mid-July until October, over twenty of his articles were printed on the first page of the newspaper, each headed by the title, "The Rising Tide of Asiatics in B.C." The headlines in the first were,

Chinese Garden of Eden is found in Dry Belt by World correspondent.
Properties of unexampled fertility that might maintain scores of white families.
Why soldiers are idle.
Invasion of Mongolians produces tragic situation for men who fought.

The land, Cowper said, had been transformed from a desert of sand and sage and snakes. "It was B.C. brains, energy and money which conceived and carried it out.... The only fly in the ointment is that most of the land is now providing a living for Chinese while hundreds of our returned men are wearing out shoe leather on Vancouver streets or struggling to carve homes for themselves from forest jungles on the coast range."

All through his travels, the reports were the same: Ashcroft, Kamloops, Vernon, Armstrong, Enderby and Kelowna—land left by white settlers who went to fight in France had been taken over by Chinese. Further down in the Fraser Valley the situation was even worse, for here Japanese "soldiers" had taken over complete control of the berry industry. The Chinese, said Cowper, were at least content to keep to themselves, but the Japanese were a political menance. And they stretched all the way down the Fraser to its very mouth at Steveston where the fishery again was completely controlled by the Nipponese. As the writer wandered along a dyke on Lulu Island, the constant chatter of Chinese and Japanese children speaking their native tongues made him feel as if he were in a foreign land.

In his 16th article, Cowper presented a mass of statistics to illustrate the alarming proportions of Chinese immigration. In 1918-19, there was a total of 4,333 entries; in 1919-20, 544, and in 1920-21, 2,435. In addition, in the previous year, 1,445 Chinese merchants had been allowed into the country without paying the head tax. Another great worry, he said, was the marked increase in both Chinese and Japanese birth rates.

All through this endless flood of anti-Orientalism, the Chinese remained their impassive selves, never protesting. Although their dress was now western, they maintained their national customs: the celebration of New Year, the game of Fan Tan, the Chinese opera and opium smoking. And even in 1921 they still used the chicken oath in court. In October of that year, Hoey Duck was a witness in the case against Nick Kogos, who was accused of arson. On the lawn before the court house (which is still standing between the Hotel Vancouver and the Pacific Centre) a six-foot, six-inch provincial policeman held a white leghorn's neck upon a block of wood. Hoey Duck read the oath from Chinese characters printed on a piece of paper while joss sticks burned close by, "then the Celestial brought down a ferocious looking cleaver and the chicken got the axe." The paper oath was burned before the robed court officers and Hoey stated he knew nothing of the Kogos fire. (Kogos became a successful businessman. A reproduction of the Parthenon on his former shoreline estate in West Vancouver is a prominent landmark.)

There was a brief respite for the Chinese toward the end of 1921; a general election had been called. Sir Robert Borden, prime minister since 1911, had resigned in July 1920 to be replaced by Arthur Meighen, whose government had steadily deteriorated. The country was asked to choose between the Conservatives' Arthur Meighen and the Liberals' William Lyon Mackenzie King. The new Liberal leader had been described by Harry Stevens, now minister of trade and commerce, as "a dismal failure," while Margot Asquith, visiting from London, somewhat surprisingly termed him "the most impressive personality" she had met on this side of the Atlantic.

There were no outstanding issues nationally, the most useful ammunition the Liberals could muster being the unemployment figures and the huge losses of the C.N.R. Provincially, the Asiatic question was not a major subject of debate, though Harry Stevens found himself continually on the defensive when the matter was raised. The Liberals won by a small overall majority, though with the split between the Conservatives and Progressives, they held by far the largest number of seats. Harry Stevens was returned, along with Meighen's minister of agriculture, Simon Fraser Tolmie of Victoria.

"The new Premier," said the *World*, "is not showy or sensational, but able, honest, sane and public spirited." It would remain to be seen whether he was also, as Harry Stevens put it, "a dismal failure." The problems of the country, at any rate, were now placed upon the broad, though low-altitude, shoulders of Mackenzie King, who had so often visited British Columbia to settle the everlasting problems of labour and the Asiatic. They were still the problems of the province.

Early in 1922, another great campaign against the Oriental was begun, culminating in the appearance of British Columbia's 13 M.P.s (Liberals, Conservatives and Progressives) before Charles Stewart, the new minister of immigration. They demanded total exclusion of all Orientals from the province. Stewart was most impressed with the unanimous opinion of members from all parties; he expressed his personal sympathy and promised an early consideration of the problem.

In May 1922, the Member for New Westminster, W.G. McQuarrie, introduced a bill to exclude all Orientals from the country. He quoted figures to illustrate the extent of Oriental involvement in British Columbia's industry, pointed out that the provincial legislature had requested the abrogation of the Anglo-Japanese Treaty, and emphasized that many public bodies were in favour of total exclusion. In the past ten years, he said, the numbers of both Chinese and Japanese had doubled and their birth rates had been increasing spectacularly. In 1910, for instance, the Japanese birth rate was one per 252 white births, but in 1921 it was one per 17.

Mackenzie King, as a result of his negotiations with the Japanese and Chinese following the 1907 riot in Vancouver, had been more personally involved in the Asiatic problem than any other previous premier. British Columbia members probably wondered how he would approach the situation. When he rose to speak on the immigration bill, he said that it was not a local or provincial matter; it was a national and international one. Although it was partly racial and religious in its nature, it was first and foremost an economic concern. (Up to this point, British Columbia members must have wondered if he was in favour of exclusion or against it.) In his opinion, the premier went on, the influx of an inferior class of person to Canada would inevitably have the effects of lowering the standard of living. (He was in favour of exclusion—surely.) The head tax had been ineffective, he said, but he did not believe in exclusion; he believed in restriction. (And their hopes were dashed). The bill was defeated and one including the term "effective restriction" was passed.

The next day, the Liberal-oriented Vancouver *World* produced a bitter editorial stating that British Columbia members were ignored, in spite of their unanimous opinion. "B.C. is no longer a white province but the domain of brown and yellow races," shouted the editorial, and Attorney-general A.M. Manson agreed. "We want B.C. to be a white province," he said.

Those few who had lived in the province for 30 or 40 or 50 years had become accustomed to the failure of anti-Oriental legislation, though they had hoped for more on this occasion. The Asiatic Exclusion League rallied its forces and approved of a new crest in the form of a lapel button, in which the letters "B.C." were symbolically coloured white against a blue background. The Women's Institution attacked "the yellow races." The provincial Minister of Mines, William Sloan, ably supported by A.M. Manson, presented a resolution for the consideration of the Dominion government to the effect that the government of British Columbia was in favour of complete exclusion. Like countless others, it was duly passed and forwarded to Ottawa, to be laid aside as the others had been.

In the first week of February 1923, A.W. Neill, the Independent member for Comox-Alberni, arose in the Dominion House to introduce a bill which would indirectly exclude the Chinese. There was no chance of its being successful, but the House made its usual gesture of discussing the familiar arguments. On February 22, however, Charles Stewart, the minister of immigration, stated that the government had been in communication with the Chinese ambassador in Washington and the Chinese consul-general in Ottawa, who had just returned from discussions in Peking. It had been generally agreed that no more Chinese would enter Canada, the exceptions being consuls, merchants and students. Thenceforward, there would be strict regulation of Chinese already in the country, Vancouver and Victoria would be the only ports of entry, and a controller of Chinese immigration would be appointed. The Republic of China had agreed to these stipulations and there was no ill will. The greatest stumbling block, trade, would not be affected.

The government presented a bill to this effect, but as it slowly progressed through its committee stage, its three readings and its debate in the senate, it became apparent that British Columbians did not consider it an exclusion act. It was merely another form of restriction. Consuls, merchants and students? They had gone through all that before. The New Westminster City Council passed a resolution—seconded by a future mayor of that city as well as of Vancouver, Fred Hume—demanding complete exclusion. Simon Fraser Tolmie said the bill would leave the country wide open to Chinese merchants. The Dominion government had never given British Columbia satisfaction, he said, and no party was to blame more than the other. It had all resulted in "jellyfishing." He concluded: "I want to say that the country and its representatives must wake up if we are to preserve Canada as a white man's country to be enjoyed by future generations." The Tolmie name had been part of British Columbia's history since his father, Dr. William Fraser Tolmie, arrived at Fort Vancouver in 1833 at the age of 21 years, just 25 years following the appearance at Musqueam of the man after whom he named his son. Simon was born on Vancouver Island in 1867. He, more than anyone else, should have remembered that when his father arrived on the west coast, it was Indian, not white man's, country.

There were numerous objections to the bill, including one from J.S. Woodsworth, the Labor member from Winnipeg and future leader of the C.C.F. Party, who said that it would not help the workingman—even now, Canadian money was moving to China to build industry to take advantage of cheap labour.

Another great flurry of objections occurred in Vancouver when it was discovered that the immigration sheds were full of Chinese children between the ages of 12 and 17 years of age. It was said that they were all admitted, tax-free, as students. After visiting one of the local schools, an angry mother commented, "The place is thick with Chinese. . . . Our best schools are stuck full of foreigners and our own children have to be taught in basements and in makeshift classrooms." A woman's organization and the Asiatic Exclusion League sent another protest to Ottawa; nevertheless the bill was passed.

The new act was indeed only a restrictive one in the sense that it allowed consuls, merchants and students into the country, though in effect it was an exclusion act. The great irony of the affair was that British Columbians did not recognize it as such and therefore could not enjoy the ecstacy of the moment. Christmas had come—but it was just like any other day. Tillie the Toiler continued to wave her willowy hips, sheathed in an ankle-length gown, before the frustrated eyes of her office partner, Mac, and Dorothy Dix continued to smile benignly from beneath her rat's nest hairdo. Maggie continued her unsuccessful attempts to bring a little culture into Jiggs' life and Babe Ruth conveniently found himself suffering from his regular springtime malady when the drudgery of spring training rolled around. It was as if nothing had happened.

Four days after prorogation of parliament, the *World* summarized the achievements of the past session. It did not even mention the new immigration act. Since 1860, while there were still two colonies on the west coast, there had been attempts to restrict the Chinese. Now that they were virtually excluded, no one seemed to notice, though there were few of the old pioneers remaining. Dr. J.S. Helmcken, never an anti-Orientalist, had died just three years before the passage of the act, at the age of 96 years. And Joe Martin? When Charles Stewart announced in February 1923 that an exclusion act would be forthcoming, Fighting Joe had just been discharged from the Vancouver General Hospital. At that time he achieved another milestone in his colourful life: he was the first person in Vancouver to be treated with the new drug, insulin. But before the Chinese bill was debated, Joe was back in hospital, where he died from the complications of diabetes in March 1923.

The remainder of that year saw a continuation of the fight against the Oriental, led largely by the demagogic Attorney-general and Minister of Labour A.M. Manson. Brought up in Ontario on "Scots porridge and Presbyterianism," as the Vancouver *Sun* later put it, Manson would later spend 26 controversial years on the British Columbia Supreme Court and, as chairman of the Mobilization Board during the Second World War, would strike fear into the hearts of those who had the spectre of conscription hanging over their heads. In 1923 Manson was riding roughshod over the province, excluding women and music from beer parlours, closing blind pigs, purging the Vancouver Police Commission and waging a war of attrition against the Chinese. Excluding them was not enough to keep British Columbia a white man's country, he said.

The Chinese were still not free from persecution. There had been 39,587 enumerated in the census of 1921. They were spread from ocean to ocean: 14 in Prince Edward Island; 315 in Nova Scotia; 185 in New Brunswick; 2,335 in Quebec; 5,625 in Ontario; 1,331 in Manitoba; 2,667 in Saskatchewan and 3,581 in Alberta. British Columbia, with a total population of 524,582, had a Chinese population of 23,533, almost 4.5 per cent of its total. Canada's largest city,

Montreal, with a population of 618,500, had 1,735 Chinese residents, while Toronto, with a population of 522,000, had 2,134. Vancouver's population was 117,217, of whom 6,484 were Chinese, while Victoria had 38,727 citizens, including 3,441 Chinese.

To those who had their families with them, exclusion was no great disaster; it might even relieve the pressures of anti-Orientalism. But there were many merchants and labourers with families in China. They had a choice of returning to their homeland or waiting patiently for the immigration laws to be relaxed. Most of them remained. And white children of the '20s and '30s, knowing nothing of politics, trade and commerce or immigration laws, wondered what manner of men these were, who would leave their wives and children in distant China.

CHAPTER X

1923 to the present

*"Some Very Disagreeable Decisions Will Have
To Be Faced Here In British Columbia.
I Am Thinking of The Chinese."*
Bruce Hutchison. 1943

Those years between 1923, when the Chinese exclusion act was passed, and 1945, when the Second World War ended, were valuable years for the Chinese of British Columbia. Indeed, their fortunes began to swing upward during the First World War, when they took advantage of the times to acquire land, control the market gardening of the province and, perhaps more than anything, make the first meagre inroads into the wholesale and retail marketing business of Vancouver, Victoria and other small towns of the province. The exclusion act, by relieving the pressures of anti-Orientalism, gave the Chinese an opportunity to consolidate their position in the community, with a minimum interference from the whites.

Time, too, was on their side. Over these years, a new generation of both white and Chinese were born and, to a large extent, raised and educated together in an atmosphere which, though by no means entirely convivial, was relatively free of the constant agitation caused by the everlasting attempts to legislate the Chinese out of the country and by reports of the arrival of yet another two or three thousand Chinese immigrants. The average annual number entering the country for the 11-year period ending in March 1922 was 2,294. From 1924 to 1947, only eight Chinese were admitted as immigrants. The new generation would take years to reach maturity, and another war would intervene to assist the process, but the recognition of the civil rights of British Columbia's Chinese was only a matter of time.

There were visible signs of improvement in relations in the early 1920s. Chinese, Japanese and a mixture of white nationalities attended such primary schools as Charles Dickens, Central, Cecil Rhodes, Henry Hudson and Laura Secord, later moving on to Britannia or Vancouver Technical high schools, where they wallowed together in the mud of the rugger and soccer fields. The Japanese, always treated more respectfully by the whites, had a baseball team, the Asahis, as early as 1921, and by 1924, one of a long series of fine Oriental soccer teams, the Chinese Students, was entered in the second division of the local league in Vancouver. It was this type of activity which would do more to mend relations than the combined actions of politicians, Asiatic Exclusion Leagues and Retail Merchants Association.

It was necessary, however, that political parties and labour organizations become involved before legislation to change the laws of the country could be passed. The first faint indication of this appeared in 1921, when a new wave of anti-Orientalism was sweeping the province. Orthodox unionists accused the Chinese of creating unemployment, but a group of die-hard socialists pointed out that there was unemployment even in those regions where there were no Chinese. More specific evidence of change occurred in 1928, when the Canadian Labor Party, an affiliation of various unions, was virtually destroyed, firstly by the appearance of communists in their midst and secondly by the unexpected passage of a resolution calling for enfranchisement of Orientals. The resolution was promoted by Ernest Winch, a strong socialist and one-time president and secretary of the Vancouver Trades and Labor Council, later an M.L.A. representing the Canadian Commonwealth Federation Party. In an attempt to rescue the disintegration of organized labour, a referendum later voted to repeal the resolution, although many members were still in favour of Oriental enfranchisement.

This temporary move by the labour socialist groups to support the Chinese was indeed a reversal of policy. From the very beginning it had been the workingman who had opposed them. Now, in 1928, there arose the first faint flicker of support for them. In past years, big business in the form of the C.P.R., the G.T.P., the Dunsmuir Mines, the Fraser River canners and many others, were against exclusion, but only because they were bound to profit by cheap labour. Early socialists such as Ernest Winch had nothing material to gain. They could not even hope to gain politically since, in general, the province was still very much anti-Oriental.

Organized labour, however, was not the only group which experienced a change in policy. In 1929, a provincial statute established a Trades License Commission, and soon the Retail Merchants and the Canadian Manufacturers' Association were clamouring for the Commission to use its influence to curb the spread of Orientals into the business community of Vancouver. Remember the Canadian Manufacturers' Association? They had cheered Sir Wilfrid Laurier enthusiastically when, in speaking to their Toronto convention in 1907, the prime minister had stated that it would be simply panic to allow a riot in Vancouver to affect trade with the Orient. At that time, the Chinese were a poor, labouring class; now they were becoming businessmen. In 1928, there were 79 Chinese greengrocers in Vancouver, 77 of whom were outside Chinatown. There were only 14 such businesses run by whites. Of the 37 shops listed as groceries, 19 were outside Chinatown, and of 37 Chinese laundries, 34 were in white man's territory. The Chinese had even spread into the tobacco business. Ninety-six licenses were granted and 35 were outside Chinatown. Chinese were all very fine when they toiled with pick and shovel or when they weeded their gardens on the river flats or even when they operated their little shops and laundries in Chinatown, but when they began to spread into the retail business outside the narrow confines of their quarter, the white businessman recognized a threat to his security, just as the workingman had recognized the threat to his security many years earlier.

There was little opportunity for further growth in the depression days of the early thirties. R.B. Bennett, with the durable Harry Stevens in his cabinet, became prime minister of the country, while Simon Fraser Tolmie chose an unfortunate period to lead the government of the province. China, in a virtually constant state of turmoil since the Opium Wars of 1839, was now fighting the Japanese in Manchuria. In spite of the depressed state of the economy, British Columbia Chinese began collecting money in order to mobilize a force of 1,000 recruits and a fully equipped aeroplane corps for their homeland. Their campaign received little sympathy from the white population. School teachers' salaries were being reduced by ten per cent, the District of Burnaby went into receivership, many families were on relief, and in Vancouver, Uncle Billy Hassell was auctioning off strange and wonderful items for his radio Santa Claus Fund—one of the more popular being Mayor Louis D. Taylor's famous red tie.

And the province was trying to save money in every conceivable way. It attempted to persuade China to take over the care of 70 mental patients who could not be deported and who were costing the government $25,000 a year. It agreed to pay the cost of transportation of any unemployed Chinese who wished to return to his homeland, reasoning that this was cheaper than paying them relief money.

By 1933, however, the electorate hoped miraculously to improve the economic situation by virtually annihilating Tolmie's Conservatives and electing the Liberals under Thomas Dufferin Pattullo. In that election, seven members of the new Canadian Commonwealth Federation (C.C.F.) won their first seats. They were now firmly espousing the cause of the Chinese, and in the Dominion election of 1935 this became an important issue. In a full page advertisement in the *Province*, together with photographs of all their Lower Mainland candidates—including G.G. McGeer, Ian Mackenzie, A.M. Manson and Tom Reid—they stated that a vote for the C.C.F. would be a vote for Chinese: "50,000 Orientals in B.C." it read. "C.C.F. Party stands pledged to give them the vote. The Liberal Party is opposed to giving these Orientals the vote. Where will you stand on election day? A vote for any C.C.F. candidate is a vote to give the Chinaman and Japanese the same voting right that you have! A vote for a Liberal candidate is a vote against Oriental enfranchisement." Whether the plea worked to their advantage is impossible to say; W.L. Mackenzie King and his Liberals won nationally and the province returned five Liberals, five Conservatives, four C.C.F., one Reconstructionist and one Independent.

The following year, the Chinese market gardening business was again attacked. Earlier, the objections had been over the growing of vegetables. More recently, their invasion of the retail business was protested, but now in 1936, it was said that Chinese were gaining control of the wholesale market. In 1922, there had been only one Chinese in this business, but now there were 21. The white wholesalers on Water Street found that they could get their hands only on imported vegetables, largely from California. During the depression, it was said, Chinese financiers had organized wholesale companies which controlled the farms and they had since strengthened their position by making interlocking agreements with the 500 truck farmers of the Lower Mainland. The wholesale outlets, in turn, controlled the numerous retail outlets. In the West End, Kitsilano, Point Grey and Fairmont Districts there were 69 Chinese and 77 Japanese retail stores selling fruit and vegetables. In addition to this, there were 155 Chinese vegetable peddlers who sold from door to door in Vancouver alone, to say nothing of many more in Burnaby, North Vancouver, New Westminster and Vancouver Island.

There was no doubt now that the Chinese had entered into the field of big business, and yet the Chinese farm labourers were still in a state of virtual serfdom. They were controlled by labour brokers, just as the railroad and cannery workers had been for years. The broker fed and clothed the worker, made cash advances to him during the winter months and even sent money home to China for him. No wages were remitted directly from the farm owner to the labourer; the broker received a lump sum from the organization for whom he had a contract and he managed the affairs of the labourer.

This state of affairs provided a fecund soil for the next—and last—of the little anti-Chinese demagogues. His name was Clive Planta, Independent M.L.A. for Peace River—some 750 miles from the troubled delta land of the Fraser, and about as far away from the scene of the action as one could get and still remain in the province. In the latter half of the thirties, his name was a household word.

Planta spent the early hours of several mornings, late in October 1936, following the Chinese produce trucks from the gardens in Delta, Lulu Island and Burnaby to the various wholesale headquarters in Vancouver and from there to the city market near the C.N.R. depot on Main Street. Soon after this, he described the results of his nocturnal sleuthing to the legislature—the filth, decay and squalor of these wholesale headquarters where vegetables, eaten by whites, were handled. On two occasions he asked for a Royal Commission to investigate the situation, and when both failed, he continued his campaign by storming through the Lower Mainland, speaking to such organizations as the Kiwanis Club, the Potato Growers of the Fraser Valley, the East Delta Potato Growers and the Junior Board of Trade.

Perhaps his inflammatory speeches had some effect. The British Columbia Coast Vegetable Marketing Board established the price of potatoes and set a quota for each grower. Every sack of potatoes to enter Vancouver was to be tagged, to attest to its legality. The Oriental gardeners refused to have anything to do with this, and Clive Planta was driven on to greater effort. "The Chinese violate every law in British Columbia and every regulation of the municipality," he shouted at a meeting of the Local Council of Women.

In the early morning of the first day of March 1937, Chung Chuck, a Ladner potato grower, eased his heavily laden truck onto the Fraser Avenue Bridge, only to find his way blocked by a large timber, behind which stood five burly white potato farmers and an inspector for the marketing board. They were there, as the *Province* put it, to stop "the spud bootlegging activities of Chinese growers." According to white interpreters of the incident, the inspector told Chung to unload his untagged potatoes, and the infuriated Chinese climbed out of his truck swinging a club. He was disarmed and in the melee, the inspector suffered a cut on the head, said to be inflicted by a knife. Chung Chuck fled, leaving his truck and untagged potatoes to the tender mercies of the wounded inspector and the five potato farmers. The Chinese then brought charges against the six, claiming he had received cuts, bruises and torn clothes from his tormentors.

An editorial in the *Province*, referring to the Chinese as "An Oriental Menance," declared that the farmers were merely trying to help the potato board to obtain a market for Canadians, "as against the increasing tide of ruthless Chinese competition." Twenty years ago, the editorial went on, "lowly John Chinaman" leased a parcel of land from its white owner, produced his vegetables by hand and peddled them through the streets of the city. Now big corporations owned large farms equipped with modern machinery, but still manned by the cheapest Chinese labour, who worked from dawn till dark. The corporations were directed by "smart young Orientals born in Vancouver and claiming the rights and privileges of citizenship." The trucks were owned by Orientals and driven by Oriental chauffeurs to Oriental warehouses and Oriental retailers, "where the salesgirl is very apt to be a brilliant young Chinese graduate of the University of B.C." The editorial ended somewhat pathetically on a note of defeat. "It is a changed situation indeed."

Most of these facts appear to have been true. Whether they were or not—and whether Clive Planta, the potato board or Chung Chuck were right or not—does not matter now. The important facts were that British Columbians were slowly realizing that the Chinese were in business to stay and that they were no longer an impoverished mass of labourers, lacking the intelligence of whites. In the previous century, it had been said that the Chinese were useful only for menial tasks and were quite incapable of being educated. By 1937, the *Province* accepted quite naturally the fact that there were "smart young Orientals" and "brilliant Chinese graduates."

Clive Planta, though he continued his campaign, was a man of the past. Adult British Columbians of the day, however, would never completely rid themselves of their feelings of uneasiness and suspicion of the Oriental races living amongst them. And as the Second World War approached, they began to worry more and more about the Japanese. It was said they produced almost five times as many children as did the Chinese, presumably since there were only an estimated 2,525 Chinese women in the province while there were many more Japanese women. Indeed, Bruce Hutchison, writing from Victoria for the *Province*, believed that the Chinese population was dropping as rapidly as the Japanese was increasing. This was welcome news in one sense, but Hutchison added a word of caution: the drop in the Chinese population was only a dip in the graph; there were many young girls in Chinatown who would soon be old enough to marry, at which time the population would again soar.

Although there continued to be a mild degree of tension over the market gardening business, the worst was over. Among those Chinese who were spreading out into the white community, some were becoming westernized. Others remained in Chinatown to carry on their ancient way of life. In April 1938, the bones of 1,000 Chinese, deceased for at least seven years, were enclosed individually in linen bags and packed neatly away in cedar caskets labelled suitably for transportation to their homeland. And as late as 1942, there were still some Chinese who demanded the chicken oath in court. (The unfortunate victim that year in Cranbrook was a Buff Orpington rooster.) But even in Chinatown there was a certain degree of occidentalization in progress. The Chinese Mission, just a few months after the war began, reported a considerable change. "It is no longer true that Chinese work for so much less and live on a so much lower standard than other working people," the report read. "The standard of living, as regards health and cleanliness shows a marked improvement over a number of years. The Chinese are spending more on home comfort in this country and demanding higher wages from their employers."

The Second World War affected the lives of every citizen. For the Chinese, it was the beginning of the last chapter in their desultory quest for equality. Indeed, it had hardly been a quest at all; they had been too busy defending themselves, too busy keeping out of trouble, to seek equality. With National Registration and conscription, together with their value in war industry and the armed forces, they saw their opportunity to move to the offensive. If they could be conscripted, they said, they should be allowed to vote. It all seemed quite reasonable. Much of the campaigning was carried on by the young people of the community. In 1942, the Chinese Youth Association of Victoria presented a long brief to Premier John Hart, pointing out that the province's 23,000 Chinese were solidly behind the war effort, many Chinese were in the armed forces or in war industry and the community had given great support to the country's war loan drives—but that the Act of 1875 forbade them the vote. They also pointed out that the legal and pharmaceutical professions were closed to them and that they could not be employed in public works. A further complaint was that (like Victoria's coloured community of the 1870s) they were not allowed to serve on juries.

The Chinese Youth Associations of the Interior and of Vancouver as well as the Ninghing Benevolent Association under Foon Sien all campaigned vigorously for the franchise. They were supported by a number of service clubs, but perhaps their most avid supporters were the members of the C.C.F. Party—whose progenitors, the workingman and the socialist party, had been their most bitter enemies. If it had been the national C.C.F. Party who demanded the vote for the Chinese, one might have passed it off as being another manifestation of easterners' not understanding British Columbia problems—but this was not so. The 15 C.C.F. members of the provincial house were solidly behind the Chinese, as was the C.C.F. Dominion member for Vancouver East, Angus McInnes. Even some of the trade unions were cooperating with the Chinese—who were now complaining that they were not allowed to make income tax deductions on dependents in China.

The old established parties, however, were still in power. Most of their members had lived through some of the worst days of anti-Orientalism—the riot of 1907, the frequent arrivals of Chinese immigrants, the bitter days following the First World War. To them, anti-Oriental laws had always existed. Thus, in 1943, Attorney-general R.L. Maitland took issue with M.J. Coldwell, leader of the C.C.F. who, he said, was trying to force British Columbia to give the franchise to Chinese. This was a provincial matter, Maitland insisted, and it was one which had been a problem in British Columbia since the earliest of times. The provincial policy had developed as the result of long study and experience. It had been decided long ago that "it was not wise to grant the franchise to Asiatics." Furthermore, Maitland went on, such bitter subjects should not be raised during the war. "It is up to us to decide who gets the vote in British Columbia," he said. "The Dominion can decide on their own vote."

The younger generation, born in the 1920s, were quite ignorant of all that had gone on before. If they had stopped to consider, they would have recalled their own transgressions. Remember Jim, the back door Chinaman? He was still there in the 1940s, and remained until the importation of California vegetables drove him from his market gardens. But the child of the '20s and '30s could recall the friendly, smiling face, so often adorned with solid gold teeth, which greeted him faithfully and regularly at the back door at the same hour of the day on the same day of the week, year after year. He had pleasant memories of the gifts "the Chinaman" would present, with beaming face, to his best customers at Christmas or New Year's —burning hot sugared ginger in little blue boxes, "Lai Chi" nuts which rattled round in larger blue boxes, or lily bulbs for spring planting. He could recall exasperating memories of being caught behind a Chinese flivver travelling at ten m.p.h. on a narrow, pot-holed road; shameful memories of stealing apples or oranges from the open Model Ts or Chevs parked in the back lane; of hiding in the bushes and shouting insulting little rhymes at his mother's favourite "Chinaman" (Chinkee Chinkee Chinaman, sitting on a fence. Try to make a quarter out of fifteen cents); or memories of the more daring small boys who faced the Chinaman squarely in the security of his back yard and shouted, not knowing what it meant, "Chinna-mucka-hyoo!"—then ran like hell.

Those same small boys did not notice that Chinese children did not swim in Victoria's Crystal Pool, that Chinese fellow students did not receive free milk dispensed by the school board, nor did they know that the school dentist did not send complete reports to Chinese parents. And when those same small boys grew their way into high school or university, they did not realize that the Chinese beside whom they worked or studied or played on the soccer or rugger field or on the baseball diamond could not be employed on public works, could not toil on Crown land and could not vote. They did not think it strange to see a Chinese in the king's uniform, and when John Chan or Sam Louie were reported missing overseas, they felt just as badly as they did when similar reports were made of the deaths of Jim Harmer or Pat Flynn.

It would take time, but certainly changes were slowly taking place. The newspapers began to support the Chinese in their quest for enfranchisement, albeit with some reluctance. On one occasion they pointed out that for years Canada had nursed along her relations with Japan, and as late as 1941, the year Japan attacked Pearl Harbor, Canada had sent them scrap metal. This was in sharp contrast to the shabby treatment the Chinese had always received.

Bruce Hutchison, a Vancouver *Sun* columnist by 1943 (later editorial director for the same newspaper) perhaps best reflected the feelings of British Columbians. He believed that justice could be done to the Chinese only by giving them the vote—though he considered this a "very disagreeable decision." Everyone, he said, agreed with President Roosevelt's Four Freedoms. "But the general idea seems to be that the sacrifices and concessions would be made by someone else; not by us. It certainly does not occur to most people in these parts," he said, "that some very disagreeable decisions will have to be faced here in British Columbia. I am thinking of the Chinese of British Columbia."

Hutchison went on to say that Asiatics could never be assimilated. "That is a law of nature which our parliamentarians cannot repeal. Therefore the Chinese cannot reasonably expect us to encourage a large immigration of their countrymen into Canada. It is not merely a question of numbers. It is a question of pride. It is the danger of discrimination. . . . Either we must make friends with these people (of China) and give them a chance in the world or we must fight them eventually."

Four hundred Chinese ultimately joined the armed services, including several women in the Canadian Women's Army Corps, but it was not until mid-1944 that Chinese were conscripted. The reason for the delay, it was said, was that conscription would only bring a new rash of demands for the franchise, as indeed it did. Premier Hart, however, announced that there would be no discussions of the matter at the present.

When the war finally ended a year later, there was a startlingly different attitude towards the Chinese than there had been after the First. Labour, in the form of both the Vancouver Trades and Labour Council and the C.C.F., was all in favour of Chinese enfranchisement. The other enemy of the past, the war veterans' associations, also completely supported the Chinese.

In spite of this change in attitude, the Chinese were hardly overwhelmed with generosity. Yick Wong, the publisher of the *Chinese Times*, stated in 1946 that it would be more difficult for the Chinese than for any other group of immigrants to achieve equality due to the almost hereditary discrimination British Columbians had developed for the Chinese over the foregoing 80 years. This attitude was amply demonstrated by an editorial in the Vancouver *Sun* on the day that Yick Wong began a nationwide campaign against racial discrimination. "We shall declare at once our great friendliness for the Chinese as a people and as individuals," the editorial began quite blandly. "They were the earliest Oriental immigrants to this Province, they have lived decent lives amongst us, they are fine people to get along with." But the editorial writer was completely incapable of suppressing his age-long attitude of white superiority. "Economically they create no problem. They are not above the tough jobs which must be done by somebody. They are excellent house-boy servants, they go in for stoop labour on farms on a scale no Caucasian will attempt, and they possess to a remarkable degree that interesting trait of being able to mind their own business. There is still a limit, of course, to the numbers we can assimilate economically. . . . " The editorial went on to point out that the chief source of dollar exchange for China came from the $100 million sent from Canada and the United States, that Canadians cannot own a foot of land in China and that there was a great deal more to discuss before Chinese were given the vote.

In spite of their ingrained demeaning attitude towards the Chinese, it became apparent to British Columbians in 1947 that the Dominion was about to amend its immigration laws. The precise number of Chinese in the country at that time was not known, though the 1941 census had shown a total of 34,627, a considerable reduction compared with the 46,519 in 1931. This was the result not only of absence of immigration but the paucity of women. In British Columbia, for example, there were 16,220 males and only 2,399 female Chinese, a ratio similar to that of the other provinces. Possibly the Dominion had this in mind when, in 1947, they allowed wives and unmarried children into the country. It was nothing sensational, but the Chinese accepted the meagre gift and immediately prepared to ask for new concessions.

By mid-1947, some 2,000 Chinese had departed for their homeland, many to return with their wives and children whom they had not seen for many years. Others awaited patiently the arrival of relatives by the long sea route, while still others, perhaps with less patience and more money, met wives and children as they stepped from the *Empress of Hong Kong*, Canadian Pacific's new airliner which had replaced the old ocean steamers of the past.

The provincial government was a much more difficult bastion to conquer. It was not until 1949, while the Liberal-Conservative coalition was in power, that the Chinese were presented with their franchise. Surely it made little difference in their daily lives; but it was another step forward in their quest for equality. Others followed slowly, though they had begun as early as 1942, when the newspapers began reporting a long series of "firsts": the the first Chinese to be commissioned in the army, the first male Chinese admitted to the bar, the first female Chinese admitted to the bar, the first Chinese delegate to the British Columbia Fruit Growers' Convention (Peter Wing), the first Chinese to hold an office in a Board of Trade (Peter Wing) and many others.

And one by one the old anti-Oriental laws were erased from the statute books. Probably the last was the Chinese clause in Crown leases. It was dropped in March 1951 in accordance with instructions received from the attorney-general, but the old order-in-council of 1902 was not formally rescinded until September 1958.

But to Foon Sien, the president of the Chinese Benevolent Association, the immigration laws were still most discriminating. By 1959, he had travelled 11 times to Ottawa, to plead for a more liberal policy. Although a number of minor changes were made, it was not until 1967 that Chinese immigration was placed on an equal basis with that of other nationalities. The new act, still in force, recognizes three categories of immigrant. The Dependent Category places little in the way of the close blood relative, though there is a long list of those qualifying as close blood relatives. The Nominated (or distant relative) and the Independent (those with no relatives) Categories are given a certain number of points for such items as age, training, occupation demand, language capability, pre-arranged employment, etc. with admission requiring 50 points. It is virtually an open immigration policy, and Chinese are treated no differently from anyone else. Foon Sien, an immigrant of 1910, saw his long struggle end successfully before he died at the age of 70 years in 1971.

The relaxation of the immigration laws in 1947 resulted in the admission of 21, 76, 803 and 1,746 Chinese annually between 1947 and 1950 inclusive. The very liberal changes of the law in 1967 increased Chinese immigration to a level similar to that of the peak in 1882, when Andrew Onderdonk brought in 8,083. From 1968 to 1970, annual admissions numbered 8,328, 8,272 and 5,377. Over the same years, the numbers remaining in British Columbia were 3,070; 2,617 and 1,588.

The number of Chinese in Canada, as shown by the 1961 census, was 58,197, with a ratio of 1.6 males to one female, a marked change from the eight to one ratio of 1941. By province, there were 445 in Newfoundland, 43 in Prince Edward Island; 637 in Nova Scotia; 274 in New Brunswick; 4,749 in Quebec; 15,155 in Ontario; 1,936 in Manitoba; 3,660 in Saskatchewan; 6,937 in Alberta; 24,227 in British Columbia; 100 in the Yukon and 34 in the Northwest Territories.

These are likely to be the last accurate figures available, since the 1971 census reverted to an almost Victorian form of etymological delicacy by inquiring only of one's "cultural group" or "mother tongue." This is looked upon with favour by the Chinese community. Though they are proud of their racial origin, they wish to be known as Canadians, rather than Chinese Canadians. Unless Oriental features preclude one from being Canadian, the great majority are as Canadian as English, French, Scottish, or Ukranian Canadians. There are a few of the old, traditional Chinese remaining and these form one of the three subcultures existing in the community today, the others being the westernized group consisting of the sons and grandsons of earlier immigrants and the new immigrants, largely from Hong Kong.

But even the lives of the traditional group have changed since the Second World War and the immigration act of 1947 which allowed the admission of wives and children. Prior to this, the Chinese lived in Chinatown and seldom left its ill-defined borders. With the arrival of wives and children, they moved into the suburbs of Chinatown—which then changed from a residential to a commercial quarter. The gambling houses, theatres and joss houses have almost disappeared, and television, bowling clubs and service clubs have replaced them. There are no longer elaborate funeral processions, other than for a very prominent member of the community. The bones of deceased Chinese are no longer returned to their ancestral home and the sumptuous celebrations of the Chinese New Year are a thing of the past. Amongst the elderly Chinese who immigrated prior to 1923, the only marks of their past existence are their Chinese dishes and their language; many still speak only their Oriental dialect.

But today you can meet the sons and grandsons of the Chinese who shuffled ashore from the great white Empresses in the early part of the century, virtually penniless, wearing their queues, paying their head tax and being faced with numerous discriminatory practices. You can meet them in virtually any profession, either inside Chinatown or outside. Gordon Cumyow, like his father, Won Alexander, acts as an interpreter and serves the poor and helpless in Chinatown. Dr. Wah Leung, Dean of Dentistry at the University of British Columiba, was born in Victoria, as was the Vancouver lawyer and former M.P., Douglas Jung. One of Vancouver's leading impresarios is David Y.H. Lui, whose father was from Hong Kong and whose mother belonged to a well established Victoria family. A leading west coast artist is Raymond Chow, who looks out from his home in Delta upon the land his grandfather farmed.

And then there was Eng Wing, who left his native Canton in 1901, to settle in Kamloops. He became a houseboy, but as he learned the English language, he progressed to the position of cook, restaurant operator and general store merchant. In 1911 he returned from a visit to China with a wife and raised a family of seven in the Kamloops area. The eldest, Peter, born in 1914, joined his father in the grocery business, married a Revelstoke native, Kim Wong, and became an active member of the Kamloops Board of Trade in 1934. From that time to the present, Peter Wing has held a long series of public and professional offices in the community. Whereas in 1875, when "the Heathen Chinee" elected Councillor "Lummond" mayor of Victoria, it was feared that Kwong Lee himself might soon be chief magistrate of the city and that "next year all the council will be filled with gentlemen with pigtails," not only was Peter Wing elected alderman of the City of Kamloops in 1959, but was re-elected in the following two aldermanic elections, and in December 1965 became mayor of his native city. He retained this office in the next two elections, finally retiring in 1972. Peter Wing, the son of a Chinese immigrant who had served as a houseboy, was an alderman for six years and mayor of Kamloops for six years.

The old politicians would find it difficult to believe. One of the few who lived on to see it all was H.H. Stevens. He had come to Canada in 1887 at the age of nine and to Vancouver at the age of 16 years. As a child he had heard Sir John A. Macdonald speak before a political rally in Peterborough, Ontario, and he had ultimately sat in the House of Commons with Sir Wilfrid Laurier and Sir Robert Borden. He had been in the cabinets of Arthur Meighen and R.B. Bennett. And Harry Stevens had fought in the Boxer Rebellion in 1899, had stood on Granville Street and watched the Asiatic Exclusion League parade in 1907, had been pelted with stones and coal by the East Indians on the *Komagatu Maru* when he attempted to board the ship in 1914. Like every politician of his day, H.H. Stevens was strongly anti-Oriental, though he was by no means as acrimonious as his acquaintance, Dr. H.W. Fraser. The sentiment, however, was so strong within him that, even up to his death at the age of 94 years in June 1973, his strange bitterness towards the Asiatic races appeared merely dulled by the passage of half a century.

Amor De Cosmos, Arthur Bunster and John Robson would no doubt have responded in the same manner. If they had been born a hundred years later and the emancipators of the postwar period had been born a hundred years earlier, their opinions on the Oriental question would have been reversed. The men of one age cannot be condemned, those of another praised; they were all products of their times—with the exception, perhaps, of the distant voice of

James Fell who, in 1876, had the courage to point out the unpopular truth of the Opium Wars to the gathered throng in Victoria's Theatre Royal.

The rattle of James Watt's tea kettle has been replaced by the pound of the diesel and the whine of the jet, and the Opium Wars have been replaced by a more subtle form of economic suzerainty. The dismal tale of the Chinese in the sea of sterile mountains has a happier ending.

Chronology

CHAPTER I

1843 - Fort Victoria constructed.

1846 - 49th parallel chosen as western boundary of British North America.

1849 - Vancouver's Island established as a British colony.

1858 - April—first rush of gold seekers from San Francisco.
   - May—Amor De Cosmos arrives in Fort Victoria.
   - June—the first Chinese arrive from San Francisco.
   - August—mainland established as the Colony of British Columbia.
   - December—first edition of De Cosmos' *British Colonist*.

1859 - New Westminster established by Royal Engineers.

1860 - Kwong Lee first advertises in *Colonist*.
   - Kwong Lee's wife first Chinese woman to arrive in the colony.
   - increase in Chinese arrivals, mostly from Hong Kong.
   - ten dollar poll tax for Chinese proposed but defeated.

1862 - Billy Barker discovers gold in Cariboo's Williams Creek.

1863 - Amor De Cosmos elected to colonial Assembly.

1864 - James Douglas retires as governor of two colonies. Chinese contribute $100 to welcoming fund for new governor of Vancouver Island, Arthur Kennedy. Frederick Seymour governor of mainland.

1865 - head tax on Chinese again debated.

1866 - union of the two colonies, the capital in New Westminster.

1867 - confederation of Ontario, Quebec, New Brunswick and Nova Scotia.

1868 - Victoria chosen as permanent capital.
   - Barkerville fire.

1869 - death of Governor Seymour and appointment of Anthony Musgrave.
   - Chinese welcome Governor Musgrave to Barkerville.

1871 - Chinese employed in Nanaimo coalfields.
- Bunster proposes $50 Chinese head tax in last Colonial legislature.
- British Columbia joins confederation.

CHAPTER II

1871 - De Cosmos, Bunster and Robson elected to first B.C. legislature.
- De Cosmos elected to Dominion parliament.
- increase in anti-Chinese sentiment.

1872 - Robson proposes $50 Chinese head tax and prohibition of Chinese from employment on provincial and Dominion works, both defeated, in first provincial legislature.
- political patronage begins with appointment of J.H. Gray.
- Sir Francis Hincks elected M.P. for Vancouver District by acclamation, after defeat in Ontario.

1873 - Anti-Chinese Society formed in Victoria.
- Sir John A. MacDonald resigns over Pacific Scandal. Bunster elected M.P.

1874 - increasing discontent over failure to construct the railroad.
- Robson proposes head tax, Bunster a queue tax, both defeated.
- Chinese construct Grand Trunk Road to Hope.
- Drummond elected mayor of Victoria by the Chinese vote.
- Edward Blake refers to B.C. as "a sea of sterile mountains."

1875 - Chinese barred physically from voting in Nanaimo.
- motion to bar Chinese from employment on Victoria city works passed.

1876 - Chinese Joss House opens in Victoria.
- James Fell defends the Chinese in a Victoria public meeting.
- Governor-general Lord Dufferin visits Victoria.

1877 - Strike in Dunsmuir mines broken by militia and American strike-breakers.
- Death of Sir James Douglas.
- Hastings townsite established on Burrard Inlet.
- The Queensland Act first discussed.

1878 - Bunster proposes C.P.R. labour clause stipulate worker's hair length.
- Bill to exclude Chinese from provincial works passed.
- Bill levying $30 licence on all Chinese passed, leading to general strike of Chinese in Victoria.

1878 - Sir John A. Macdonald elected in Victoria, in absentia, after defeat in Ontario.
- Workingman's Protective Association formed in Victoria.
- B.C.'s second "Separation Memorial" sent to Queen Victoria.
1879 - De Cosmos presents bill for peaceful separation of B.C.
- Sir John appoints Select Committee on Chinese Labor and Immigration.
- Onderdonk purchases contracts to construct 127 miles of C.P.R. in B.C.
- Premier Walkem fails to get anti-Chinese clause in C.P.R. contracts.

CHAPTER III

1880 - Construction of C.P.R. in B.C. begins in April.
- White and Chinese labourers from San Francisco arrive in June, and Chinese labourers from Hong Kong arrive in July.
1881 - Bunster attacks Sir John over Naturalization Bill.
- Chinese labourers arrive in larger numbers.
- Shortage of Chinese labour in Victoria.
1882 - Noah Shakespeare elected mayor of Victoria.
- Peak of Chinese immigration (8,083) from San Francisco and Hong Kong.
- Sir John states Chinese will not become permanent settlers.
- De Cosmos and Bunster defeated in Dominion election; Shakespeare elected.
- U.S. bill prohibits immigration of Chinese.
- Governor-general Marquis of Lorne visits Victoria.
1883 - Scurvy and beri-beri spread amongst Chinese railroad workers.
- Chinese killed in riot at C.P.R. construction site.
- Shakespeare proposes $50 head tax in Dominion house.
- Chinese immigration decreasing; anti-Chinese sentiment increasing.

CHAPTER IV

1884 - Unemployment and starvation amongst Chinese.
- Chinese labourers break strike in Dunsmuir mines.
- Provincial Chinese Regulation Act passed, later disallowed.
- Provincial act to prevent Chinese immigration passed, later disallowed by the Dominion.
- Knights of Labor organized in Victoria.

- First Royal Commission on Chinese immigration.
- W.C. Van Horne visits Burrard Inlet.
- Construction of E. & N. begins, financed by Dunsmuir.

1885 - Province again passes act to prevent Chinese immigration, later disallowed by Dominion.
- C.P.R. agrees not to use Chinese on Coal Harbour extension.
- First Dominion head tax on Chinese set at $50.
- Anti-Chinese parades in Victoria.
- Dominion Franchise Act excludes Chinese, at suggestion of Sir John.
- Failure of Chinese businesses, including Kwong Lee's.
- Governor-general Marquis of Lansdowne visits.
- West and east portions of C.P.R. joined at Craigellachie.

1886 - Destitution amongst Chinese.
- Incorporation of City of Vancouver.
- Province inserts anti-Chinese clauses in all private bills.
- Chinese construct C.P.R. extension to New Westminster.
- Vancouver destroyed by fire.
- First tea ship arrives from the Orient.
- Sir John visits Victoria.
- Chinese population decreasing.

1887 - First train arrives in Vancouver.

CHAPTER V

1886 - The Chinese play decisive role in election of Vancouver's first mayor.
- The Knights of Labor campaign against Chinese in Vancouver.

1887 - January 8: Chinese clearing Vancouver's Brighouse estate escorted to Victoria steamer by whites.
- February 24: Chinese from Victoria arrive to clear Brighouse estate and are attacked by whites.
- February 25: Chinese on False Creek given notice to depart.
- February 28: Provincial legislature passes bill to send 35 provincial constables from Victoria to Vancouver and suspend local magistrates.
- March 19: Special constables return to Victoria.
- Almost 200 killed in Vancouver Coal Company mine explosion; Chinese blamed.

CHAPTER VI

1887 - Chinese clear Brighouse estate and are grudgingly accepted.
- Ships carrying Oriental trade arrive in Vancouver; Victoria by-passed.

1888 - U.S. suddenly passes absolute exclusion bill, causing increase in Chinese immigration to B.C.
- Edward Blake visits Victoria's Chinatown, Vancouver's Stanley Park.
- First of many attempts to amend Coal Mines Regulation Act to prevent Chinese from working underground. Defeated.

1889 - Two strikes in Dunsmuir mines.
- Death of Robert Dunsmuir. James Dunsmuir takes over mines.
- Governor-general Lord Stanley visits.

1890 - Provincial government amends act to bar Chinese from working underground. Ignored by Dunsmuir. Later disallowed
- Dunsmuir mines on strike.
- B.T. Rogers offered bonus and tax concessions for sugar refinery in Vancouver, provided he employ no Chinese.
- Request to raise head tax to $100 refused.

CHAPTER VII

1891 - Coal Mines Regulation Act amendment again defeated.
- Complete exclusion of Chinese refused by Sir John.
- Death of Sir John A. MacDonald.
- The great white Empresses appear.
- Increased Chinese immigration.

1892 - Socialist Tom Keith's anti-Oriental amendment postponed. First to include Japanese.
- Keith's bill to raise head tax to $500 defeated.
- Smallpox epidemic begins among Chinese immigrants.

1893 - Keith's anti-Oriental amendment defeated.
- Keith's request to raise head tax to $500 defeated.
- Punch's request to raise head tax to $100 passed, refused by Dominion.
- Economic depression, unemployment and increasing Chinese and Japanese immigration.

1894 - Keith's anti-Oriental amendment ruled out of order.
- Visit of Wilfrid Laurier, accompanied by Joseph Martin.

1896 - Sir Charles Tupper becomes fifth prime minister in five years.
  - Separate schools an election issue in Canada; Asiatics an issue in B.C.
  - Laurier promises that, if elected, he will accede to B.C.'s Chinese immigration requests.
  - Laurier elected prime minister.
  - Li Hung Chang visits Vancouver.
  - Anti-Asiatic sentiment increasing.
1897 - Numerous anti-Asiatic bills proposed in B.C.
  - Chinese and Japanese arriving in greater numbers.
1898 - More anti-Asiatic bills proposed in B.C.
  - Joseph Martin elected and appointed attorney-general of B.C.

CHAPTER VIII
1899 - Many anti-Oriental bills passed in B.C., including request to raise head tax to $500.
  - Failure of B.C. members to obtain anti-Oriental legislation.
  - Dominion disallows all B.C. anti-Oriental bills since they include Japanese.
  - The threat of naturalization of Chinese and Japanese.
  - B.C. proposes Natal Act.
1900 - Lt.-governor McInnes dismisses Semlin; Martin premier.
  - Increased Japanese immigration.
  - Laurier increases head tax to $100, effective 1901; refuses to consider Natal Act.
  - B.C. passes Natal Act, disallowed by Dominion.
  - Murder of Police Chief Alex Main.
1901 - Dunsmuir closes mines rather than submit to strikers.
  - Employees of Dunsmuir and Vancouver Coal Company unite.
  - Second Royal Commission on Oriental affairs.
1902 - B.C.'s new Natal Act disallowed by Dominion.
  - Oriental immigration continues.
  - Chinese Empire Reform Association active in Vancouver.
1903 - B.C.'s new Natal Act again disallowed by Dominion.
  - Thirteen B.C. anti-Oriental bills disallowed by Dominion.
  - Laurier increases head tax to $500 effective 1904.
  - McBride premier of B.C.; organizes government along party lines.

1904 - B.C.'s new Natal Act disallowed by Dominion.
- Chinese immigration drops.
- Kang Yu Wei visits B.C.

1905 - Imperial Privy Council disallows B.C.'s Coal Mines Regulation Act.
- Dunsmuir sells E. & N. to C.P.R.
- Construction of Grand Trunk Pacific begins.
- Violence against Chinese in Salmo.

1906 - Violence against Chinese in Penticton.
- Immigration of East Indians causes concern.

1907 - B.C. passes Natal Act; Lt.-governor Dunsmuir refuses assent.
- Increased immigration of Chinese, Japanese and East Indians.
- Asiatic Exclusion League organized in Vancouver.
- Anti-Asiatic riot in Vancouver.
- Commissioner W.L. Mackenzie King settles Japanese claims, discovers conspiracy amongst industrialists.

1908 - B.C. passes Natal Act with Dunsmuir assent; Act declared inoperative by courts.
- Commissioner W.L. Mackenzie King settles Chinese claims; discovers opium legally manufactured, sold and smoked in B.C.
- Dominion prohibits importation, manufacture and sale of opium.

CHAPTER IX

1909 - Grand Trunk Pacific complains of inability to import Chinese labour.

1910 - Canadian Northern and Kettle Valley Railway bills pass with stipulation that white labour only be used.
- Louis D. Taylor of the Asiatic Exclusion League mayor of Vancouver.
- Laurier explains his Oriental policy in Vancouver speech.
- Fourth Royal Commission on Chinese immigration reveals subterfuge, incompetence, patronage, and smuggling of Chinese and opium.
- Chinese immigration again increasing.

1911 - All B.C. Liberals in Dominion election defeated as a result of immigration scandal.
- Robert Borden elected prime minister.
- Rebellion against Manchu Dynasty in China.

1912 - Republic of China established.
- Chinese immigration continues to increase.
1913 - Strikes and riots at Nanaimo mines.
1914 - New Dominion Naturalization bill stipulates five year residence and adequate knowledge of French or English.
- East Indians and *Komagatu Maru* affair.
- World War I.
1915 - 1918—Anti-Orientalism continues in spite of little immigration.
1916 - Thousands of labourers from China cross Canada to France.
1917 - Amalgamation and nationalization of G.T.P. and Canadian Northern.
1918 - Armistice.
1919 - 21
   Increased opposition to Orientals and Europeans from veterans and businessmen.
1921 - Fruit and vegetable business in control of Chinese and Japanese.
- Mackenzie King elected prime minister.
1922 - B.C. passes resolution in favour of complete exclusion.
1923 - Dominion passes immigration act, in effect excluding Chinese.

CHAPTER X
1924 - 47
   Eight Chinese admitted as immigrants.
1928 - Canadian Labour Party passes resolution urging Oriental enfranchisement.
- Increase in Chinese businessmen outside Chinatown opposed by Retail Merchants and Canadian Manufacturers' Association.
1933 - C.C.F., supporting Chinese cause, elect seven members to B.C. house.
1935 - In Dominion election, Liberals charge a vote for the C.C.F. is a vote for Oriental enfranchisement.
1936 - Chinese gaining control of wholesale market gardening.
- Clive Planta begins campaign against Chinese market gardening.
1937 - Violence over Chinese trucker's untagged potatoes.
1939 - World War II. Chinese join armed forces voluntarily.
1942 - Chinese protest lack of franchise, their restriction from cer-

tain professions, and anti-Chinese clauses in government contracts.

1944 - Chinese conscripted.

1945 - World War II ends.

1946 - Labour, C.C.F. and veteran's organizations favour Chinese enfranchisement.

1947 - Dominion allows Chinese wives and unmarried children to enter.

1949 - Enfranchisement of Chinese in B.C.

1951 - Anti-Chinese clauses in Crown leases dropped.

1956 - Douglas Jung elected M.P. for Vancouver.

1958 - Peter Wing elected mayor of Kamloops.

1967 - Chinese immigration placed on an equal basis with other nationalities.

Sources Other than Newspapers

1. Willmott, W.E. "Approaches to the Study of the Chinese in British Columbia," *BC Studies*, No. 4 (Spring 1970).
2. Cheadle, Walter B. *Cheadle's Journal of Trip Across Canada 1862-1863*. Edmonton: M.G. Hurtig, Ltd., 1971.
3. Baillie-Groham, Mrs. *Fifteen Years Sport and Life in the Hunting Grounds of Western America and British Columbia*. London: Horace Cox, 1900.
4. Ibid.
5. Canada, Report of the Select Committee on Chinese Labor and Immigration, Journal of the House of Commons, Vol. XIII, 1879.
6. Canada, Ottawa. Report of the Royal Commission on Chinese Immigration. Printed by order of the Commission, 1885.
7. Willmott, op. cit.
8. Personal communication to author.

Index